MAX STARKLOFF

AND THE

FIGHT FOR DISABILITY RIGHTS

Merry Christmas,
Uncle Joe!
Charlie Claggett
12-24-14

CHARLES E. CLAGGETT JR.

WITH RICHARD H. WEISS

MISSOURI HISTORY MUSEUM

ST. LOUIS

DISTRIBUTED BY UNIVERSITY OF CHICAGO PRESS

ISBN 978-1-883982-79-9

Library of Congress Cataloging-in-Publication Data
Claggett, Charles E., Jr.
  Max Starkloff and the fight for disability rights / Charles E. Claggett Jr. ;
with Richard H. Weiss.
    pages cm
  Includes index.
  ISBN 978-1-883982-79-9 (hardback)
  1. Starkloff, Max. 2. Quadriplegics--United States--Biography. 3. People
with disabilities--Legal status, laws, etc.--United States--History. 4. People
with disabilities--Civil rights--United States--History. I. Weiss, Richard H. II.
Missouri History Museum, issuing body. III. Title.
  RC406.Q33C52 2014
  362.4'3092--dc23
  [B]
                                        2014027210

Missouri History Museum
PO Box 11940, St. Louis, MO 63112
Distributed by University of Chicago Press

Printed and bound in the United States by Thomson-Shore, Inc.

·Table of Contents·

·FOREWORD·

By William H. Danforth

When Colleen Starkloff asked me to speak at her husband's memorial service on January 4, 2011, I spoke about how Max Starkloff affected me. I can think of no better way to start my foreword for this book than to paraphrase my remarks on that occasion.

It is an honor to be speaking about Max Starkloff, a hero of St. Louis and, more, a hero for our entire nation. Imagine a person becoming quadriplegic at age twenty-one. Imagine the devastating physical and psychological changes that would be expected, back in the 1950s before Max had shown the way. The world would have expected to hear no more of him other than confinement, obscurity, and probably early death with few attending his service. Now, fifty-two years later, this church is filled with those who admire and love Max Starkloff and have drawn comfort and inspiration from his abundant and overflowing life.

He married, lived with Colleen, raised a family, and founded two innovative, first of their kind, service organizations: Paraquad, to make independent living possible for the disabled, and the Starkloff Disability Institute to open workplaces to the disabled so as to lower their unnecessarily high unemployment rate. Along the way he was the major founder of the National Council on Independent

Living, becoming a national leader, spokesperson, and role model for the disabled, meeting presidents and testifying before Congress. And always, he aimed to benefit others.

I can hardly imagine the determination, the self-discipline, the intelligence, the vision, and the lack of self-pity that it took to transcend all expectations and to set a shining example for us all, disabled or not, of an inspiring life of service and significance. Max was our touchstone. We admired him; we loved him.

Some have said, "How sad it is that Max is gone." I understand and share that sentiment, but there is another way to look at his passing. That is: "How fortunate we are to have had Max for so long." Who could have expected in 1950 that Max would live another fifty-one years? He suffered from one health problem after another, especially from lung infections. I suspect that we would not have had him for as long without some near miracles.

First there was Max himself, his determination, his character as strong as steel, his amazing mental stability, his intelligent management of his life and affairs. Then there were the near miracles of those who surrounded him, the love, care, and support of his friends and admirers, his physicians and therapists, his family, and, most especially, his own special miracle worker, his beloved Colleen.

Finally, I give thanks for the life of Max Starkloff. It could never have been long enough, but it was sufficiently long to change our city and our nation for the better, sufficiently long to have provided fuller lives for thousands and inspiration for thousands more, including those of us here today. Max's life will remain forever our blessing.

My impressionistic take on Max Starkloff leaves me anxious to know more, to know when he decided to give his life to improving the lives of the disabled, to understand better his trials, his disappointments, his ups and downs along the way that most of us humans know well; I'd like to learn more about those close to him, his wife, Colleen, their children, parents, and siblings. I feel the same way about Abraham Lincoln. Most of us have heroes. Maybe if I understood how Max came to be the Max that I remember, I could even make my own life better.

I am thrilled that his friend and mine, Charles E. Claggett Jr., a person who worked closely with Max in his later years and chaired his board, decided to write a knowledgeable and in-depth story of Max's life and history. Charlie is observant, perceptive, and a gifted writer. We are fortunate.

I believe that this book will give its readers the same inspiration that so caught those of us who knew Max during his life. Thus, the Starkloff influence will live on through the work of Charlie Claggett.

·Author's Note·

Istarted working with Max Starkloff late in life, when I was in my fifties and he was in his sixties. In many ways, I can say that I spent a half century of my life preparing for that encounter. And my dad helped me do it.

I am the son of the late Charles E. Claggett Sr., who, for a decade beginning in the late 1950s, was president and chair of the Gardner Advertising Company, a St. Louis agency with offices in New York, Hollywood, and six European cities. Though Gardner no longer exists, it is legendary, in large measure because of my dad. He worked for Gardner for thirty-seven years, pioneering the concept of market research, which he applied to promoting products as disparate as Ralston Purina cereal and dog food and Jack Daniel's whiskey. Those of you of a certain age may remember his ad for Purina Dog Chow, with the tagline "So complete, all you add is love."

Most people would say that my dad suffered from a disability. But *suffered* is absolutely the wrong word. Dad contracted polio when he was five years old. Even so, he never thought of himself as crippled, handicapped, or in the current parlance, disabled. The disease nearly destroyed the muscles in his legs. But there he was as an adolescent climbing the flagpole in front of his house using only his arms. When Dad reached the top, he would hold his legs out parallel to the ground. He went on to captain the gymnastics team at Princeton, specializing in the flying rings and rope climb.

Dad was slated to be on the U.S. team in the 1932 Los Angeles Summer Olympics. But officials disqualified him, saying his disability gave him an advantage over the other able-bodied competitors because he had less weight in his lower body to hoist in such events as the rope climb.

There was nothing my dad couldn't do . . . or so it seemed to me when I was growing up. My dad would tell me about the time he would sit on a mat and go into a handstand by pulling his legs through his arms. And I would say with great childlike authority, "That can't be done." And he would say, "OK, I'll show you."

At this point, my dad was about forty years old, a chain-smoker, and no longer fit as an Olympian. Nevertheless, I watched as he took his cane, made his way to the living room, removed his tie, put his hands on the floor, and went into a handstand just as he had described. As all the cigarettes and pens fell out of his pant and shirt pockets, I was thinking, "Wow."

Dad was my hero. But not so much that he could keep me from being an indifferent student. Actually, a very bad student. I went to the same private prep school that Dad attended, St. Louis Country Day School, and I flunked out of the seventh grade. By then I was pretty well convinced that I was dumb as a rock. Of course, it didn't occur to me that if I studied just a little bit, I might get better grades. It wasn't until my parents sent me off to boarding school (Suffield Academy in Connecticut), with its structured environment, that I thrived. I later attended the University of Denver (DU), where I studied radio, television, and film.

By then I no longer felt stupid. In fact, I was pretty full of myself. After graduation from DU, I didn't know what I wanted to do except that I didn't want to follow in the footsteps of the legendary Charlie Claggett.

I remember sitting at home on the porch the summer after graduation with my feet up on a table when my dad approached:

"What are you going to do with the rest of your life?"

"Well, Dad," I said, putting my hands behind my head. "I think I'm going to take it easy for a while and think about it."

"Well, that's a good idea. But you aren't going to do it here."

"What do you mean?"

"We're done here," Dad said. "I paid for you, and now you have to go out on your own and earn your own living."

"Well, like when?"

"Like right now."

I moved to Boston, where I got my first job with a local film company, and one or two years later I moved back to St. Louis, where I started my career as a copywriter at D'Arcy Advertising in 1972, following in my dad's footsteps. Twenty-seven years later, I had worked my way up to managing director and chief creative officer. Like Gardner, D'Arcy had a storied history of its own, starting with its first account, Coca-Cola, in 1906, and adding Anheuser-Busch in 1914. In 1979 I had the good fortune to be an associate creative director at D'Arcy when Anheuser-Busch needed a new campaign for Budweiser beer. I was part of the team that created "This Bud's for you" and helped develop the campaign and the commercials that launched it.

D'Arcy enjoyed a seventy-nine-year relationship with Anheuser-Busch, but in 1994, our agency lost the Budweiser account, and many of us moved on. I began writing a novel. And it was around 2003 that Max Starkloff got in touch with me. Max and I had known of each other through my dad. Charles Claggett Sr. was one of the first board members of Paraquad, the organization Max founded to advocate for, and serve, people with disabilities.

I am sure Max got all the valuable marketing advice he needed from Charles Sr. until Dad's death in 1998 and so had no need of my services. I was proud of Dad for his work, and sympathetic toward it, but up to that point I never took much of an interest in the disability rights effort that Max was leading here, nationwide, and worldwide.

In 2003, Max and his wife, Colleen, reached out to me at the suggestion of my cousin, Dr. William H. Danforth. Danforth told the Starkloffs, who were starting a new nonprofit, that they needed another infusion from the Claggett bloodline.

Now that you know my story, you will understand why Max Starkloff's story resonated so strongly for me. Those in the literary world say that readers will identify with characters who are at once relatable and exotic. Relatable in that the characters have traits that you can identify with. Exotic in that they possess superhuman powers that you only wish you could have. Mixing the two can be intoxicating.

Here was a man who in many ways was so much like me . . . and my dad. Like me, Max was an indifferent student in his youth, fun loving, and a bit full of himself. Like my dad, Max was indefatigable. Maybe even more so. Here was a man who lost the use of all his limbs in a car accident at age twenty-two. When he emerged from an institution sixteen years after his accident, he was able to create an organization that enabled thousands of other disabled individuals to escape institutionalization, reclaim self-esteem and dignity, and live independently. What Max accomplished was as improbable to me as the little miracle my dad performed on the living room floor with his handstand.

Every reader brings his or her own biography to a book. I wouldn't have written this one if I didn't think there was something in your life, everyone's life, that could relate to Max. He is as ordinary as any one of us, and yet extraordinary in what he accomplished.

As you read, you will find that Max had to muster massive amounts of grit and willpower to accomplish what he did. But you will also find that he did so in large measure so that he could have what many of us have and sometimes take for granted—a wife, children, a pet, a nice house, and a job to go to and to come home from. How he got there and helped so many others get there is a remarkable story that I have spent nearly a decade compiling.

You may consider me a biased narrator. I am the chair of the board of the Starkloff Disability Institute, after all. But I am going to assert that this work is not hagiography—an uncritical account that treats the subject with undue reverence. Max wouldn't have wanted that. His body of work includes false starts, digressions, and failures, as well as grand successes. On a personal level, friends and family could tell you that he could at times be more than difficult, while also being a visionary to whom it was impossible to say no. For me, that makes the tale all the more compelling. Perfect people are boring subjects.

In sharing this account, I am indebted to Max's mother, the late Hertha Starkloff, who, while spending so much of the latter part of her life caring for Max, wrote a detailed manuscript that allowed me to re-create key moments in Max's life. Other scenes are drawn from detailed interviews that I conducted with Max before his death and with other members of Max's family (most particularly his wife, Colleen; sister, Lecil; and brother, Carl), his friends, and the professionals who provided personal assistance or worked alongside him as he helped shape the history of the Disability Rights Movement.

So here is Max, as I knew him, and as his family, co-workers, and those who are both disabled and nondisabled knew him. The imperfect, yet remarkable, Max.

This book is dedicated to mothers of children with disabilities.

·INTRODUCTION·

On August 9, 1959, twenty-one-year-old Max Starkloff's world was one of pretty women, race cars, sports, parties, and fun. Handsome, athletic, and six feet five inches tall, Max was a charmer. With humor and a smile, he could almost always get his way. Everyone liked him. His peers respected him. Girls adored him.

On August 10, Max awoke to a different world. After his accident, as a "C3 through C5 quadriplegic," he entered a world of ignorance, prejudice, isolation, and discrimination. The medical community believed a spinal cord injury of this magnitude would certainly result in death in just days or months, and they behaved accordingly. A Catholic priest gave Max the last rites. If he lived, he was destined for a lifetime of institutionalization.

There was little assistive technology in 1959. Rudimentary electric wheelchairs, but no computers, no touch-tone telephones. Sidewalk ramps, or curb cuts, were nonexistent, as were public accommodations of any kind for anyone on wheels. An eight-inch curb or step was as effective a barrier to a person in a wheelchair as an eight-foot wall.

The only public laws regarding people with disabilities were designed to discriminate, such as Chicago's Municipal Code 36-34, which forbade anyone with a deformity "to be allowed in or on the public ways or other public places in this city." The common attitude at the time was that people with disabilities were "non-

MAX, SUMMER 1956.

people," helpless, better off dead, and as such were to be hidden from public view, confined to institutions, pitied, or ridiculed. At one time, Max's sister quietly prayed that God would take him and spare him a life "as a vegetable."

The only jobs available for disabled people were mindless, menial work in "sheltered workshops" that paid far below what non-disabled workers received for performing similar tasks. This was the world Max and other people with disabilities faced in 1959, a world where his chances of living a "normal life" were about the same as landing on the moon.

Decades later, Max's world would include a beautiful wife and three children, a nice house, and a high-profile job. He died on

December 27, 2010, at age seventy-three, having lived more than a half century beyond the automobile accident. But he was more than a survivor. At his memorial service on January 4, 2011, at Saint Francis Xavier College Church in St. Louis, he was remembered as one of the country's leading disability rights activists. Max's life story is the history of the Disability Rights Movement. This is his story and the story of millions of people with disabilities in the twentieth century.

• CHAPTER 1 •

"PRAY OUT LOUD"

Jim Morrison was driving home from a party in Defiance, Missouri. It was about 11 p.m. on a hot August night as he drove his parents' 1950 Plymouth four-door along the dark, winding country road. The windows were open, and Chuck Berry was singing his new hit song "Maybelline" on the AM radio.

Jim, twenty-two, had left the party early along with a number of others because he had to get to his summer job in St. Louis the next morning. He was between semesters at Parks College, where he was finishing his engineering degree. He drove down a hill and slowed for a sharp turn at the bottom when his headlight beams illuminated his friend Patty Wilkerson running on the side of the road toward his car waving her arms. She wobbled, wearing only one shoe, and looked frantic. Then he saw the overturned car, a 1959 Austin-Healey Sprite, his friend Max's car. Its headlights were still on, pointing at a weird angle off into the trees. He quickly slowed and pulled over about thirty feet from the car, leaving his high beams on. The Sprite, a convertible, was lying upside down at a right angle to the road. Patty, Max's passenger, had been thrown free and, miraculously, was unharmed. She was sobbing, shaking uncontrollably as Jim ran to help his friend. "He ca- . . . can't move," she cried. "I tried to help him."

Jim got down on his knees and peered under the car. He could see Max's body underneath, pushed beyond the driver's seat into the back of the small car. "Max, are you all right?" Jim asked.

"I can't feel a thing," came his friend's whispered reply.

Without thinking, Jim, a stocky 175-pound, former high school linebacker, squatted on the driver's side and started to lift the nearly 1,500-pound sports car. He managed to raise it eight inches off the ground, then realized he couldn't put it down without crushing his friend. "Then I really got scared," he remembered, "and just kept lifting.[1] I got it up on its side where it was stable. Max was hanging down, and he just sort of spilled out." Max, lucid throughout, remembered rolling out on his face and not being able to breathe. He was afraid he would suffocate. He heard someone say, "Roll him over."

"I grabbed him by the shoulders," Jim said, "and dragged him away from the car to the side of the road." Jim had been working during the summer as a lifeguard at a St. Louis hotel and had taken first aid training. "I remember pinching Max's hand and asking him if he could feel it, and he kept saying no. He was calm and coherent the whole time. I knew what it meant. I tried to keep his body straight, and keep him from going into shock. I put my jacket over him to keep him warm and tried to keep him awake and talking."

The Missouri State Highway Patrol received the call at 11:15 p.m., and Trooper Roy Bergman arrived at the scene forty minutes later. Max had been lying on the road for almost an hour. "I remember how I thought about the two young adults apparently enjoying the evening in a cute little sports car," Trooper Bergman recalled forty-five years later, "and how it all stopped with this tragic event."

Mary Ann Lubbe, one of Max's friends, arrived on the scene moments ahead of the Highway Patrol. She remembered how "Max kept saying, 'Pray out loud. Pray out loud.'" Mary Ann and Max were both devout Catholics. Other people from the party started arriving. According to Mary Ann, "People were pulling their cars off the road, hopping out, and running around yelling, crying, or just staring off into space." She remembered seeing Dr. Emmet Kelly, the host of the party, directing traffic, intoxicated. He was wearing powder blue Bermuda shorts and a Hawaiian shirt. "I felt I had to keep talking to Max," Mary Ann said, "so I held his hand and kept praying . . . Hail Marys, the Act of Contrition, anything I could think of. It seemed like days went by before the ambulance arrived. And Max just kept saying, 'Pray out loud. Pray out loud.'"

The ambulance medics, careful to keep Max's head, neck, and back in the same position, gently rolled him onto a board. They placed rolled towels on either side of his head, neck, and torso, then pulled belts tightly across his head and body, immobilizing him. The ambulance left for St. Joseph's Hospital in St. Charles. Mary Ann accompanied Max in the ambulance. Nearly fifty years later, she still remembered the sound of the siren on that long, dark ride: "For years after the accident, every time I heard sirens, my mouth would dry up."

Max's friends followed the ambulance from the scene of the accident and were piling out of their cars as Max was being wheeled into the emergency room. "I went right in there with him," Mary Ann said. "Dr. Kelly, in his Bermuda shorts and Hawaiian shirt, began ordering the hospital staff around as if he was in charge, but the hospital staff didn't know who he was, much less that he was a doctor. I remember thinking how funny he looked with his little bird legs. They're looking at him with this expression, 'Who the hell are you?'"

At some point during the confusion in the emergency room, Dr. Kelly had the presence of mind to ask Mary Ann to call Max's

1959 NATIONAL DODGE AMBULANCE. PHOTO COURTESY OF TONY KARSNIA.

mother, Hertha. Bravely, Mary Ann went to the phone. It was approximately 12:45 a.m. "Mrs. Starkloff, there's been an accident, and Max has been hurt. We're at St. Joseph's Hospital in St. Charles, and Dr. Kelly is here. You should come immediately." Hertha Starkloff was jolted awake. "I'll be there," she said. It was her fifty-third birthday.

When Mary Ann returned to the emergency room, plans had changed. "Call Mrs. Starkloff and tell her we're going to St. Mary's," barked Dr. Kelly. St. Joseph's was not equipped to handle spinal cord injuries. Mary Ann rushed back to the pay phone and reached Max's mother before she and Max's nineteen-year-old sister, Lecil, had left to make the forty-minute drive to the hospital. "I remember," Max said later, "the hospital people asking *me* where I wanted to go. I didn't know which hospitals treated people with spinal cord injuries and which didn't, and apparently they didn't either, so I chose St. Mary's because my uncle was a doctor there."

AT ST. MARY'S HOSPITAL

Hertha and Lecil Starkloff met the ambulance when it arrived at St. Mary's. It was 1:30 a.m. Two and one-half hours had elapsed since the accident. Hertha had made two calls before leaving home. One was to her best friend, Martha Engler, who agreed to meet her at the hospital. The other was to her brother-in-law, Dr. Max Starkloff. Dr. Starkloff, fifty-six years old at the time, was an internist at St. Mary's and an instructor in internal medicine at Saint Louis University, where he earned his M.D. in 1931.

A large man with an impressive résumé and heritage, Dr. Starkloff was the grandson of Dr. Max C. Starkloff, St. Louis's revered health commissioner from 1895 to 1933. During the great influenza epidemic of 1918, one of history's most deadly epidemics, the elder Starkloff, along with U.S. health officials, watched as the flu killed hundreds of thousands of people in Europe, then moved across the Atlantic and began its deadly sweep across Boston, Philadelphia, New York, and Chicago. Starkloff persuaded St. Louis mayor Henry W. Kiel to declare an emergency and grant the health commissioner exceptional powers. When the flu arrived in St. Louis, Starkloff made an unprecedented move: He shut the city down. Schools, theaters, public transit, and all nonessential businesses were closed until further notice. He was visited by groups of angry businessmen who predicted economic disaster, but he remained firm. When the epidemic had run its course, Chicago and

MAX C. STARKLOFF, M.D. HALFTONE PHOTO-
GRAPH, 1900. FROM NOTABLE ST. LOUISANS.
MISSOURI HISTORY MUSEUM LIBRARY.

Kansas City had lost half their populations. St. Louis's death toll was the lowest in the country for a city of its size: 3,641.

Dr. Max C. Starkloff died in 1942. His grandson and namesake, Dr. Max Starkloff, was not without influence in St. Louis, and particularly at St. Mary's Hospital. At approximately 1 a.m. on Monday, he proceeded to call the best specialists in the city. When his nephew arrived at St. Mary's Hospital at 1:30 a.m., the emergency staff was ready and waiting.

"It was a totally different scene from St. Joseph's," Max recalled. He remembered a heavyset nurse who was also a nun running alongside as they wheeled him in. "Ceiling lights were pass-

Dr. Max Starkloff, "Uncle Max," who
treated Max the night of the
accident, shown here with his wife,
Ardath, ca. 1965.

ing overhead. It was like the opening of *Ben Casey*." Then the cart
stopped and his mother and sister came into view.

"Mother, I goofed," said Max.

"Don't worry, Max. You're here now. Everything's going to be
OK," Hertha said.

Someone wheeled Max away. Hertha realized she and Lecil
were gripping hands.

"Come on, Mother, sit down," said Lecil, taking her arm.

In the emergency room, Max remembered seeing his uncle
talking with three other doctors. He saw a wood drill and felt a
numbness in his head. A priest was called in to give him the last

rites. "I don't need those," said Max. The priest replied, "We'll do it just as a precaution."

But Max said he knew better. "Back then, it meant death."

To stabilize his spinal column, two holes were drilled into Max's skull, one on either side, in order to attach Crutchfield tongs. The tongs enabled doctors to gently decompress Max's vertebrae by connecting the top of his skull to a rope attached to a twenty-five-pound weight at the head of his bed. His inert body was laid out on a Stryker frame, a large canvas structure that stabilizes the spine and permits the patient to be turned every two hours to prevent bedsores. The frame, new at the time and built for a person of average height, was too short for the six-foot five-inch Max, causing his feet to stick out beyond the end. It would have to do.

At about 3 a.m., Dr. Starkloff and three doctors approached Hertha and Lecil in the waiting room. Starkloff introduced Dr. Edmund Smolik, a neurosurgeon. Known in the hospital as "the Doctor," Smolik was usually trailed by two interns, who he introduced to Hertha as his assistants, Dr. Henry Lattinville and Dr. Francis Nash. "This is bad, Mrs. Starkloff," Smolik said. "The first

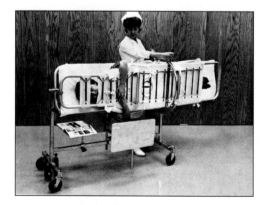

STRYKER FRAME, CA. 1959.
PHOTO COURTESY OF STRYKER.

X-rays show partial dislocation of the third, fourth, and fifth cervical vertebrae. He's paralyzed from the neck down. We rarely see someone with this type of spinal cord injury survive longer than a few days."

Dr. Smolik considered three factors in his prognosis: the location of the lesion, the extent of the lesion, and the patient's age. While the X-rays that Smolik and his associates reviewed at the time showed dislocation of the vertebrae, what the technology could not reveal was the degree to which the spinal cord itself had been affected. Whether it had been partially or completely severed could only be determined by watching Max over the next few days to determine his range of feelings and movements or by doing a laminectomy, a procedure where portions of one or more vertebrae are removed in order to decompress the spine and expose the spinal cord for visual inspection. Advocated by some neurosurgeons and shunned by others, it was considered a risky procedure because the patient's neck had to be hyperextended while in traction in order to pass a catheter through the larynx to provide enough oxygen to prevent permanent brain damage. It was also shown in many studies to render little improvement if the spinal cord had been cut.[2] Smolik thought it best to wait and observe Max.

The third factor, Max's age, was the only thing he had going for him. Being only twenty-one years old improved his chances for survival. What Smolik feared most, however, was pneumonia or respiratory failure, as the nerves that control the diaphragm lie in the second, third, and fourth cervical vertebrae.[3] The higher up the spine the cord is severed, the more muscles and internal organs are affected, as they no longer can send and receive impulses from the brain. If the nerves to the diaphragm were damaged or severed, it would mean that Max's breathing would become shallow and vulnerable to total failure, causing outright suffocation, pneumonia, or permanent brain damage due to lack of oxygen.

For the time being, Dr. Smolik had stabilized Max and done everything he could. Now, whether Max lived or died would depend on Max. His system had gone into spinal cord shock, a condition during which all sensory, motor, and involuntary functions below the level of the lesion are suspended.[4] It would be several weeks before anyone could know the true extent of Max's injury, if he lived that long.

Hertha fought through the numbness to pull herself together. "Have you called Carl yet?" asked Dr. Starkloff. Carl was Max's brother, who was studying to be a priest at Regis College in Denver. Four years older than Max, he had decided to join the Jesuits in 1952 and was preparing to work in a Catholic mission on an Indian reservation in Wyoming. Carl remembered being roused out of bed early in the morning to take an important phone call. He took the call at a pay phone in the hallway. He heard his mother's voice: "Carl, Max has been in a terrible automobile accident. The doctors don't think he will live." Carl said nothing for a long while. He felt faint.

"Wait a minute, Mother, I have to sit down." He sat on the floor to collect himself. Then he said quietly, "I'll be home tomorrow." The normally reserved young novice hung up the phone and felt a surge of anger. "That fuckin' sports car!" he yelled.

Max's father, Carl E., also arrived that morning. His second wife, Lee, recalled that it was about 3 a.m. and that Carl received "a formal greeting" from Hertha. "She didn't want him there at all." Hertha had divorced Carl in 1953 when Max was fifteen years old. How long Carl stayed or whether he even saw Max is not known.

MAX'S FATHER, CARL E. STARKLOFF, CA. 1967–1968.

THE SECOND DAY

Hertha and Lecil made their second visit to the hospital later the morning of August 10, expecting the worst. They were greeted by a hospital now in full swing: nurses in crisp white uniforms wheeling carts, doctors conferring in white lab coats with stethoscopes sticking out of their pockets, nuns in full habit, and staff moving quietly around them under bright florescent lights. The distinctive hospital smell of disinfectant assaulted their nostrils. They noticed none of it. Max had been moved from the emergency room into one of the small hospital rooms on the intensive care floor. Upon reaching the room, the two women paused outside the door, knowing that the next few moments would require every ounce of strength they had. They looked briefly at each other, took deep breaths, and stepped inside.

Max was lying face up on what looked like a canvas frame suspended between poles on wheels. Above his head was a mirror positioned so he could see people in the room. Large prongs, attached to the sides of his partially shaved head, connected via a rope to a twenty-five-pound weight hanging at the head of the frame. His arms were outstretched on separate tables on either side. Small sandbags had been placed, one in each hand, to keep them from curling. A suction tube entered his nose from a large bottle next to the bed.

Hertha and Lecil, not wishing to convey any sense of panic or alarm, greeted Max in the same calm voices they might use at a church social: upbeat, chirpy, and melodious. "Good morning, Maxim. How are you feeling this morning?" "Fine," came a whispered reply. The two women moved into the small room cautiously, so as not to disturb any of the equipment. Trying not to look nervous, they adjusted themselves, smiled, and kept their chins up. "I can't see you," said Max, "unless you lean over me."

At this point, Max still believed his condition was temporary. "When you don't have pain, you don't realize how serious it is," Max would tell his mother weeks later. "You naturally think it's only temporary. I was scared, but I wouldn't let myself think about it for fear I might give up." While no one had told Max that he had only a few more days to live, he began to sense, as the day wore on, the seriousness of his injury by the way the doctors, nurses, and everyone else acted around him. That morning, however, the combination of hearing his mother's and sister's cheery voices, as well as his own constant reassurances that his condition was only temporary, boosted his spirits.

After a few more pleasantries, he stared up at them, then asked, "Mother, will you scratch my nose?" Hertha scratched it without thinking. She recalled later: "A friend came to see me, and as I walked out of Max's room, I suddenly realized that *I had had to scratch his nose because he could not.* 'Emily,' I said to my friend slowly, explaining the situation to her so that I myself would understand better, 'He couldn't scratch himself. I had to scratch his nose.' He had asked me to do it so casually. The sobs must have come. I don't remember. I only remember [Emily's] arms around me."

The second threat to Max's life was revealed to Hertha and Lecil that morning. One of the nurses, after positioning Max's arms along his sides, carefully placed what looked like a catcher's mask without the screen on Max's face, securing it with elastic bands over his ears and around the back of his head. Then she placed a large canvas frame, similar to the one upon which Max was lying, over Max, placing his face in the hole. She then strapped the top frame to the bottom frame, forming something like a sandwich with Max immobilized in the middle. Once everything was secure, she stood at the foot of the bed and rotated the frame along the long axis of his body to position Max on his stomach, and then she locked it in place.

The Crutchfield tongs, rope, and twenty-five-pound weight providing traction at the center of the axis at the head of the bed would remain stationary. When facedown, Max could look only at the floor through the hole in the canvas, his head supported and cushioned by the padded mask. The nurse then removed the top frame and set it aside, then proceeded to examine and massage Max's heels, buttocks, and back.

Max would be turned, or "rotisserized" as he came to call it, every two hours every day and night for thirty-nine days, approximately 468 times while in traction. When Hertha asked why her son had to be turned every two hours, she was told it was to prevent bedsores. A bedsore, or decubitis ulcer, can develop in a matter of hours. Common to people who can't move, the sore is caused by bone pushing against a surface, such as a bed or chair, cutting off the blood flow to the skin. The tissue dies, and an open wound develops. If left unchecked, it continues to enlarge and fester. Before penicillin, pressure sores killed quadriplegics within days. Even with penicillin, a wide-open sore could take months to heal and was always prone to infection.

The third deadly condition for people with spinal cord injuries is bladder and kidney complications. Explained to Hertha by Dr. Edward Cannon, Max's urologist, Max's catheter would have to be flushed twice a day. His urinary output was being measured and maintained by his drinking prescribed amounts of various liquids. He was being given laxatives and enemas to ensure a regular bowel. And he was being fed a diet high in protein and vitamins with an appropriate caloric content. From now on, all bodily functions would be monitored, measured, recorded, and appraised. Food in. Waste out.

Hertha and Lecil began to learn the rhythm of the busy hospital. Max was turned. Dr. Starkloff stopped by frequently, reassuring Hertha that everything possible was being done. Drs. Smolik, Lattinville, and Nash "moved among us as ghosts," Hertha recalled. "One of them was always there. My reaction toward them varied from hour to hour: gratitude, supplication, anger."

Hertha quickly forbade any discussion of Max's case in his presence. "I told them his personality must not be hurt in any way, and they never said a word. They let me be haughty; I suppose they saw with experienced eyes the hidden plea in that last sentence, which really said, 'Protect his personality. Keep his thinking straight. Please, please let nothing happen to the real Max.'" Hertha and Lecil struggled to keep up lively chatter and appearances. Hertha was determined not to let Max cross the thin line that separated hope from self-pity.

By the first afternoon, more of Max's friends had heard the news. Patty Wilkerson arrived late in the morning. "After the accident, I just wanted to be there," Patty said. "Max and I had a bond." While Max and Patty had never dated, they had been good friends since childhood. "On arriving at the hospital, I was scared. Like, what do you say? But when I saw Max, we just picked up and we were two kids talking about kid things. It was important to be together." Patty spent hours lying under Max's bed.

"I'm sorry," said Max. "I'm sorry I goofed." He had nearly killed them both. The day of the accident, Max had been racing his Sprite at a gymkhana in Washington, Missouri, sponsored by the Sports Car Club of America. He had removed the mandatory roll bar just before driving to the party, and neither he nor Patty had used seat belts that night. Ironically, had they been wearing seat belts, Patty would most likely have been killed or paralyzed. "We had not even been drinking," Patty explained. "We were going so slow, Louie Meddler passed us, and I remember saying, 'Those guys are so drunk. They are in trouble.' Then *we* were in trouble."

Mary Ann Lubbe also visited Max that afternoon. "In going to visit, I never knew what to say." She did find someone who was entirely self-possessed at Max's bedside, however: Hertha. Mary Ann and many of Max's friends did not know the half of Hertha's story, but it goes a long way in explaining how Hertha responded

HERTHA STARKLOFF IN 1935.

with both equanimity and passion to Max's plight. It also illu-
minates how Max found the strength to endure, persevere, and,
ultimately, thrive.

•CHAPTER 2•

MAD MAX

Hertha Beck was born in New York City in 1906. She had worked hard for a degree in journalism at the University of Missouri but quit before graduating. It was during the Great Depression, shortly after the stock market crash of 1929, when she met Max's father, Carl E. Starkloff. Carl was a bright, charming, young attorney fresh out of Saint Louis University law school and brimming with optimism. He swept Hertha off her feet and married her on June 1, 1931. The couple lived in St. Louis, where he worked as a trial lawyer and she as a secretary at Pevely Dairy.

In 1936, Carl accepted a part-time position with the Binkley Manufacturing Company, and they moved to Warrenton, Missouri, a rural farming community of about twelve hundred people located fifty-eight miles west of St. Louis. By then they had a three-year-old son, whom they named Carl. Max followed on September 18, 1937, and then Lecil was born three years later on April 18, 1940.

Smart and attractive, the young Starkloff couple made friends easily in Warrenton, and Hertha settled into a small-town life of raising children and keeping house. While Warrenton was close enough to the St. Louis area to receive its newspapers and radio signals, it was quite rural. The main street was about five blocks long and went down a hill, ending at the Binkley plant. Founded in 1934 by Carl Starkloff's longtime friend Bill Binkley, Binkley Manufacturing quickly became a leader in roll forming, a process in shaping steel parts.

The house at 402 Walton Street in Warrenton was built by Carl E. Starkloff.

Young Carl remembered his life in Warrenton as being a lot like the life depicted in the book *To Kill a Mockingbird*. It was a simple life. He remembered his family as being poor. His father often was paid in produce, since his clients were poor also. Carl remembered eating a lot of fresh fruits and vegetables, which his mom always had in plentiful supply. Candy was a special treat because it was expensive. The children usually wore no shoes in the summer and ran around with little supervision. The kids played baseball all summer, encouraged by their father, who once played professionally. Hertha had young Carl and Max baptized as Evangelical Lutheran in 1939 in her mother's St. Louis apartment. They never attended a Lutheran church, but they attended a Methodist church until 1945.

Max had fond memories of life at 402 Walton Street in Warrenton. At age four, and dressed only in his underpants, he and Lecil (then aged two) drove a car belonging to one of their parents'

CARL E. STARKLOFF IN 1935.

friends through a neighboring field and into the neighbor's house. This may have started Max's love of cars and driving. When Max was nine, he and a friend climbed aboard a train as it lumbered by their house and took a trip to Truesdale, a town one and a half miles away. They walked home and never told their moms about it.

Up the road, the Bebermeiers, who owned the drugstore in town, had a field on which grazed a bull. Max remembered going to see the bull when he was two. The bull charged. Seeing it all happen as if in a nightmare, Hertha ran out to save her son, but she wasn't fast enough. She watched as the bull ran toward little Max, then stopped abruptly just inches from him, looked at him for a minute, then turned away.

Lecil remembered being as young as two and a half and walking all over town with her "big brother Max," who was at that time all of five years old. She said that Max was very protective.

TOP: LECIL AND MAX IN 1942.
BOTTOM: LECIL AND HERTHA, DATE UNKNOWN.

She remembered Warrenton as being very safe: "We would walk into town to the Vita Theatre to see a movie, and walk home at night when it was dark. Other than seeing ghosts and goblins, I was never afraid."

HARD TIMES

By 1947, the Starkloffs' "idyllic life" in small-town Warrenton had begun to turn sour. At the age of nine, Max saw his father slap his mother during an argument. He had seen them fight before, and he knew his father sometimes came home drunk. Carl, Max, and Lecil learned that their father would sometimes act like two different people. "He could be very loving and supportive," recalled Lecil. "He enjoyed history and politics, and loved to play sports. He was funny, and a good cook." "He could be very funny and charming," noted Carl, "and good hearted." But, as Lecil added, "We knew they were always having problems. He was not a good provider. He didn't know how to save money. And there was always the drinking and the women."

Max was ten years old in 1947 when his mother was diagnosed with breast cancer. He had been attending the public school in Warrenton for four years. He and Lecil were sent to spend the summer with their great-grandmother, Genevieve Baldwin Starkloff, in St. Louis. Genevieve and Dr. Max Carl Starkloff, the former St. Louis health commissioner, acted more as grandparents to young Carl, Max, and Lecil. Dr. Max Starkloff's only daughter, Adele, married Dan O'Madigan around 1901 and had three sons, Max (Uncle Max, also a doctor, who treated young Max after the accident), Dan, and Carl (Max's father). When Adele's husband, Dan, died an early death, she fell into frail health and sent Max and Carl to live with her parents, who later

THREE GENERATIONS OF STARKLOFFS, CA. 1912: DR. MAXIMILIAN CARL STARKLOFF, ST. LOUIS HEALTH COMMISSIONER (SECOND FROM L) WITH HIS DAUGHTER, ADELE O'MADIGAN, AND HER THREE SONS (L TO R), MAX, CARL, AND DAN. DR. STARKLOFF'S FATHER, DR. HUGO MAXIMILIAN VON STARKLOFF, IS IN THE CENTER OF THE PHOTO. YOUNG MAX AND CARL WOULD LIVE WITH THEIR GRANDFATHER, THE HEALTH COMMISSIONER.

changed the boys' last names from O'Madigan to Starkloff (see Family Tree, page 370).

Lecil stayed with Max at her great-grandmother's house while her mother was in the hospital with breast cancer. "Our grandmother was very hard on Max," Lecil recalled. "One hot day, we went out to play in the rain. As we were used to doing in Warrenton, we took off all our clothes and went out to dance in the rain in our underwear. Seeing us, our grandmother became very angry and took it out on Max." Lecil, already close to Max, remembered this moment as one that drew them even closer together. When Hertha recovered, they returned to Warrenton. She had her right breast removed, plus the lymph nodes under her right arm. Typically, she never complained.

By 1948, Hertha and her children had been brought into the Catholic Church by the Reverend Joseph McMahon, SJ, who had helped see her through her battle with breast cancer. She had wanted her children to attend Catholic schools, so she moved Max and Lecil from the Warrenton public school to St. Mary's school in Hawk Point. Max started in the sixth grade. Carl was ready for high school, so she sent him to Saint Louis University High School (SLUH) in St. Louis. To do this required having Carl live with the Starkloff grandparents.

Thinking that it might benefit their marriage, Hertha and Carl decided to build another house, this time in a St. Louis subdivision called Oakbrook Forest. But life did not get better for the Starkloffs even as they moved into their new home in 1949. Max, now eleven years old, having spent only six months at St. Mary's school, had to move to another new school, St. Joseph school in Clayton, Missouri, a suburb of St. Louis. This was the same year that Hertha endured another bout with breast cancer and had her left breast removed. Meanwhile, Carl Starkloff Sr.'s alcoholism and womanizing worsened while he continued to squander the family's money.

By 1950, anticipating financial ruin, Hertha had taken a part-time job in the real-estate firm Spalding Kennedy. Max continued to struggle. That fall as his brother Carl started college at Saint Louis University, Max suffered the humiliation of seeing his friends go into the eighth grade while he had to repeat seventh. Conditions at home continued to worsen. Unable to afford their

MAX, A FAMILY FRIEND, LECIL, AND HERTHA AT THE DINNER TABLE,
MINOQUA, WISCONSIN, 1954.

new house in Oakbrook Forest, the family moved into another
home at 7140 Pershing.

Less than a year later in August 1952, young Carl left home
for good and entered the order of Jesuits at the age of nineteen.
An extremely strict order, the Jesuit policy dictated that novices
detach from their families. Carl would write home frequently
during his four years at the seminary in Florissant, Missouri, but
he remembered visiting his family only once. Carl looked back on
his first year with the Jesuits as "a turmoil," knowing what was
happening to his family at home.

By fall 1952, Carl Sr. and Hertha had separated. Carl moved
out. Hertha soldiered on. Max began his freshman year at Saint
Louis University High School. Two priests who taught at the

school, Father Bob Doyle and Father David Hagen, took a particular liking to young Max and helped him get through his freshman and sophomore years. But it was a struggle. "Max had such a
reputation in high school," recalled Gay Chadeayne. "If there was
trouble, he was in the middle of it."

DIVORCE AND A MOVE

Max was fifteen years old when his parents finally divorced in
early spring 1953 after twenty-two years of marriage. By the fall
of that year, desperate to cut expenses, Hertha sold the home at
7140 Pershing and moved herself, Max, and Lecil into a small
Dutch Colonial bungalow at 7217 Lindell. She had thirty-five
dollars in her bank account. She was now working full-time for a
different real-estate firm, Edward L. Bakewell. Carl Sr. married his
second wife, Lee, sometime late in 1953, not quite one year from
the date of his divorce. Marrying a second wife, unfortunately,
proved not to be the antidote to his alcoholism.

By his mid-sophomore year, Max was in a tailspin. Hertha,
feeling increasingly desperate, persuaded Max's brother Carl to
"get tough" with Max. Both Max and Carl had strong memories
of what happened next. Carl threatened to beat Max up if he didn't
study harder, and he did it so convincingly that Max started to
cry. Seeing this, Carl's pugilistic facade completely collapsed, and
both started to weep. All of it was to no avail: the special attention
from two teachers, his mother's pleading, his brother's threats. In
spring 1954, Max was asked to leave Saint Louis University High
School. He would have to enter the public school, University City
High, that fall.

Three of Max's friends at the time, Dan Nolan, Jack Lane, and
Dick Chappuis, had many memories of their high school years

Carl and Max at 7217 Lindell, ca. 1955.

with Max. "We were in the confessional all the time because of 'impure thoughts,'" Jack remembered. Dan recalled that, after a party at a friend's house, "we got hungry, and a whole bunch of us went to Lee's Grill. The place was packed and we couldn't get in. Roger started chasing the paperboy with scissors, and someone called the police. We were put in jail. Richard called his father, who said, 'I don't care if you rot there.' Finally at 11:30 the next morning we said, 'We gotta go to Mass,' so they let us out."

Jail was a frequent visiting spot for Max and his friends when they were fifteen and sixteen. Max reminisced about skinny-dipping at an exclusive country club: "As we were splashing around in the pool, somebody remembered that we'd left our wallets in the car, and when we ran to the car, there were the police—with our wallets!" The boys called their parents from jail. After coming to bail Max out, Hertha made him walk home.

Max hated University City High School. He looked down on his public school classmates. He missed his old pals at SLUH but continued to see them over the weekends. "We had a great group," remembered SLUH classmate Jim Morrison. "Gio's Bar was a favorite hangout. At Gio's, nobody carded anyone. If you could reach the bar, you could drink. There was an all-night store on Brentwood where we could buy a quart of beer for 25 cents, no questions asked." Cars were an obsession. "We used to drag race from Brentwood to McKnight," recalled Max, "on the Red Feather Express." It was the east-west highway that split the county and later became Interstate 64.

GROWING UP

In 1955 when Max graduated from University City High School, he stood six feet five inches and wore size 13 shoes. A year later, he

PFC MAX STARKLOFF, 1956.

enlisted in the Marines and spent the next three months in boot camp in San Diego. "He needed discipline," commented Lecil. "He was always looking for a father figure. The Marines gave Max structure, matured him, and Max liked it." Max admitted that "it was scary but fascinating." He met people from all walks of life. While in the Marines for two years, Max played Amateur Athletic Union basketball and become a karate instructor. "When Max got out of the Marine Corps," Jim Morrison added, "he was a lot more mature than a lot of us were. He was wild when he went in, and a lot tamer when he came back."

After leaving the corps in late April 1958, Max got a construction job as a laborer with Bangert Brothers Paving. It was hot, sweaty, dirty work, but it provided a paycheck. Once Max had earned his first or second paycheck, he bought a sports car, a used MG TD. He especially liked driving fast on winding roads. One thoroughfare, Litzsinger Road in the St. Louis suburb of Ladue, has a number of S turns. Max once crossed the double yellow line to take one turn on the inside and encountered an Alfa Romeo coming the opposite direction. The other driver, thinking faster than Max, swerved to his left and passed him on the wrong side of the line. Max hit a tree. The front of the sports car was pushed in, and after that the car tended to overheat. He took it to a dealer and sold it for eight hundred dollars.

In fall 1958, Max started night school at Saint Louis University to get a college degree. He quit his asphalt job and got a job as a stock boy in the local department store, Famous-Barr. A few months later in March 1959, he got a job at National Lead Company, a paint manufacturer. Impressed with young Max, managers told him he had a future with the company and offered to pay for his education if he would stay.

THE AUTHOR IN A 1959 AUSTIN-HEALEY SPRITE. MAX WOULD HAVE SAT
FOUR INCHES TALLER. CAR COURTESY OF PETER F. BENOIST.

Heady with success and looking forward to a bright future, Max
bought another sports car, a new Austin-Healey Sprite. Introduced
in May 1958, the Sprite was an inexpensive, no-frills two-seater
with a forty-three-horsepower engine and drum brakes, which,
according to some were "barely up to the task" of stopping the
car. The headlights, which sat on top of the hood, were originally
designed to retract, rotating under the hood so the smooth under-
side would face up and lie flush. In an effort to cut costs, however,
the retracting mechanism was eliminated, leaving the headlights
sitting up on the hood and giving the car a bug-eyed appearance.
It quickly became known as "the Bugeye."

Max outfitted the car with seat belts and a roll bar so he could
race in gymkhanas. There are very few Bugeyes around today. On
roads now clogged with hefty SUVs, the Bugeye looks more like a
toy than a real car. It is only eleven feet long, four and a half feet
wide, and two feet ten inches high. Given Max's height, he would
have towered eighteen inches above the top of the car. He took
great pride in his wheels.

Max's older brother, Carl, however, took an instant dislike to Max's taste in cars. "I always worried about those sports cars," he said. Hearing about Max buying a new sports car, Mike Sheridan, a Jesuit friend of Carl's, told him with spine-chilling foresight, "I think we're going to see that sports car with its wheels in the air. It scares me."

•CHAPTER 3•

MAX WILL SURVIVE

By the time of Max's accident, Hertha Starkloff had earned a reputation as a hardworking, effective real estate agent. She had survived two bouts with breast cancer; an abusive, alcoholic husband; and a divorce. Through her own strength of character and devout faith, she had pulled her life together in seven short years, working full-time, raising three children, and succeeding with no help from anyone outside the family.

Max's high school friends described her with awe. "She was a lioness. One gutsy lady. I really liked her," recalled Mary Britton. To Patty Wilkerson, she was "like a general in the army. She just kept paving the way." It was this woman who now focused her considerable resolve and faith on her hospitalized son, Maxim, who doctors said might live until the end of the week, at most.

"Hello, Hertha, Lecil," said Dr. Edward Cannon, entering Max's room the first day after the accident. Good-looking, tan, and always meticulously dressed, Cannon had once been a Starkloff neighbor. He had a booming baritone voice that could be heard everywhere, according to his daughter, Genie Cannon Newport, and he was always in a good mood. Forty-six years old and at the top of his game, Dr. Cannon was widely regarded as one of the finest urologists in the area. "How are you doing, Max?" He asked Hertha and Lecil to leave the room while he examined and flushed Max's catheter and dealt with his bowel. Years later, Max would say that Dr. Cannon would always ask about his bowel, "even when he saw me in a shopping center!"

Lacking feeling below the neck, the quadriplegic has no way of knowing when his or her bladder is full. Left untended, it will continue to fill until the urine it contains is forced out into bodily tissues, essentially transferring the body's waste into the bloodstream. When this happens, the result is severe kidney disease and, ultimately, kidney failure and death. As soon as Max's spine was stabilized, the neurosurgeons would have stepped aside and turned Max over to Dr. Cannon. He would have inserted a catheter, a painless process for Max. While catheters are effective in emptying the bladder, they are still foreign bodies rendering the bladder and urethra vulnerable to invasion by bacteria and subsequent infection. Max would use a catheter for the rest of his life.

Kidney and bladder stones were another threat. As Max's body chemistry reacted to the shutdown of his nervous system, it did not take long for his body's water content to go out of pH balance. Alkalinity would overcome acidity, causing the formation of stones in his kidneys, bladder, or both, stones that can cause outright kidney failure or further complicate the flow of urine from the body. Uremia (the accumulation of waste toxins in the blood) and pulmonary failure were then the leading causes of death among both para- and quadriplegics.[1]

Early the next morning, August 11, 1959, Hertha and Lecil met Sister Helen Holzum, also known as Sister Gerard Marie, for the first time. Sister Gerard was a physical therapist. She was from a large farming family in Leopold, Missouri. Max described her as "plain looking, a hearty farm girl." She stood five feet nine inches tall with dark hair and a broad face that framed a warm smile. She had large, bright eyes and an easygoing manner. When she applied her therapeutic skills, she was strong but gentle. She was

SISTER HELEN HOLZUM, AKA
SISTER GERARD MARIE.

extremely caring and spoke rapidly in a deep, soft voice. And she took an instant liking to Max.

One of Max's friends said to Hertha outside the room, "I hope you'll understand, Mrs. Starkloff, but Mother made me come down and see Max. I told her I'd rather see Max dead than paralyzed, but after you're with Max you know you're nuts for ever having thought that." That afternoon one of Max's friends, Dan Nolan, asked Hertha if she had called Max's girlfriend, Marty Carr, a Maryville University sophomore currently spending her summer vacation with her family in Chicago. Max had met Marty at a Kentucky Derby party in 1958, after he had gotten out of the Marines, and they had developed a serious relationship. Marty, at five foot three inches, and Max at six foot five, had made an interesting but handsome pair. A Shirley MacLaine look-alike, Marty was always noticed at parties. In all the confusion, Hertha had forgotten to call her. Dan, seeing Hertha's hesitation, volunteered to call her himself. A little later, he returned to tell Hertha, "She's coming down tomorrow."

Max's brother, Carl, arrived sometime that first afternoon, having traveled twenty-three hours by train from Denver. After greeting his mother and sister, he walked over to Max, knelt down, peered up into Max's face, and said, "Hi, Gertrude!"

"Hi, Ape!" came the response. "Are you here, too?"

"What a lousy way to get attention," chided Carl.

TOGETHER WITH MAX

The Starkloff family was finally together. Their ship had sunk beneath them, and now they had all found their way into the same lifeboat and clung to each other for strength. "So there I stood with all of my three children," Hertha recalled. "I was able to see what I had helped produce. Each one was thinking of the other; each moment had to be light so that no one would be the cause of any pain to anyone else. There was a feeling of security now because all of us were together."

Carl was telling his family about his trip home in a Pullman car, a luxury by Jesuit standards, when Max suddenly gasped, "I can't breathe!" Hertha went for help. Nurses instantly appeared and with practiced efficiency held an oxygen mask to his mouth and nose. Within minutes, Max's breathing became less labored.

The experience was a reminder to everyone in the room how helpless they all were. Hertha said later that she, Lecil, and Carl could only stand and watch, as if in a trance. No one became excited. "That was the amazing thing about this entire situation. You had confidence in Max; it was as simple as that. No matter what happened, you had confidence in God because Max did. You didn't let yourself get carried away by misfortune, because Max didn't." At one point, there were so many well-wishers flooding the hall outside Max's room that Dr. Max Starkloff took Hertha aside. At six feet four inches tall and 250 pounds, Starkloff towered over Hertha. "You've got to realize, Hertha, how serious this is. The doctors and nurses are doing everything they can, but there's a good chance that Max won't survive this. We have to have that room cleared for the medical staff." According to Lecil, Hertha took Dr. Starkloff by the arm and ushered him into a nearby stairwell. "And you've got to realize," she answered with a steely gaze, "that Max is going to survive. And furthermore, I don't want you to ever say that to me again. And certainly not to Max!"

When visiting hours were over, Max's friends slowly said their good-byes and left the hospital. The doctors had left for the evening, and Max and Hertha found themselves momentarily alone. Max said, "I know they don't expect me to live. But that doesn't mean you give up hope." Hertha told Max that a lot of people were praying for him. At the end of the day, as he would do each night until he returned to Regis College, Carl would kneel beside Max's bed, bow his head, and say his evening prayers with Max.

Marty arrived bright and early the following day. When she saw Max in traction, according to Hertha, "there were no tears, not an expression of alarm anywhere on her face. She was as the rest of us, just glad to be with the guy." Soon more friends arrived. Mary Britton brought her record player. Dan Nolan, Jack Lane, and Dick Chappuis arrived. And of course, Patty Wilkerson was there. Lecil remembered, "Max's friends just poured into the hospital. People would sit on the floor. Max loved John Philip Sousa marches, so we played them on Mary's record player. It was almost a party atmosphere all the time."

Each day, sometimes several times a day, Sister Gerard would exercise each of Max's limbs. First she would start with his arms, working from the shoulders down to his fingertips. Then she would go to work flexing his legs, feet, and toes. Her exercises were designed to restore function and prevent atrophy due to the absence of voluntary muscle contraction, and also to prevent contractures, or deformities of the joints. She would also take Max through a series of deep-breathing exercises several times every day to avoid pulmonary complications. Max, liking Sister Gerard and wanting to do whatever he could to improve his situation, cooperated with her in every way.

Between long bouts of physical therapy, rotisserizing, active bowel and bladder maintenance, and routine visits from nurses and doctors, Max was seldom alone. As word of the accident spread among Max's friends, they began to visit. "I always knew Max had many friends," recalled Hertha, "but I didn't know they mounted into the hundreds." "Especially girl friends," added Carl.

There was also an abundance of young Jesuit scholastics, friends of Max's and Carl's. Four or five Jesuits, or "Jebbies" as they were called, would visit Max every day. Max described them as "fabulous. They were young, funny, supportive; a joy to be around." At one point, they came to Carl and promised financial support, telling him "we help our families." And Max recalled that they never missed an opportunity to intimidate the staff, making it known that "they owned the hospital," not completely accurate but effective at the time. At first, Max's young high school friends were nervous and unsure of themselves. They entered the room tentatively and stood inside the door, uncertain of what to say. "How are you, Max?" they would ask. Then they would be surprised and relaxed by Max's casual response. Always the host,

Max quickly put his young visitors at ease. "Fine, how are you?" would come the standard reply. If he was lying on his stomach and could only see the floor, Max would say, "Get down here where I can see you," and, like Patty Wilkerson, they would lie under the bed looking up at Max, who looked down on them, a disembodied face suspended in midair. "Do you know everyone here?" Max would ask. And shortly there would be stories, jokes, and laughter.

When Max was on his stomach, his friends would gather under the Stryker frame, tell stories, and hold cigarettes up so Max could take a puff. There was always music, chatter, and laughter. When a nurse entered to take Max's pulse, the kids would fall silent. After she recorded the information on a clipboard at the foot of the Stryker frame, she would step over the young bodies sprawled under the frame as she departed.

"What's going on in here?" Dr. Otakar Machek said as he entered the room. Machek, forty-one, a native Czech, had earned his medical degree at Charles University in Prague. A Baruch scholarship brought him to New York in 1948, where he studied and taught at the New York Medical Center of Physical Medicine and Rehabilitation under Dr. Howard Rusk, the man widely regarded as the father of rehabilitation. He joined St. Mary's Hospital as medical director of physical medicine and rehabilitation in 1953, a position he held until he retired in 1993.

At the time of Max's accident, Dr. Machek was working hard to improve the hospital's fledgling rehabilitation program. Armed with the best credentials in the country, he was plowing new ground in a specialty that was considered young and untried within the medical community. In 1958 there were only 150 hospitals with comprehensive rehabilitation programs.[2] Most likely, St. Mary's program, then six years old, was not considered comprehensive at the time of Max's accident. The medical specialty of physiatry was the new kid on the block, having been recognized by the American Medical Association as an accredited medical specialty in 1949, only ten years before Max's accident. According to the website of the Association of Academic Physiatrists, "a Physiatrist is a physician who creatively employs physical agents as well as other medical therapeutics to help in the healing and rehabilitation of a patient. Treatment involves the whole person and addresses the physical, emotional and social needs that must be satisfied to successfully restore the patient's quality of life to its maximum potential."[3]

Dr. Machek, a hard-nosed former Air Force pilot, spoke with military bearing and a harsh-sounding accent. He was smiling at the kids clustered under Max's bed but trying to look stern. "This *is* a hospital, you know."

"Dr. Machek, these are my friends," said Max, introducing them.

"Pleased to meet you," said Machek, "and you're welcome to stay, however, we need to tend to Max right now, so I have to ask you to step outside just for a minute." A nurse lifted the needle off the record. The room fell quiet, and the visitors quickly did as they were told.

Outside Max's room, the atmosphere in the hallway was more somber. Hertha, Carl, Lecil, and her boyfriend, Steve, were sitting in the hall, looking exhausted, having had only a few hours sleep since the accident.

"Do you think he will live, Mrs. Starkloff?" a friend asked.

"That's up to God," replied Hertha, "but I know the doctors are doing all they can. Will you keep him in your prayers?" she asked the group.

"Yes, ma'am," they replied, crossing themselves.

When visiting hours were over, Hertha found herself alone with Max. It had been a busy, active day with so many visitors, nurses, doctors, and nuns going in and out of Max's room. By contrast, Max's room now seemed very quiet. She was reminded of the other half of Max's day, when he was alone with his thoughts. "Max," she said, "what do you think about when you're alone?"

Max thought for a moment. She noticed his lips often quivered due to the shock to his nervous system. Then he spoke in a soft voice, "I sleep when I get the chance, but there's always so much going on. They're either giving me shots or medicine or milk shakes—I never want to see another milk shake again!" It was all the food he could eat the first week. "Or they're turning me," he continued. "At night, one of the nurses usually sits beside me and gives me a cigarette until I go to sleep. Did you ever see so many good-looking nurses, mother?"

"Never."

"Or I'm getting therapy. Sister Gerard brings one of the nuns to visit, and then the priests come in. The time flies, really."

Max's friends continued to come and go during all hours of the day as their schedules and summer jobs permitted. Not having seen Gay Chadeayne at the hospital, Mary Britton called her at her summer job as a doctor's receptionist. She knew Gay and Max had been close and wondered why Gay had not visited Max at the hospital.

"I don't belong there," Gay told her friend. "I'm only going to make things worse. And besides, I have to work." She was terrified to see Max, having heard rumors about his condition and not knowing what she might do or say when she saw him.

"It's not like that," Mary reassured her. "He's the same old Max from the neck up. I know how you feel. I felt the same way, but somehow when you're with Max, he makes all your fears go away. I don't know how to describe it."

"I can't. I just can't," said Gay. "I hope Max understands." Max and Gay had dated briefly before she met Tom Noonan, whom she married in 1960. She always maintained, however, that she and Max had "a secret love affair" when they were fifteen and had remained close friends ever since. It would take Gay four weeks to muster up enough courage to visit Max.

The routine of hospital life continued as Max was poked, changed, turned, massaged, and evaluated. He remained optimistic and cooperative, and he enjoyed the visits from his friends and family. After a routine physical therapy session by Sister Gerard, Hertha stopped her in the hallway. "How's he doing, Sister?" Hertha asked. A look of worry crossed Sister Gerard's face. "He isn't responding, Mrs. Starkloff," she said. "He may not respond for two or three months. He may never respond. We just have to wait and see."

FRIENDS IN NEED

That afternoon, Marjorie Stephens, one of Hertha's associates from Laura McCarthy Real Estate, came to the hospital. She didn't ask to see Max but instead led Hertha calmly down to the solarium at the end of the hall.

"Hertha," she said, looking her directly in the eyes, "I'm going to come straight to the point. I know you have no money unless you sell a house. Your place is beside Max right now, and I want to help you in every way I can." She placed a check in Hertha's hand, and Hertha gratefully accepted it without looking at it.

"Thank you, Marjorie," Hertha said softly. "You have no idea what this means to us." When Marjorie left, Hertha looked at the check. It was enough to pay her household bills for a month. This was not the only help she would receive from Laura McCarthy Real Estate and its agents. Another agent friend, Ruth Seibel, whose son had been killed in an automobile accident one month earlier, came to see Hertha at the hospital. Fearing that the visit would reopen old wounds, she didn't stay long, but she offered her support, both emotionally and financially, to Hertha. Hertha's bosses, Harriet Strickler and Laura Smith, also gave money to Hertha. They came to visit her at her house, and Hertha remembered thinking later, "They must have thought me slightly demented the day they came over to the house to give me the check because I told them, 'This hasn't really been all tragedy. The beauty of people has taken the edge off it.' The goodness of others made me strong enough to say the right things to Max, Carl, and Lecil."

When Carl was not at the hospital, he spent his time in prayer and meditation. He felt the weight of his family upon his shoulders: his divorced mother not only having to support her family, but also now having to pay mounting hospital bills. Should he leave the order and get a job to help make ends meet at home? His mother sensed his concern: "I knew he was contemplating leaving the society, his beloved Society of Jesus. It had taken him two full years to make up his mind to enter, and now that he'd been in it seven years, he knew it was his life, the vocation for which he'd been born." She prayed for guidance.

That evening, Hertha and Carl visited a nearby restaurant for their first dinner outside the hospital in three days. "I'll hate sports cars for as long as I live," said Carl, staring at the menu. "Max doesn't, Carl," Hertha said, desperately trying to find the right words to say. At last she said, "Carl, did you ever stop to think that perhaps Max loved sports cars too much? You know yourself . . . if you let anything control you instead of you controlling it, you're in grave danger of losing your sense of values. Rather than lose one single person God has destined for heaven, he permits something to happen to jar that individual into clearer thinking. He lets us use the free will with which we're born until we get out of line, and then somehow he sets our thinking straight."

She paused. "All Max's life it's been nothing but cars," she continued. "He's been a scamp in school. He's always had a high IQ but never worked at it. He's gotten by on the happy accident of charm and he was blessed with a genuine love for human beings; but his mind, his eyes, his hands were delighted by cars only. This wasn't his first accident, you know, Carl. God practically had to kill him in order to knock some sense into that stubborn skull of his. Evidently he's destined for more in life than concentrated thought on cars, or God would not have permitted this to happen." She hesitated, then squirmed with embarrassment. "Here I am philosophizing to you when you've had years of it."

"No, go ahead," Carl replied. "Keep talking."

"Sweetie, I know that everything that affects Max affects you. You've often told me that. But first and last, your life is dedicated to God unless he lets you know otherwise. As for the practical end of this accident, your Uncle Max is helping here at the hospital. There are no doctor bills, and I know Uncle Gus [Hertha's brother, August Beck, who lived in Canada] will do all he can. For the present, my own friends are helping me. The present is all we can think of now, isn't that right?" Carl nodded and permitted a slight smile. They ordered their dinner and talked of good friends, Max's and Hertha's, and how each visit and phone call was a gift in itself. Then Carl added reassuringly, "Father Fischer said he'd watch the situation, too, and will advise me." Father Joseph P. Fischer was the provincial of the Society of Jesus in St. Louis, a man for whom Carl had tremendous respect. With Father Fischer as his spiritual guide and mentor, Carl felt relieved that he wouldn't need to make this tremendous decision by himself.

"Carl," Hertha said, "Think back. All your lives, I've tried to train each one of you to be true to yourself, because only that way can you fulfill what God has meant for you. Now if your superiors thought your vocation wasn't that of being a priest, they would tell you so: They've told others. If by any chance you don't want to be a priest, that's a different thing. Remember, I've always said I didn't care if you wanted to be a ditchdigger, just so you'd be a good ditchdigger and happy with your choice. You cannot spend your life doing something you were not meant to do, or else things happen to you on the inside. Anyway, have you thought what it would do to Max if you gave up your life's work because of him?"

When they returned home, Hertha suddenly had a flashback. In her mind she saw Max coming from the kitchen, his head barely clearing the doorway, and tearing up the stairs hurrying to dress for a party. Other pictures of Max raced through her mind. Sounds and images from the past: he and Lecil teasing, laughing, or infuriating one another; Max's mischievous and teasing laugh that made you laugh in spite of yourself. He could not laugh aloud now because the accident had weakened his lungs. She remembered Max as he left to join the Marines, and even then, at eighteen, although he must have felt uneasy and apprehensive, he smiled and waved a rolled-up magazine at her and Lecil at the station and ran toward the train. Max would never run again!

Hertha could hold it back no longer. As she recalled later, "the sounds torn from my throat were horrible. They were loud and wild, and I didn't care. Those cries coming from a broken heart drifted down the entire street of our pleasant neighborhood." Carl held his mother compassionately and said nothing.

Returning to the Starkloffs' home later that evening, Marty called her parents to tell them she would be staying longer than planned. She walked into the kitchen where Hertha and Carl were talking. "I know my mother must think I'm crazy. She said that when I come home she'll make me happy again, and when I said I'd never been happier in my life she didn't say a word. I guess she was stunned. No one understands unless they're here, Mrs. Starkloff."

DO YOU WANT THIS BOY TO LIVE?

Hertha, Carl, Lecil, and Marty arrived the following day, August 14, prepared for the worst. This was the day they would learn whether Max would live or die. Seeing Dr. Machek, Hertha approached him with a combination of dread and optimism. Quietly, Hertha thanked God for what she had: a son who was not only alive, but whose mind and speech were intact. She thanked him that she and her children were together and were being carried on by the prayers and companionship of hundreds of friends.

Hertha liked the direct way Machek met her eyes, and she appreciated his straightforward approach. When recalling her first impression of Dr. Machek, she said, "I think I was most aware of the set of his shoulders, of the wide mouth, firm and generous; the clipped, unhesitating way he spoke in his Czechoslovakian accent. I soon learned that the words 'can't,' 'won't,' 'don't' were viewed by him of small or no account. I learned to love him and respect him deeply for his frankness toward me, toward anyone, where the good of Max was concerned." She believed he cared intensely for Max and was doing all he could; all that science could to preserve his life.

Hertha asked: "Do you think now that Max will live, Dr. Machek?" It was a simple question to which Machek gave a simple reply. "Yes." he said. But then Hertha thought she saw something in his eyes, a searching quality that asked her, "Do you *really* want this boy to live?"

She knew that Machek's answer was a *qualified* "yes," a "yes, if . . ." *if* Max didn't contract pneumonia, *if* Max didn't have renal failure, *if* Max didn't succumb to infections from bedsores, if . . . if . . . if . . . She knew that Max still required intensive critical care. And then there would be the adjustment Max would have to make, both physical and mental, to his new life if he lived. Dr. Machek knew that another leading killer of quadriplegics was suicide through starvation. But none of these concerns were spoken. Upon hearing the answer she so desperately hoped to hear, Hertha said simply, "Thank you, Doctor," then turned and walked to the chapel to thank the Blessed Mother. Hertha thought and prayed. "So far, so good. One day at a time. Max stretched on that frame either on his back or on his stomach was still our Max, completely warm, alive, hopeful, fighting."

Hertha and Lecil visited the hospital coffee shop later that morning to have lemonade. Like Carl, Lecil also had been concerned about her mother and sharing part of her financial burden. "Mother," Lecil said, "I've decided I'm not going back to school." She spoke quickly so her mother couldn't interrupt her. "It's silly. Maryville is expensive. I'm going to try to get a teaching job." Lecil, a dean's list student, had given her decision a great deal of thought and analysis.

"But you love Maryville," said Hertha.

"I wouldn't love Maryville now with all those expenses staring you in the face. Anyway, it isn't as though I want to specialize in anything. I'll just be getting married anyway. I can always do lots of reading at home. I plan to speak to the nuns to see if I can get a teaching job."

Hertha quietly counted her blessings. She recalled later, "Lecil, without a pang or backward glance, became a woman, eager to accept her share of responsibility." Within weeks, the Sacred Heart nuns found her a position at a nearby Catholic girls school, Villa Duchesne.

That afternoon when there were a number of people in the room and Max was on his stomach, he said abruptly to his mother, "Get everyone out of the room. You stay and talk to me." Without a word, everyone simply left. Hertha began talking about everything and nothing when Max stopped her and said, "Mother, what do I have to look forward to if I live?"

Hertha described how she was feeling at that moment: "That was one of the times when I was two people. As though I were another figure unassociated and detached standing in a corner, I saw myself seated on the floor beneath him, looking out the window searching for the proper words."

She addressed her son slowly, "Maxim, not any of us has anything certain to look forward to but eternity, darling. It's just that you must learn it so young. Look, a second before the accident, you thought you had the world in your hands, and then suddenly your life's plans were changed. And yet, Max, so much that is beautiful was born of this. God permits tragedies to happen because it brings out the beauty in people. Did you ever guess you had so many friends?'"

"I didn't know people cared that much," Max admitted. "When I get home, Mother, we'll have to have a big party for them. We've got to do something for them."

"Max, you're doing more for them than you know by your example. It's the most extraordinary thing I ever saw," Hertha said. "Everyone feels awful about you, and yet there's no unhappiness. I guess it's because each one is carrying the other, and you're the one who's doing it because you refuse to let them feel pity for you." Whether consciously or unconsciously, Max knew that to accept pity from anyone meant that he was surrendering his will to fight.

"Maxim," Hertha chose her words carefully. "Everyone has arms and legs and hands, but God doesn't give too many a lovable personality, levelheaded thinking, and a sense of humor, but he's [given] all that to you, and that's most important."

Max looked at her as if deciding. "Well," he said, "that's enough of that. Let's turn on some lights. Where is everyone?"

Carl prayed and made up his mind the next day. He would continue in the society and return to take up his duties at St. Stephen's Mission in Wyoming. It was, he believed, the right decision. That, however, did not change the fact that his good-bye to Max might be the last. He went into Max's room alone while the rest of the family waited in the hall. After chatting briefly with Max, he knelt by the bed to pray. Max, lying on his back with arms outstretched, also prayed quietly. Both men knew that their futures were in God's hands. They said good-bye, and Carl turned. Without looking back, he left the room, drawing to a close what he later described as "the worst ten days of my life." The strict rules of the order would prevent him from returning for a full year.

FOOLED THEM ALL

"Uncle Max said I'm going to Desloge, Mother," Max said with a grin. "I guess I fooled all of them, now that I'm still alive. Desloge is supposed to have a better rehabilitation center and is better equipped for quadriplegics." His mother noted the ease with which Max used the word "quadriplegics" just twelve days since the accident.

Firmin Desloge Hospital was a larger facility, better equipped, and, like St. Mary's Hospital, was also owned by the Catholic Church. With the help of the church, and with the help of her brother-in-law, Dr. Max Starkloff, Hertha was able to make more favorable financial arrangements with the hospital as well.

The news of Max's impending move made Hertha apprehensive. She couldn't imagine how they would move a man the size of Max while he was in traction and not hurt him. "When are they going to do that?" she asked hesitantly.

"It's going to be interesting to see how they're going to manage, isn't it?" asked Max, as if he was looking forward to watching a grand piano being moved down a flight of stairs.

"St. Mary's is so pretty, and the nurses so much fun," said Hertha. "They can't give you the same personal attention at [Firmin Desloge], Max."

"Who cares about that?" said Max. "I'll go anyplace or do anything they tell me so long as they can help me." Hertha felt her apprehension begin to melt away under Max's confidence and positive attitude.

When Sister Gerard heard the news, she broke into tears. "I know I'm doing what I shouldn't," she sobbed. "I'm letting my heart get involved with my work. I do that with some patients," she explained through tears and a half smile. "But I'll be going on

FIRMIN DESLOGE HOSPITAL, 1325 S. GRAND AVENUE. PHOTOGRAPH
BY JOSEPH HAMPEL, 1946. MISSOURI HISTORY MUSEUM.

retreat next week, and I'll offer up all my meditations and prayers
to God to be transferred to Desloge." She looked directly at Hertha. "I know I can help him," she said firmly.

Moving day—twenty-two days after the accident—dawned
hot and humid in St. Louis as both the outside temperature and
humidity reached into the 90s. Max's family and friends and the
staff of St. Mary's began to orchestrate his move to Desloge Hospital, a mile east of St. Mary's. Hertha, Lecil, Steve, and neighbor
Charlie Grimm were on hand to move all Max's hospital belongings out to the car: TV, radio, record player, records, books, bottles
of holy water, flowers, and cards—three weeks' worth of daily ac-
cumulations. Max listened with interest as the doctors, nurses, and
attendants held a conference over him. Someone had to carefully

hold the cord of weights as Max was rolled with a minimum of jostling into the elevator and then into the ambulance.

As they slowly moved Max through the emergency room doors to the waiting ambulance, the muggy air wrapped itself around them like a moist, hot towel. Hertha was fretful about the move. She worried about leaving the excellent care of the St. Mary's staffers she had come to know and respect, especially Sister Gerard, Max's physical therapist. She feared Max would become lonely and withdrawn, as many of his friends were beginning to return to school. Max's girlfriend, Marty, had left for Chicago earlier that morning.

The medics carefully lifted Max into the ambulance, secured him, and departed for Desloge. Hertha and Lecil, their car loaded with Max's hospital possessions, left shortly thereafter. It was not a long drive, but they might as well have been traveling from St. Louis to New York City. St. Mary's was a small- to medium-sized hospital by 1959 standards. Desloge was much bigger. Housed in a tall, imposing French Renaissance building constructed of pink stone with copper mansard roofs, it was one of the largest and most prestigious hospitals in the region.

When Hertha arrived at the ambulance entrance to Desloge, Max had already been wheeled inside for processing. Waiting for her was the nun in charge on Max's floor. Like all the nuns, she was wearing a white habit. Her bonnet framed her face and was made of starched white linen with wings that jutted out. She wore a floor-length robe with long, baggy sleeves. A starched white bib covered her chest. On her feet she wore polished black shoes with black stockings. Around her waist was a rope sash from which hung a rosary. A large, overbearing woman, the nun in charge carried a book of hospital rules and a strict demeanor. She introduced herself to Hertha and Lecil.

"Now, Mother," the nun in charge said consolingly, stroking Hertha's arm, "we will be very careful with Sonny!" Sonny?! This earned the nun in charge the nickname "Sister Sonny" for the duration of Max's stay at Desloge.

"We must see that he gets plenty of therapy so that as little spasticity as possible will develop." This was the first time anyone had mentioned anything about spasticity.

Hertha wanted to shake the nun, but she said nothing. Lecil watched her mother with concern, knowing Hertha was anxious and upset. They followed Sister Sonny into the hospital. Hertha's first impressions of Desloge were not good. Overall she felt that it wasn't as attractive as St. Mary's. Max's room was tiny, dull, and stiflingly hot, as it lacked air-conditioning.

"Hi, sweetie," both women chirped in their cheeriest garden party voices as Max was brought into the room. "How was the ride down?"

"Fine," came the standard reply. "I didn't see much but at least I got a ride through town, and it was fun hearing the cars racing past me on the highway."

"This room isn't as pretty as St. Mary's," Hertha began. But Max interrupted her.

"I don't care," he said matter-of-factly. "I can't see anything but the ceiling anyway. As long as they're able to help me, is all I care about."

Max lay on his back on the Stryker frame. On the floor beside him stood a large bottle with the catheter tube disappearing under the sheet. Hertha and Lecil began bringing in Max's things. They placed plants on windowsills, taped Mass cards and comic cards on the walls, placed the radio on the windowsill, and put the record player on one of the tables. Lecil's boyfriend, Steve, brought in the

TV set and placed it on another table. They put smaller items such as candy, cookies, and Max's electric razor in the dresser drawers. Lecil placed a pair of prism glasses, provided by a priest named Joe O'Brien, on top of the dresser. The prism glasses enabled Max to watch TV lying on his back. Steve and the two women busied themselves tidying, moving, organizing, decorating—trying to drive the dreariness and despair out of the small room.

Within the hour, two orderlies came to the door and announced that it was time to turn Max. They were strangers to the family and exuded an air of indifference. This only confirmed Hertha's fear that Max would not get the care and attention that he had received at St. Mary's, care and attention he desperately needed in order to live. She stepped outside into the hall with Lecil and Steve.

Lecil was almost in tears. "I wish we hadn't had to leave St. Mary's," she said. "It's so cold here."

Without saying what she was thinking, Hertha tried to bolster her daughter's spirits. "It's bound to be a more-impersonal hospital, Lece. Clinics just are that way."

"Sure, Lecil," said Steve, also hiding his true thoughts. "It'll be fine after we get used to it. Max doesn't mind. He's more interested in getting well than in anything else."

The two orderlies left Max's room, their attitude of indifference unchanged. One of them looked at the family clustered in the hall and shrugged his shoulders, as if to indicate that they could re-enter the room if they wanted to.

Upon entering, they found Max facedown. "This darn mask!" he was saying. "They haven't got it right. They didn't even know how to turn me!"

Hertha's apprehension was boiling into anxiety. As Hertha recalled, "And to my fingertips I knew that it would not be long before everyone in charge of Max was going to find in no uncertain terms precisely what I expected of them."

After a few more snafus, Hertha finally lost it. "You all act as though you think Max is dying, so what's the use of straining yourselves," she said to Sister Sonny out in the hall. "Well, he isn't dying. He's very much alive. And you're going to do everything in your power to keep him alive, Sister. At St. Mary's his care was thorough and concentrated. You're going to live up to your reputation as a rehabilitation center as long as my son is here!" Mentioning St. Mary's often, Hertha discovered, "was like mentioning a rival sweetheart to a lover. It got results."

Sister Sonny, four nurses, and an intern arrived shortly and began to go to work on Max. According to Hertha, "there was no small talk, no halfhearted effort, just efficient cooperation." For the first time that long day, Hertha began to feel some sense of confidence in Desloge as well as a sense of relief that Max was being cared for properly. When they left, Max looked up at his mother and smiled. "That was fun!" he said.

When Dr. Machek saw Hertha later in the week, he took her aside in the hall. "I've never seen anyone react to an accident of this kind as Max does," he said. "He's remarkable." According to Hertha, he then looked her straight in the eye, as he often did, and said, "You know, Mrs. Starkloff, Max is going through hell. But his mind is active. He is an extremely intelligent young man, and he is practically crucified. The mind wants to do things his body cannot." Later that evening when things had quieted down, Hertha asked Max if he ever experienced periods of frustration, and if so, how he handled them. "Well," he answered, "that's when I whistle or sing or just let out a shout. Or I make the nurses' lives miserable," he smiled.

• CHAPTER 3 •

IMPROVEMENTS

Max's treatment began to improve after the first day. Sister Sonny still carried the rule book, however. The biggest infraction was the visiting hours Max's young friends did not observe. When she tried to enforce the hospital's visiting rules, the first people to object were Max's young Jesuit friends, who reminded her once again that "they owned the hospital" and respectfully told her that they would come and go as they pleased.

On one occasion, Dr. Machek had to set Sister Sonny straight. Seeing the conflict one afternoon, Machek took her aside and convinced her gently but firmly that Max was an exception. "You cannot tell a young man twenty-two years old when to go to sleep, Sister," he told her. She started to interrupt him several times but he looked in another direction and continued talking. "Also, we cannot leave Max, whose mind is well and active, to any possible brooding. His friends are to be permitted to come and go freely, within reason, so that when he is alone and awake in the middle of the night, he will have them to think about and not himself. Is that right, Sister?" Without giving her an opportunity to answer, he walked away.

One of Max's visitors soon after his move to Desloge was Gay Chadeayne. More nervous and reluctant than most of Max's friends, it had taken her almost four weeks to work up her courage to visit. "I kept thinking I was only going to make things worse," she recalled. But then Max made her feel comfortable and at ease in his small room. She remembered taking the streetcar from her job as a doctor's receptionist to visit Max every other day after work. "I came to depend on her," Max recalled. "She loved to play the guitar and sing to me in the room."

Hertha's comfort level with the hospital continued to improve as Max's first week in Desloge wore to an end. The following week, on Monday, September 7, she planned to return to work. She had taken almost a month off. Now, as financial problems and concerns about Max's future continued to mount, she felt she needed her real estate commissions. "I was surprised and glad to feel eagerness in getting back to work," she wrote in her manuscript. "The very thought of walking into the office, checking property on our weekly tours with quick-witted women, calling prospects, submitting contracts, was invigorating. I nourished that enthusiasm because now more than ever it was important that I make a good living." She would, of course, continue to visit Max every evening and would call his room before leaving the office to ask him what he would like for dinner. "I could have anything I wanted," Max recalled. "If I wanted something homemade or if I wanted a Steak 'n Shake burger or a club sandwich from Busch's Grove, she would find a way to get it for me." Hertha wanted Max to have "a normal environment" as much as possible, and she was probably concerned about his weight. During his stay in the hospital, Max would lose seventy pounds.

The spasticity that Sister Sonny had forewarned Hertha about when Max first arrived at Desloge began slowly, although no one remembered exactly when. Max recalled that his toes and fingers began moving uncontrollably at first. When he pointed this out to one of the nurses, she told him it was just involuntary muscle movement and was normal. "But the muscles are working," Max pointed out, grasping at any small shred of optimism. He was told that they were working, but that they were not being controlled by the brain because the nerve pathways had been severed. In other words, he should not interpret spasms as any sign that he might someday regain control of his muscles. Still, he held on to the hope that he might walk again.

One day the following week, when Hertha visited Max after work, his door was closed so she sat on the stairs across the hall to wait until whatever was being done to him was completed. Soon a young orderly came out of the room, saw Hertha, and smiled. He was slim, neat, and professional. Hertha found his smile very pleasing and smiled back. He walked over to her and said, "I'm on my way downstairs to get another toothbrush and some toothpaste for Max, Mrs. Starkloff."

"What is your name?" Hertha asked the young man.

"Ernest Brothers," he said. His gaze was direct and respectful. There was an air of self-confidence and dignity about him that Hertha liked. She recalled, "Of almost all who attended Max at Desloge up to this time, this young man was the one toward whom I felt a spontaneous warmth of friendship."

Ernest Brothers was twenty-one, had a wife named Joy who had graduated from Harris Teachers College, and had a five-month-old daughter. His voice had a hushed quality. Hertha, always observant, noticed his hands. "Long, slim fingers with strength in the palms. They would know how to give a rubdown, how to handle a patient. He told us later that he wanted to study to become a therapist." When Hertha entered Max's room, she mentioned Ernie and how impressed she was. "He's great," answered Max. "He gets me turned in nothing flat."

Hertha learned to be very grateful to the nurses for their patience and understanding with Max. "He must give you a hard time now and then," she said to one nurse out in the hallway. "Not really," the nurse replied. "His bark is worse than his bite. And we know why he does it."

One evening when Max felt like watching television, one of the nurses and one of the orderlies came in to help Hertha place the set so he could watch. This required placing the television at a height that Max could see while wearing his prism glasses. First a large table had to be cleared and dragged into position. Then a smaller table was placed on top, and on top of that a small stool. Finally, with great effort, the TV was hoisted up on top of the stool. The project usually took about fifteen minutes before the set was turned on and the prism glasses were placed on Max's nose.

"I don't think I want to watch after all," Max announced, once the laborious process was completed. The nurse turned indignantly to Max and then stopped, seeing the grin on his face.

"I thought you meant it," she said, softening. The stiffer the nurse, the harsher the hazing, and eventually all the nurses who got to know Max learned that laughter could make their jobs a lot more pleasurable. Those who didn't get Max's sense of humor always left his room wearing a bewildered expression.

Hertha later wrote about those early weeks in Desloge: "Max was never a Pollyanna in his attitude or outlook, nor was he resigned. There was no forced cheerfulness, but neither was there a prolonged despondency. There were times when he lay on his frame, his lips in a straight line, his eyes closed to everything but his own inward struggle, and at those times we continued our chatting, quietly among ourselves. We didn't try to 'cheer him up' because in the final analysis this was his battle to conquer, but over and above the small talk our thoughts, our passionate desire to help him must have emanated around him, giving him strength."

During the week of September 14, Hertha noted in her manuscript, "Six weeks: forty-two twenty-four-hour days spent in traction! There weren't even four walls for him to look at. He was turned on his stomach and saw a drab, tired brownish linoleum unrelieved by any pattern; then after two hours he was turned over and saw a dull white ceiling broken only by the light fixture."

"There's a moth in that light globe that's been there since I've been here," Max said to his mother one day, "I wish to God they'd get him out."

Hertha noted, "Did he associate himself subconsciously with that moth, I wondered? He's certainly just as trapped." Hertha asked him how he'd slept.

"Last night I felt like whistling," he said. "So I did. The nurses tried to shut me up but couldn't. I just kept it up until I was tired and then I felt a lot better." He smiled at his mother with a twinkle in his eye. "Some of the nurses come in to me and say, 'Max, you can talk to me. I'll understand.' What should I talk about? I'd rather whistle or sing, or just plain order them around."

•CHAPTER 4•

EX-TRACTION

Hertha's business associate Marjorie Stevens called her one evening to ask if she thought Max would be interested in selling insurance. Marjorie's son-in-law, Walter, was a district manager with Aetna insurance. Hertha had been praying for just such an opportunity. She never expected it would come from Marjorie, a woman she never thought would understand their situation.

"Oh, Marjorie," Hertha exclaimed, "Max has always wanted to sell. Only it used to be cars. What do you have in mind?"

"Well," Marjorie explained, "I simply told Walter about Max's accident and what courage he's shown, and Walter really became quite excited when I suggested that Max might sell insurance for Aetna."

When Max heard the news, he said, "When can I start?"

"Well," said Hertha, "I think Walter thought it best to wait until you were out of traction."

"Out of traction? What's that got to do with it?" said Max. "There's nothing to keep me from talking, is there?"

When Hertha told Marjorie about Max's reaction to the job, both women laughed with delight. Marjorie told her that Walter would send his assistant, Art Meyers, to the hospital to interview Max. Training would follow and, later, when Max was able, there would be an exam he must take. In the meanwhile, any prospects Max might have, Art would take care of personally so Max would be able to keep the entire commission.

"There's so much good that's come out of this, Mother," Max told Hertha later. "There's Marty, a real job I can be proud of, and friends you've made through my friends."

"More than that, Maxim," said his mother. "It's knowing that however hard God's will is, if we accept it, he rewards us in his own good time. It's not just the job, Max, it's that Marjorie thought of it; it's that Art Meyers is willing to give up hours to doing your work."

Dr. Machek delivered more good news to Max one morning during rounds: He would be getting out of traction on September 22. When Max told him that September 18 would be his twenty-second birthday, Dr. Machek said simply, "Then we'll have to have you out of traction on your birthday."

When Hertha heard the news, her reaction was, "Then, let's have an ex-traction party!" She checked first with Sister Sonny, who reluctantly gave her permission, "although her eyes were round as she gave it to me, as though never in the world would she be able to arrive at a conclusion regarding these Starkloffs." And then the invitations went out.

A few days before the ex-traction/birthday party, the family received more good news. Max's therapist from St. Mary's, Sister Gerard, appeared, smiling and triumphant, her prayers answered. The Sisters of Mercy had transferred her from St. Mary's to Desloge. Hertha noted, "It was like the reuniting of the family to have Sister Gerard again who had started with Max at St. Mary's."

The morning of September 18 dawned early as Max was wheeled on the Stryker frame into one of the hospital's examination rooms to have the Crutchfield tongs removed. Dr. Smolik, Max's neurosurgeon, was present, as well as his two assistants, Drs. Lattinville and Nash. It was a momentous occasion, as just six weeks ago none of them had expected Max to live this long. But the doctors weren't fooling themselves. The odds of Max surviving over the next few months were still stacked against him.

After taking many X-rays, they removed the tongs, swabbed the two holes with antiseptic, and inserted cotton into each one. They wheeled Max back to his room for a rest later that morning, then returned him to physical therapy for his afternoon session, a routine that would continue for the next ninety-seven days.

While Max was in physical therapy, Hertha, Lecil, Steve, and some of Max's friends prepared his room for the party. Hertha was expecting about forty guests. Lacking a cooler, they decided to fill "a strange tub" in the foyer of Max's room with ice and beer. Seeing this, Sister Sonny was horrified. "The Lord never meant for a urinal to hold ice and beer," she exclaimed. Hearing this, Hertha wondered out loud to Steve, "Urinal! Whatever uses a urinal that size? An elephant?"

Steve, who had a summer job with a sign company, brought in his favorite electric sign for a headache remedy, which he left leaning against the wall intending to hang. Dr. Machek, entering the room in his starched white coat, asked Hertha what the sign was for. When she explained that Steve was planning to hang it in Max's window, he said simply, "I'll hang it." Hertha offered him a cold beer, which he accepted. He then lit a cigar, climbed up on a chair, and proceeded to hang the sign.

Max was exhausted but exhilarated when they returned him to his room at about 4 p.m. His first post-traction day in therapy was also his first day out of the small, claustrophobic room in eighteen days. He would now be allowed to lie in a conventional hospital bed, one that could be elevated at the head so he could look straight at people. Seeing all his friends amidst the balloons and decorations in the small room, he grinned, "as though he were riding through the Arc de Triomphe," noted Hertha.

Shortly after the party began, Hertha was told by one of the nurses that she had a phone call. When she walked out to the nurses' desk, she saw Max's girlfriend, Marty, who had schemed with Hertha to surprise him on his birthday. "I loved the way Marty flirted with Max," Hertha recalled. "Tiny as the room was and overflowing with people, with all the poise in the world she would lean toward Max and murmur pleasing or amusing things to him. I could tell, because the one-sided grin came to his face often, and his eyes were full of delight as he watched her."

While Max no doubt received many cards and gifts, one of the biggest gifts was from his future brother-in-law, Steve Saller, who gave him a telephone for his room. While Max couldn't physically answer the phone, with assistance he could keep in touch with family and friends.

The following evening, Dr. Machek stopped Hertha in the hall as she approached Max's room. "The X-rays show that Max's spine has straightened amazingly," he told her. Her spirits brightened, "What about the cord?" she asked eagerly. But the expression on his face revealed the answer. "No one has seen the cord, Mrs. Starkloff," the doctor reminded her gently.

HEART TO HEART

Marty stayed for a week, spending the nights with college friends in one of the dorms at Maryville College. Her presence at the hospital was a relief for Hertha and Lecil. With Marty visiting Max, they felt they could catch their breath. One Friday evening as Hertha was returning Marty to Maryville, the two women talked in the car in the university parking lot for over three hours.

MARYVILLE COLLEGE, MERAMEC STREET AND NEBRASKA AVENUE.
PHOTOGRAPH, DATE UNKNOWN. MISSOURI HISTORY MUSEUM.

"It was a date night [for the students]," recalled Hertha. "We'd been talking of incidental things, getting to know one another better. At last, the cars began rolling up the driveway. Several of them were sports models, and of course I pictured the many times Max had driven up this same driveway with one or another of the Maryville girls. It was a trend of thought in which I dared not indulge."

"We certainly make an odd-looking pair here at this time, don't we?" Hertha asked Marty. Then, feeling that Marty needed to talk, she asked, "Marty, you must be weighed with confusing thoughts and emotions. Will it help any if I suggest that you try not to entertain them any more than you need to at this time?"

"It's all so strange the way this happened, Mrs. Starkloff," Marty said. "A long time ago when I knew Max loved me, I was mad at myself because I didn't love him back in the same way. I remember one time when we were sitting in a booth, and I tried to explain the way I felt about him but was too confused to put it clearly. He was so gentle, didn't press me in any way, and I thought then he deserved the best in the world. But since the accident, I think I'm in love with him."

"Well, maybe you really aren't, Marty," Hertha replied. "You know, all women are potential mothers. You mustn't let pity creep in here and disassemble your true emotions. Max wouldn't want that, you know."

"I know, and neither would I," said Marty, looking out the window. "But I'm sure I love him. Now my problem is—am I big enough to live a lifetime with Max should he stay paralyzed? Maybe our marriage would last for two or three years because I'd finally feel cheated."

Hertha recalled the moment. "The apprehension I felt for Max's future was like a cutting wedge. This thought would be uppermost in the mind of any honest, sensible woman."

"Sweetie, this isn't the time for decisions," Hertha finally said. "You know Max loves you, and if you love Max, why don't you simply enjoy one another from day to day and not look into the future. When you go back to Chicago, Marty, I want you to promise me that you will date. If you find that you fall in love with someone else, well, that could happen if Max were well and whole. If you don't, well, perhaps your life is meant to be spent with Max. But I wouldn't try to analyze the situation right now. I don't think any of us, you, Carl, Max, Lecil or I are capable of clear thinking at this time. Timing is one of the most important factors in any decision, Marty, and this moment isn't the time for a decision that would rule your entire life."

"Mrs. Starkloff," said Marty, "I want Max to have the very best. He has so much to offer, even now; the way he never talks about himself, his patience. If he could make a living, he could always adopt children." She and Max both loved children. "I love being with him," Marty said, "Fussing around his room. We played house today while I cleaned out the drawers and he poked fun at me. He has the dirtiest grin."

"Well, we truly don't know what Max will be able to do, Marty. Dr. Machek says that . . . another ten years and who knows? He's only twenty-two; his youth and innate good health are with him, to say nothing of his constructive thinking."

Earlier that day, Hertha and Lecil had learned that Max could turn his left hand over and back again. Seeing that as a sign of regaining movement in his entire body, they all became excited and optimistic. "Does this mean he may eventually be able to move other muscles?" Hertha asked Sister Gerard. "He does that by way of his bicep, Mrs. Starkloff," Sister Gerard said. "He cannot use his fingers, perhaps never will. He has no feeling below the bicep."

Max's brother, Carl, having finished the Jesuit program at Regis College in Denver, had moved to a Native American reservation in Wyoming. He wrote letters to his mother and sister, regularly telling them about his important work. His letters were upbeat and positive as he typically would not have burdened his family with his concerns about Max, concerns better left in God's hands. However, it bothered Hertha that he did not mention Max once in his letters, a sign to her that he was hurting badly and having a hard time dealing with the situation. "I didn't care who he spoke to about Max just as long as he spoke to someone," Hertha noted. She had learned that Sister Gerard had written Carl a nine-page letter, much to her relief. "Apparently, he was corresponding with her and surely speaking of Max to her."

Toward the end of September, Lecil began her new teaching job at the private Catholic girls' school, Villa Duchesne. She taught French to first through eighth graders and worked in the office. "I didn't like teaching very much," Lecil recalled. "The kids kind of rode all over me." She also assisted one of the nuns as her secretary. "It was make-work. They created work for me." But it was a job and income the family needed badly.

Hertha continued to worry about Max's frame of mind. Lecil's boyfriend, Steve, had left for Notre Dame, and many of Max's friends were also returning to college. While Hertha knew his friends would continue to write and call, she was afraid that it wouldn't be enough.

"WILL I NEVER WEAR PANTS AGAIN?"

As September evolved into October, Hertha's and Lecil's lives evolved, as well. "Looking back to those wild days of Lecil going to school," Hertha writes, "my showing houses, working on contracts, Lece and I taking turns picking up laundry and doing the marketing, calling Max each evening to find out what he wanted for dinner, both of us rushing down to the hospital, stopping on the way to pick up his dinner, feeding him, leaving at 8:30 so that Lece could prepare her schoolwork, so that I could call prospects to discuss their problems with them—I can only say I see in my mind's eye two hands on a clock going 'round and 'round faster and faster and faster, and I am sure that there were forty-eight hours instead of twenty-four squeezed tight between the twelve numbers of that round face because so much could not have been accomplished in a normal twenty-four hours. Lece and I became a regiment of two—one aim—complete cooperation so that every drop of time might be utilized."

Max was working just as hard. Dr. Machek was applying the latest principles of physical medicine. But Max's rehab was not all work and pain. "The PTs [physical therapists] were mostly women," Max recalled. "Attractive women. And they were fun." He recalled falling asleep once on a floating device in the Hubbard tank, a warm-water tank the PTs used for muscle therapy. "When I woke up," Max remembered, "I smelled this wonderfully sweet smell. They had filled the tub with bubble bath." "It helped you forget what horrors you were living with," Max would say later.

He remembered spending a lot of time on a mat trying to work different muscles and regain balance. "They don't know what muscles are going to work," said Max, "so they get you to focus on a muscle and try to move it." Every quad is different because where the cord is severed and how much it is severed can affect any one of millions of separate nerves. "Muscle twitches and spasms would often confuse and mislead me into thinking the muscles would work, but the PTs always knew the difference."

He would spend hours trying to hold himself up with his arms only to learn eventually that his only movement would come from his left deltoid and, to a limited extent, his left biceps. Eventually he would learn to feed himself by having someone strap a fork to his left hand and using his biceps to lift the food to his mouth.

He recalled seeing two paraplegics in the hallway on his way to therapy. One never wore pants, but always had a sheet over him. Max wondered, "Will that be me? Will I never wear pants again?" If he survived, would he ever date again? Could he marry? Could he have a family? Where would he live? How could he earn a living? He had had one year in college and two years in the Marine Corps cleaning and loading armaments. No college degree and no marketable skills. What would he do? He never told anyone in his family about these thoughts that haunted him when he was alone.

Max remembered one particular visit with Dr. Machek when he and the doctor were alone. Dr. Machek was standing at the foot of this bed. He looked uneasy and shuffled his feet. "Did you ever go to bed with Marty?" he finally blurted out.

"No," replied Max.

"Too bad," said the doctor. "You should have." Dr. Machek turned on his heel and left the room. Max, alone with this bomb drop, felt humiliated and frightened.

And then there were the "nightmarish nights." The spasms continued to worsen. They spread from his toes up into his legs, came more frequently, and lasted longer. The nurses would continue to reassure him that they were "natural" and "normal," but it didn't help. According to Hertha, "Max's legs, rebelling at not being moved, of their own accord jumped crazily all over the bed and kept him awake nights. There were times when everything went wrong, and not one of us was strong. Max would be tired and completely without humor or hope, Lecil would have had a hard day with her students and examination papers to prepare, and one of my deals would have fallen through and I felt sweat on my spine because of my heavy responsibilities."

COMATOSE

At about noon on October 12, Hertha was sitting at her desk at the real estate office when she received a call. It was Dr. Machek. "Mrs. Starkloff," he began, "I received a call from [Sister Sonny] just now. We don't know what has caused it, but Max is in a coma. Dr. Lattinville is on his way."

Hertha froze, feeling numb. "A coma, Dr. Machek?" She knew instinctively that this was the beginning of Max's slide into death. "What should I do?"

"You'd better stay there until someone calls you," he suggested.

Her numbness disappeared. "Oh, no, Doctor. Please, I promise I'll be good, but I must be with Max."

After a short pause, Machek said, "All right."

Hertha hung up the phone and stared off into space. Someone came up to her to ask about a house, but she said simply, "I don't know. Max is in a coma." Within seconds everyone in the small Laura McCarthy Real Estate office knew.

When Hertha arrived at the hospital, she took the elevator to the third floor, then walked to Max's room. Outside the room she saw Sister Sonny. "May I go in, Sister?" she asked. The nun looked at her, momentarily unsure of what to do. "I won't go if you think it will hurt him," Hertha said quickly. Just then one of the nurses who Hertha had befriended exited the room. "Mrs. Starkloff," she said seeing Hertha, "I think it would be good if you saw Max. He has been calling me 'Mother.'"

Hertha entered the small room. "His face looked very young," she recalled. "His eyes were wide and unseeing, and there was that smile on his face that was a part of Max no matter if he were laughing at life or life was laughing at him." The nurse followed Hertha into the room, took a wet cloth, and began wiping his face. A large oxygen tank stood beside him. Glucose dripped into his vein. Suddenly, he seemed to look in Hertha's direction and said in a teasing way, "Hel-lo, Mo-ther." By the time Hertha could respond, she felt he had retreated back into himself.

As Hertha sat patiently in the room, Max would utter commands and pleas for help. "Someone turn me!" "Nurse! Nurse! I've got an itch." "Get that car off me, someone!" Hertha recalled, "That was Max, my son, lying before me, but no tears came. It was as though the grasp of Death had made me numb so that I could not cry and it was good, because in a moment of clarity Max might see me cry and he must not know how serious his condition was. The priest came in to give him the Last Sacraments. For a moment Max seemed to see him, a bewildered look came into his eyes as though he were thinking, 'What's going on, anyway?' so I smiled at him as though at a joke between us. The priest smiled, too, and laid a gentle hand on Max's shoulder, but he'd slipped away from us again."

When Hertha walked out into the hallway, she was greeted by sympathetic friends and hospital staff who had gathered outside the room. "I'm so sorry, Mrs. Starkloff." "I'm so sorry . . . " She saw Dr. Machek sitting at the desk at the nurses' station and went over to him. He offered no condolences, but to Hertha his face said it all. He offered only an explanation and well-worn words of encouragement: "The coma is caused by lack of oxygen to the brain, or by a spasm of the small arteries. Everything's being done. Everything's being done." To Hertha, the last words were like a prayer. "But we must be prepared for the worst," he said.

"I know, Dr. Machek," replied Hertha dully. "I know."

Dr. Max Starkloff arrived, and the large man knelt down beside her. "Hertha, we had to expect this," he said. "It had to happen." "I know, Max," said Hertha. But inside she felt she didn't know. It was as if she were watching a play and the people all around her were the actors. She felt detached, watching to see what would happen next.

When Hertha got Carl on the phone in Wyoming, his voice was tense. "We'll go into the chapel immediately, Mother. Do you want me to come home?"

"No, darling," she replied. "You'll do us more good right where you are offering up your work and prayers for all of us. God and all of us know you'd rather be here, and because of your sacrifice your prayers will carry more weight. I'll let you know if you should come home."

When Lecil finally called, her voice sounded alarmed but restrained, "What is it, Mother?"

"Lecil," Hertha told her, trying to sound calm and collected herself. "Max isn't at all well. Come down right away, darling," she said, then added, "but drive carefully."

Hertha was in Max's room when Lecil arrived. Seeing Max with his eyes wide open, unseeing, staring at the ceiling, she had no way of knowing exactly what was wrong, but she immediately greeted him in the usual way, trying not to show alarm or concern. Then she looked at her mother. As Hertha recalled, "We looked at one another and I took her from the room. I put my arms around her, and she cried, and then she looked directly into my eyes as though looking for some assurance, but finding none, she pressed her lovely mouth firm and said chokingly, 'I've got to go to the chapel.'"

Hertha got busy calling other close friends and family members from a pay phone in the hospital. She called Steve at Notre Dame, Marty in Chicago, and her brother, Gus, and prepared them for the worst. By the time she had finished, it was night.

Then she received a call from the mother superior at Maryville College (now University). "Mrs. Starkloff," she said, "Marty just called us. I went into the lounge and announced it to all the girls.

They were watching the beginning of the Veiled Prophet Ball on television, and without a word every one of them went to the chapel to pray the rosary for Max." The Veiled Prophet Ball was a lavish debutante ball held each year since 1903 by St. Louis's oldest fraternal organization. It was an honor and privilege for a young woman to make her debut at the ball, and some of the women making their debut that year were friends of Max's.

Hertha and Lecil stayed with Max into the night, wanting to be by his side as he took his last breath. He would drift in and out of consciousness, recognizing his mother or sister one minute, then sliding back into a blank stare the next. Little was said in the small room as the women prayed and tried to prepare themselves for Max's departure.

"What time is it, anyway?" Max suddenly blurted out, startling the two women. Hertha and Lecil stared at each other, not knowing what was happening.

"It's about 9:30, honey," said Hertha, trying to sound calm and matter of fact.

"Nine thirty!" exclaimed Max. "At night? What's happened?"

"You've been a pretty sick guy, Maxim," his mother told him.

He looked at the oxygen tank beside the bed. "What's this for?"

"You needed oxygen, Max."

He didn't say anything for a few minutes, trying to figure out the lapse in time. Then, apparently deciding to let it go, he asked, "Why don't we turn on the television? What's on?"

His mother and sister again looked at each other in amazement, "Why, the Veiled Prophet Ball is on. Want to watch that?"

"Sure," said Max. So they turned on the television.

"In a funny way," Hertha recalled, "he recognized a few of the debutantes he'd gone out with. He made some costumely observations in a teasing way, as a friend feels free to do. Now and again in the next hour, he didn't make much sense, but he was definitely better. At 11, the night-nurse came, and Lecil and I went home thoroughly bewildered and weary. Life and death had tossed us about, leaving us altogether mystified and eviscerated."

IDIOT WORK

Max's weight continued to drop. From 195, he now weighed 135 pounds. "You know what he needs to stimulate his appetite," Marty said to Hertha one day. "Things he likes, like celery, carrots, and really cold milk."

Hearing this, friends brought in a small refrigerator. And with it came instructions from the medical staff to record everything Max ate and drank in exact amounts. Two clipboards were placed at the foot of Max's bed. One said in large letters "Intake," the other "Output." Hertha, Lecil, and other friends were instructed to record the numbers of cubic centimeters contained in each glass of liquid given to Max, which they did. The nursing staff recorded the output.

The ready availability of Max's favorite foods and drinks seemed to work as planned. While no weight increase is noted in Hertha's manuscript, she did note, "With the advent of the refrigerator, Max's appetite grew, the too ascetic lines of his face lessened, and the teasing expression of his eyes overcame the former luminosity."

Dr. Machek postponed Max's physical therapy after the coma until Max regained his strength, probably a week to ten days. On Max's first day back, Hertha accompanied him to the physical therapy room on the second floor. She watched as Sister Gerard pushed Max gently to one side and said, "Straighten up, Max." He would struggle, his lips pressed into a grim line of determination until exhaustion overcame him. Not once did she hear him say "I can't" or see any sign of self-pity.

Hertha noted, "Days passed, and he could do no more than he did the day before. But he never gave up. There were times he became furious with himself and his helplessness, and you thought his teeth must surely splinter because of their gritting, but it never lasted over a few minutes. Tomorrow was another day. Sometimes 'tomorrow' was worse than 'yesterday' had been because the spasms during the night tired him before the day even started, but he brushed those days impatiently aside. There had to be a good 'today' coming up."

Occupational therapy (OT) or, as Hertha called it, "work for the handicapped," was a different matter. While Machek had been able to bring Desloge Hospital's physical rehabilitation up to date by bringing in trained therapists and incorporating the latest machines and techniques, Desloge's occupational therapy department, supposedly intended to prepare disabled people to make a living, was behind the times.

"They didn't know what to do," Max recalled from his one and only visit to OT. "They strapped a splint to my left arm and put a paintbrush in my hand, then asked me to stain a trivet for my mother. It was the last thing my mother would've wanted." He asked why they were making him stain a trivet for his mother and was told that it would strengthen his arm. Since he was spending his days in physical therapy strengthening his arm, he thought the whole exercise a waste of time. He noticed an electric typewriter with a cord wrapped around it in the corner. "Can I strengthen my arm on that?" he asked. "I guess so," the therapist said. Somehow, he typed a letter to Carl. "It was a lot more difficult," Max said. "It took a lot more concentration than staining the trivet."

No one ever told him in the OT room that day that he could be trained for an income-producing job. He believed it was because the doctors felt that either he was going to die or that his disability was so severe, he wouldn't be able to do anything if he lived. Because of this, nobody offered Max vocational rehabilitation, something the government mandated in 1976 for all people with disabilities. "I never knew such a thing existed until after I got home and ordered my first wheelchair," Max recalled. "And the wheelchair salesman told me about it."

Driven by Dr. Howard Rusk and others, occupational, or vocational, rehabilitation programs had been put in place during the Second World War to return disabled soldiers to the front. When penicillin and other antibiotics came into wide use in the mid-1940s, the medicines extended the life expectancy of people with disabilities. That made it imperative for the medical community to find ways to help disabled people earn a living. Blind people were hired to work in photographic laboratories. Sheltered workshops were established. "It was idiot work," Max recalled.

Even if a disabled person was able to find that work, obstacles abounded. Just a single step or an eight-inch curb would keep a person in a wheelchair housebound for life. "A lot of quadriplegics went through occupational rehab at the time," recalled Max. "Some of them died when they got home." *If* they got home. As nursing homes were considered the norm, most quadriplegics, having survived the juggernaut of infection, respiratory arrest, kidney failure, and neurological destruction in the hospital, were placed in nursing homes where life was so boring, they didn't even want to get out of bed in the morning. "Quads didn't live very long," Max recalled of the 1950s and early 1960s, "probably because they didn't want to."

• CHAPTER 4 •

THE VISIT

During the last two weeks in October, Art Meyers started coming once or twice a week to teach Max how to sell life insurance. Because Max was unable to hold a book or turn the pages, he had to depend entirely on his memory, which was one of his strengths. He learned the basic concepts, then memorized important details, fitting them into small mental filing cabinets in his brain.

He was an enthusiastic learner, seeing this as his new life's vocation. Art's company, Aetna, had an excellent reputation, and Art was a good and patient instructor. Soon Max began to practice his pitch on his visitors, and, because everyone wanted to help, he sold two life insurance policies almost at once. Gay Chadeayne was his first customer.

Hertha, who had seen her own career in real estate become successful over time, was an enthusiastic coach. "My real estate started out like that, Maxim," she told Max one evening. "Now you must knock yourself out proving yourself. There will be problems of others for you to think about, and everyone has them, and each one is important because it's important to that individual." It had been ten weeks since Max had become paralyzed, and Hertha had found him not only a job but a career, one he could perform using only a telephone.

At the end of October, Dr. Machek told Max he could go for a ride in a car anytime he wanted to, news Max relayed to his mother and sister with enthusiasm. "Well!" Hertha recalled. "That was a production. We learned to allow plenty of time for anything that had to do with Max, and it was one of the things that caused him mental anguish. In order for Max to take his first few rides, the car must be one with a reclining seat, so each Saturday for three weeks I drove to the other end of town to rent this particular car until

Sunday evening. That meant sandwiching business appointments carefully so that clients would not be aware of the frustrating contest being fought for my time. I needed clients badly whether they bought a house or not because one never knew when they might buy and one had to be the agent closest to them at their moment of decision. But on the other hand, Max needed every encouragement, and any change from his daily routine was stimulating."

Hertha knew she could not drive Max alone. She would need help getting him into and out of the car, and she felt unsure of herself with Max riding in the passenger seat. She asked Ernie Brothers to accompany her on the first ride, and his presence relaxed her and gave her confidence. On the last Sunday in October, she drove the car she had rented late Saturday into the ambulance driveway at Desloge, then went up to Max's room to help carry several pillows and sheets down. The pillows would be piled up on the seat behind Max to support him, and the sheets would be knotted together and used to tie him securely to the armrest and front seat. Ernie and another orderly were dressing Max, and Hertha was satisfied to note that his pride in his appearance hadn't diminished. "The tie had to match the shirt, the sport coat must match the pants, even the shoelaces must be tied a certain way," she noted.

It was a beautiful day when they finally set forth on Max's first car ride since August 9. Missouri's falls rival New England's in their sprays of color, usually peaking in the third weekend in October. The temperature was forty-nine degrees on a cloudless day.

"Let's go by the house," suggested Max. "I want to see the Oliveris." The Oliveris were their neighbors, and Max had often babysat Mary Kay, seven; Janet, five; and Bobby, four. When they pulled up in front of the house, Katherine Oliveri came out with her three children. The kids had heard about Max's accident, and their mother had tried to set expectations, but being children, they weren't sure what to expect. Max had always picked each of them up and given each a twirl and a hug. They approached the car cautiously, and Max waited expectantly inside. He, too, was not sure what to expect.

Mary Kay, the oldest, was the first to approach the car. Her mother guided Mary Kay to Hertha's side of the car because neither the door nor window on Max's side could be opened. The little girl tentatively peered up into the car.

"Hello, Mary Kay," said Max with a smile. She looked at him calmly with interest, then, saying nothing, turned and went into the house. It was Janet's turn next. When she saw Max sitting in the car wrapped in sheets, unable to move, she burst into tears and ran into the house. Bobby, the youngest, came galloping down the terrace of the house, took a quick peek into the car, and quickly retreated, saying, "I saw him. I saw him."

Hertha looked at Max. He didn't say anything. As she recalled, "I could tell he was hurt but was making himself accept another adjustment. Something in the expression of his eyes and in the firm set of his mouth told me that somehow he would find a way to make the little Oliveris accept him as he now was. His silence and his expression said that if he didn't dwell too much on his handicapped condition, then others wouldn't either."

When Hertha offered to pay Ernie for helping her, he declined her offer. "You don't have to pay me, Mrs. Starkloff. I'll come anytime." Then he said, "Gee, wouldn't it be great if I could just go to work for the Starkloffs?" Hertha thought, "It was as though he were lifting the curtain into our future."

Coming Home

By November 26, Thanksgiving, Hertha noted that Max could raise his left hand to his face using his biceps and deltoid muscles. When she saw Max rub an itch, she exclaimed, "Max, that's wonderful! Only nine weeks out of traction, and you can raise your arm!"

"Well, after all, Mother, I am twenty-two years old," came the dry reply.

"We must give some thought to discharging Max," Dr. Machek announced one afternoon.

"Bring him home?" Hertha asked incredulously, as if Machek had just suggested she take an elephant as a house pet. Hertha later remarked, "The full realization of Max's helplessness gripped Lecil and me as we planned to re-do the dining room into a bedroom for Max. At the hospital you had the feeling in a nebulous way that Max would somehow come out the same old Max, but now that Dr. Machek suggested Max coming home in a relatively short time, the finality of Max's limitations washed over both Lece and me, leaving us breathless and despairing. How could we manage? Lecil and I both had to work. To have someone take care of Max—where would I get the money?"

Once again, the Jesuits offered to help. "Father Fischer had told me, 'Carl's spiritual welfare is important, and in view of the fact that becoming a priest is apparently his vocation, we feel that the society is better equipped to help you financially than Carl. You must come to us when you need help.' Well," wrote Hertha, "it's one thing to be told to come, but it's another to swallow your pride and do it." Hertha listed her needs and concerns at the time:

Max needed not only a wheelchair, but a hydraulic lift that would transport him from bed to chair, or from chair to car; an arm sling that held up his left arm enabling him to use it; an electric typewriter; the expensive wonder drugs; yards and yards of foam rubber, among other things.

He would be in the world of well people again. Would he be able to accept being 'different'? Would *we* be able to accept it? Looking at Lecil, I knew that her life must not be changed any more than absolutely necessary. That would be difficult, because Lecil's generosity and compassion are boundless and, being boundless, not always discreetly aware of her limitations to help another.

Once, Lece and I caught one another's eyes and confessed that we prayed Max be spared living. Then when we were with him that evening, and enjoyed his companionship so much, his teasing and imitating, and were infected by his genuine joy for living, we felt ashamed. We had been weak and had prayed for a way out. He could face what lay before him. We had to.

Hertha and Lecil never again prayed to God that it be his will to take Max, and they continued to be impressed by his struggle to regain his life. Hertha heard him saying late one evening during a quiet conversation, "I guess there must be a reason for all this, Mother. In the beginning, I wouldn't let myself think about my condition. I waited until I got used to it so that then I could do something about it. Father Jack Campbell, SJ, told me that two of the guys have come back to the sacraments because of me. I'm interested in other things besides cars. I wasn't really doing anything with my life before, but now I'm going to have to. I was just having fun, and I was lazy. Now I'm going to have to get serious." He said it very quietly.

"Yes," Hertha thought to herself, "you are going to have to get very serious."

She told Max that she had asked Ernie Brothers to stay with Max from 9 a.m. to 5 p.m. every day after he came home. "You mean I'll have to have someone with me all the time? I'll never be alone?" he asked. It had begun to dawn on him that he would be dependent on others for the rest of his life. Hertha never answered him. But she knew he liked Ernie, and soon, judging by the affectionate exchange of jokes and jibes between the two, knew that Max was working hard to make the adjustment.

Dr. Machek was also thinking about how Max would make the adjustment. "Have you thought about how you're going to get around?" he asked Max one day. When Max said he hadn't thought about it, Machek suggested he buy an old bread van, similar to today's panel trucks, and outfit it with a ramp so Max could be wheeled into the van, secured, and driven around. It was a unique concept at the time because in those days nobody even imagined that a quad could get around in any kind of vehicle on a regular basis. At the time, Max gave it little thought, focusing instead on bigger issues. Later he would buy just such a van and in eighteen years cover over 350,000 miles.

By the beginning of December, having spent three and a half months in the hospital, Max was getting restless and impatient. "I'm glad to hear that," said Dr. Machek to Hertha. "Some people feel insecure at the thought of leaving. He will come home soon." "Soon" was the closest Hertha could get to a specific date. Scrambling to prepare her house for Max's arrival, she was frantic. She decided that *soon* meant sometime in February.

On evenings and weekends in early December when they weren't with Max, Hertha and Lecil made plans for Max's arrival. The dining room would be converted into his bedroom, as it was on the first floor and most accessible. They planned how they would create a small dining alcove in a corner of the living room and where they would distribute the dining room furniture. They would have wooden shutters built to separate the dining room from the front entry hall and kitchen for Max's privacy. Hertha scheduled the carpenters for mid-January, "along with the electrician, the light fixtures, the closet, linoleum, drapes, hydraulic lift, and air conditioner."

The wheelchair was ordered, a gift from the Jesuits. The women anticipated the pleased look on Max's face as he was carried into the house now geared to his new way of life. In the meantime, they looked forward to having Max home for one day on Christmas, at which time they planned to invite about fifty of Max's friends for a "drop-by." Lecil and Steve went out and bought the biggest Christmas tree they could find and set it up in the dining room.

Then, on December 23, "the bomb fell." "Mother, I'm coming home Christmas Day!" Max exclaimed excitedly.

"Yes, honey, I know," replied Hertha warmly, appreciating Max's excitement for the big day.

"No. I mean home, really home! I'm discharged!" Max continued gaily, "Dr. Machek was just in here, and before he left, he turned and said, 'By the way, you're discharged anytime your mother is ready for you!'"

There was no way Hertha wouldn't be ready. She would be ready for her son, "if we had to hang him from the chandelier." She elaborated: "Max, or whoever had held the phone for him, had hung up while I stood frozen in the kitchen with the receiver still to my ear. There was going to be a very tall, helpless man in the room where the tree now stood waiting for its Christmas finery. Furthermore, I knew practically nothing about the care of Max. There was no wheelchair, no wall to afford privacy, no medicine, no hydraulic lift, nothing; nothing but his old bed, which was still up in his old room. I would have to make arrangements to get Ernie sooner. I felt as though I'd been picked up sharply by a tornado and had made a spiral loop, which ended in a barrel roll."

When Hertha next visited Max, he "was all sunshine and totally oblivious to the complete confusion in which Lecil and I were suddenly placed." In the hallway outside Max's room, she wailed her predicament to Max's Jesuit friends, whose eyes lit up. "They thought it was fierce fun, laughed, and set into action." One of the Jesuits left immediately with Lecil and Steve. The three of them brought Max's bed downstairs and reassembled it in the dining room. Two other young priests returned to the hospital and emptied Max's room, pulling clothes out of the closet, emptying drawers into boxes. They took those, along with the refrigerator and armloads of records and correspondence, out to the car.

Max's friend Patty Wilkerson, who had dropped by for a leisurely visit with Max, was asked to deliver the television set to one of their priest-friends at his church. Gay Chadeayne returned the record player to Mary Britton. And Hertha herself went to Max's nurse, Noreen Gott, for a quick lesson in flushing Max's catheter. "She called my druggist, ordered catheters, ointments, Mercurochrome, rubber gloves, and drugs," noted Hertha, "and warned me to watch out for pressure sores." That was the extent of Hertha's training.

Before Max left the hospital, Dr. Machek stopped by his room for one last visit. "You'll never walk again," was all Max remembered him saying. Max left Desloge on Christmas Day in a joyous mood, having spent 138 days in hospitals. He thanked the nurses and staff who had become good friends. He was dressed neatly in a blue blazer, white shirt and tie, khaki slacks, and polished Bass Weejun loafers. Ernie Brothers and one or two orderlies wheeled him down to the emergency entrance and loaded him into Hertha's Nash Rambler, as they had done for many of Max's weekend rides.

Brothers and some of Max's friends carried him from the car up two steps onto the front porch, and then up one last step into the house on Lindell. The front door opened directly into the living room. An old, folding chaise longue had been brought in from the porch, the only chair big enough to accommodate Max's large frame, and Max was seated in it. "Going home from the hospital is a huge transition," Max would later recall. "You go from the hos-

THE STARKLOFF HOME AT 7217 LINDELL BOULEVARD.

pital where everything is done for you, and then you go home and everything changes. The bathroom and kitchen are not accessible. You're suddenly faced with not being able to do all the things you used to take for granted."

People started arriving at about midafternoon, and by evening the party was in full swing with friends jammed in every nook and cranny of the house. Lecil remembered the party as being "almost giddy" and that "everyone was happy to see Max out of the hospital. But nobody had any idea of what we were up against. There was a lot of drinking."

By 10 p.m. Christmas night, the last guests had left, except for Jerry McGlynn, Pat Connolly, Bill Kelly, and Steve Saller. Max sighed contentedly, "That was fun! People all over the place, and everyone having such a good time. I enjoyed that!" Hertha had asked Max's friends to help her get Max ready for bed. His friends lifted Max from the chaise longue and carried him to his bed in the dining room, where they discovered that Max's old bed was too small for him. The bed was purchased for him when he was fourteen years old, and Max had never given the bed's length a thought. Now that he was paralyzed and had to lie straight, the six-foot-long single bed no longer accommodated his tall body. "What did you do before the accident?" someone asked Max. "I slept diagonally," Max replied. This was one problem Hertha hadn't anticipated. She ordered a seven-foot hospital bed as soon as she could after the Christmas holiday weekend.

Next it was time to irrigate Max's catheter, a seventeen-step process that had to be conducted twice a day.[1] It was Hertha's first time, and she had been given only a few minutes' instruction before leaving the hospital. They undressed Max and apprehensively observed the catheter draining into a plastic bag strapped to

Max's leg. Hertha and Max's friends tried to keep the mood light, and she was able to complete the process "with trembling fingers" in an hour. With practice, she would be able to perform the process in about fifteen minutes.

The second evening after Max returned home, Hertha, Lecil, and several of his friends were getting him ready for bed when he announced, "I'll need a footboard or I'll get dropfoot; my feet mustn't hang over the bed." The footboard prevented shortening of the heel cord. Hertha tried using a breadboard from the kitchen, but it slipped between the mattress and frame. Max's friend Johnny Lyman offered the headboard from his own bed, and within fifteen minutes ran home and returned with the headboard, which he somehow attached to the foot of Max's too-short bed.

"And I'll need a standing board," said Max, referring to a board that enabled the hospital staff to raise Max to almost a standing position. Hertha, who 138 days before had possessed an average amount of medical knowledge, recounts this moment in her manuscript: "The standing board induces stress onto the long bones, which causes an enzyme to develop that in turn influences the calcium, phosphorus, and protein metabolism; this series of functions also tends to diminish incidents of bladder stones. The standing board used at the hospital was of course the best. Electrically controlled, it could raise the patient to an eighty-degree angle. It also cost $1,500." Hertha felt completely stymied. That night, as Hertha climbed back into bed after turning him, she had an idea for Max's standing board: "The outdoor chaise longue made of aluminum, which had collapsed and now stood in the garage waiting to be picked up by the rubbish men! It suddenly became very precious to me. With a little alteration, reenforcement, and covered with foam rubber, there was Max's standing board!"

Max had to be turned every four or five hours all through the day and night. After days of enlisting friends and neighbors to lift Max out of bed every morning and return him every evening, Max's new wheelchair and hydraulic lift arrived sometime the week between Christmas and New Year's Eve, and along with them came two problems: (1) The wheelchair was too short and had to be returned for longer parts; (2) the Hoyer hydraulic lift, designed to roll on casters under a hospital bed, wouldn't fit under Max's conventional bed. They would have to make do for a few more days. Fortunately, Ernie Brothers had begun his new job of taking care of Max. He and one or two of Max's friends would have no trouble transferring Max from bed to aluminum chaise longue and back to bed. However, it was always up to Hertha to make sure enough helpers were on hand each morning and evening to get the job done.

Hertha described her house during the first four weeks with Max home as "a chaos." The combination of Christmas and New Year's, confusion and apprehension over how to care for Max, and hosting between twelve and twenty-five visitors each day made Hertha's days long and exhausting. However, she always focused on the positive: "Even though there was a certain amount of hell connected with the confusion, Christmas mishmash, and apprehension I felt, there was real happiness, too. It was as though all of us were one person diverged into many but stemming from one unit. That one unit was our love for Max."

By December 30, Max's new seven-foot hospital bed had been assembled in the small dining room, alongside the Christmas tree, which, according to Hertha, "laughed at us and never budged an inch to give us just a little more room." The new bed enabled the hydraulic lift to function properly. Max was also able to sit in his new wheelchair, which was modified to accommodate his height. Hertha could finally surrender the old aluminum chaise longue to the rubbish men. When Max had ordered the wheelchair, he was asked whether he wanted canvas or leather. Max wanted leather and asked if he could get it in red. "No," he was told, "you get plain brown because with red you get noticed. And you don't want to be noticed." Max would never forget this. Marty also arrived on December 30 and moved into Max's former bedroom. Hertha, Lecil, and Marty had a go at operating the new equipment that evening. As nobody at the hospital had shown the women how to use the equipment, it was a hit-and-miss proposition. They missed. Hoisting Max out of his chair with the new hydraulic lift, they swung him carefully over the bed, at which point he began to fall out. Placing herself between Max and the bed, Marty tried to push him back in, but Max, even at his reduced weight of 140 pounds, was too heavy. He slid out of the harness and onto his girlfriend. "We all ended up giggling," Lecil remembered.

"There were no secrets from anyone in those first two weeks," Hertha recalled. "We conserved a great deal of energy and escaped much mental anguish by not even trying to [preserve any sense of modesty]." One situation after another could have been awkward, but everyone refused to be embarrassed for Max. "Max watched us thoughtfully," Hertha continued, "with an expression that said he knew he was being a great deal of trouble but hoped we weren't discouraged. I learned a great deal from Max those first weeks; in particular, the respect that helplessness can command if one does not indulge in self-pity. He accepted help with a quiet dignity that recognizes no embarrassment whether he was being lifted from the bed, or being fed, or having the 'bag' (that was strapped around his leg and which we learned to pat surreptitiously now and then before it might reach its dangerous capacity and explode) emptied."

With Max home, Carl began to mention his brother in his letters. "It was as though he hadn't let himself believe anything encouraging up to this time," said Hertha, "but now that Max was at home he was reassured and somewhat relaxed. At last I was satisfied because he wasn't shutting himself away from us and suffering alone." The Oliveri children also began to come around. First Mary Kay, the eldest, stopped by with her five-year-old sister, Janet, who watched Max shyly and uncertainly. Recognizing her thoughts, Max offered a small, tender grin that broke the ice. She came over to Max and tentatively picked up one of his inert hands, then let them drop. "You have fwoppy hands," she said. Max agreed. From then on, Janet would ask Max, "Can I pick up your fwoppy hand?" Bobby adjusted even more quickly. He would open the front door with a careless "Hi, Max," head straight for the candy jar, which Hertha kept in the living room, grab a handful, and leave.

As things quieted down after the holidays, the Starkloffs' lives began to take on a new rhythm coordinated around Max and his needs, as well as routine household chores such as cleaning, shopping, doing the laundry, and working at their respective jobs. Hertha and Lecil quickly divided responsibilities. Hertha would get Max ready in the morning, but with her weakened arm would wait until Ernie arrived at 9 a.m. to operate the lift and move Max into his wheelchair. Ernie would feed him dinner, undress him, put on his pajamas, brush his teeth, and move him into bed each evening before leaving.

From Saturday afternoon until Monday morning, Lecil and Hertha would share responsibilities as their schedules permitted.

When Hertha was on duty at the office, showing a house, or preparing a contract, Lecil would stay with Max. When Steve came into town on occasional weekends, Hertha would be on deck. At some point during the weekend, one or the other would do the grocery shopping, clean the house, and do the laundry.

"Hertha, you and Lecil just can't take care of Max and work, too," well-meaning friends of Hertha's would tell her. "You'll have to put Max in a nursing home." Hertha resisted the idea, preferring not to even think about it. But sleep deprivation and exhaustion were fast approaching. Getting only four to five hours' sleep each night, Hertha finally called Dr. Machek. "How much longer will I have to turn Max every four to five hours?" Hertha asked.

"He must not get you up several times a night," the doctor replied. "He must discipline himself to go back to sleep when he wakes up. If he makes a nervous wreck of his nurses, where will all of you be?"

When Max heard the doctor's advice, he reacted indignantly, "Am I supposed to lie here uncomfortable?" Max's spirits continued to decline as the excitement of moving home wore off and the reality of his helplessness wore on. Gradually, Hertha began to sense that Max's positive attitude and strength were acquiescing to resignation and inertia. He no longer took interest in learning the insurance business or in what was going on around him. Hertha wrote,

> I lay in bed that night my eyes wide open in order to imagine myself in Max's position. Suppose I had to ask to have a cigarette lighted, suppose I had to ask for every sip of water I wanted, suppose I had to ask someone to hold my legs down when they went into spasm. Ask—ask—ask,

when I'd always been virile and strong and independent. Then suppose I'd see the ones around me who were so busy working to make me comfortable, grow more and more tired, what would it do to me? It would make me feel guilty, and then because I couldn't do anything about it, I'd feel despair, and finally not being able to fight despair, I'd become indifferent. That's what I'd feel, I thought. But I can't show him pity, I argued to myself, I've got to make him feel that he must help others.

The next morning while Ernie was upstairs, Hertha had a chance to talk to Max privately. "You know," she began, "people are pretty wonderful. Generosity isn't simply our due. Being overly grateful embarrasses anyone, but being sincerely interested in another's welfare shows gratitude more than anything."

Max stared at her. "Do you think it's fun for me to lie here paralyzed and not even be able to feed myself or scratch the back of my head, or anything?" he asked, angrily.

"If you think I like to see you lying there unable to help yourself in any way, think again," replied Hertha, eye to eye.

All of Max's emotions welled up like a thundercloud inside him, and for the first time in many years, his eyes filled with tears. Hertha turned and walked out of the room. Ernie had come downstairs during the conversation and was waiting quietly in the kitchen. "I'll be back in a little while," she told him.

"Sure, Mrs. Starkloff," replied Ernie. "Max'll be alright."

When Hertha returned home later that evening, she met Ernie in the kitchen. "He didn't talk to me until about two this afternoon, Mrs. Starkloff," he said, "but I think your talking to him did a lot of good. We sort of like to play and sing during the day, but he just frowned and sort of thought today."

TURNING A CORNER

Eventually Max regained his interest in selling insurance and began reading the textbooks left for him by Art Meyers. He also started listening to the news on the radio each evening at six. "Stan Musial asked for a pay cut today," he told his mother and sister after work one day. "He asked that his pay be cut from $100,000 per year to $80,000 per year." Stan Musial was the St. Louis Cardinals' home-run slugger. Hertha noted, "As subtly as he had become self-centered and apathetic, as subtly did his eyes open and absorb. I don't know just when it started, but the fact that I don't was a good sign; a sudden turnabout wouldn't have been lasting. His patience grew, and his inherent sweetness returned to keep at bay the logical cold suggestions that he must go into a home. However, his struggle to conjure up courage and strength for the day ahead must have been man-size, for in the morning when I went into his room and he was still sleeping his face was not composed; his mouth was firm, his eyebrows drawn together."

There were nightmares. Hertha could hear Max crying out in the night as he relived the accident in his dreams. She would go down to his room, gently wake him, and reassure him he was safe at home. Then, once awake and fully conscious of his paralyzed state, he would silently show his frustration and anger. "At those times, I said nothing," recalled Hertha. "What was there to say? At twenty-two, would I have a child or a man? If I had uttered one word, he would have turned his fury on me and I would have deserved it . . . He was so dear, so brave, and I was so tired, so tired."

Max and Ernie settled into a routine each morning. Ernie would sit by Max's bed with the breakfast tray on his lap piled with memo book, insurance rate books, pad, and pencil and say, 'Now who do we have to call?'"

Hertha was upstairs one morning when Max called her from his phone. "Boy am I a salesman," Max said enthusiastically. "Am I a salesman!" he repeated. "I got two calls this morning from people who want insurance. One wants accident and the other, endowment. I'm going to call Mr. Meyers now and get all the information."

According to Hertha, Max "typed faster and neater each day with the left hand. He sat in his wheelchair at this desk, an arm sling held his elbow, which supported the metal wristband, which in turn supported a fingerlike metal extension that held up his hand at the palm. Sometimes he missed the top row of keys because there was scarcely space enough for the outstretched hand, at which he'd make a comic face at anyone who might be watching him. There was no doubt but that before my eyes there was emerging the man I had always known Max could be."

The Jesuit scholastics would visit Max almost every day. Bill Kelly and Pat Connolly were the most frequent visitors. They were always quick to help and kept the atmosphere light with constant jocularity. But one Saturday evening, even Bill Kelly halted his wisecracking when he saw Hertha's exhausted face after coming home from work. As she recalled, "One day the exhaustion that had been creeping up around me for some time reached up and swallowed me whole. Saturday, I had to show fourteen houses from one end of the suburbs to the other. That evening I had to work on a contract and take care of Max alone. I must have looked awful when I walked into the house. The expressions on Max's and Lecil's faces were of such concern I felt guilty. It took two double scotches and four phenobarbitals to put me to sleep that night, and then only for four hours. But with the prompt thoughtfulness that had been characteristic of people since the beginning of Max's accident things began to happen.

"I recalled the stern suggestion that Max must go to a convalescent home, but this time instead of furiously turning away, I was seduced. I toyed with the thought all through the early morning and felt like a person taking dope in the privacy of her room. As though inviting Lecil in on a conspiracy, I called her into my room and told her that perhaps it might be best after all for everyone concerned if we could find a nice place for Max. She looked through me and when I was finished she said quietly, 'All right; but just imagine the ambulance in front ready to take Max away. Could you let him go?'

"I imagined the ambulance, and even before the picture had developed into one of a full-sized ambulance I thrust it violently from my mind before it could carry Max away. He had improved so much, his left arm was growing stronger all the time from sheer will; his courage was great, his cooperation marked. I fell deep into despair, into this sticky net of weariness that pulled my intentions into nothingness."

"Mother, if only you would go to New York and stay with Janice and Al," Lecil pleaded. Janice Reiser was Hertha's classmate in college. "You haven't had a vacation for a year and a half, then there was this accident and more bills to worry about than you can possibly handle." Hertha relented, and the trip proved to be a balm for her.

Toward the end of her trip, Janice took Hertha to the Plaza, where the two women enjoyed five o'clock tea in the Palm Court. After the waiter brought their tea and pastries, the conversation once again turned to Max and his accident. Janice said to Hertha, "Max is so fine, so handsome, had so much to look forward to. You must have thought several times, Hertha, why did this happen to us?"

It was a question Hertha had heard many times since the accident. "No, Janice, I never did," she replied. "And I'm sure Max didn't either. You see, you can also think, why shouldn't it happen to me? We're not any better than anyone else," she continued. "Evidently, the Lord doesn't stress good looks too much, or rather, he doesn't want us to stress it or anything material too much. As for Max having had much to look forward to—he still has, probably more than before but it's on a more selfless basis. No, in spite of everything or rather, because of everything, I can see clearly that Max is making his life more worthwhile than he probably would have had he been just another good looking, pleasant young man living an average life. All this magnificent courage and well-balanced thinking he has shown would have been as a talent hidden under a basket if he weren't tried as he is being tried now."

Hertha paused thoughtfully as a violinist strolled by, and then said to her friend, "You know, Janice, each of us has a gift, be it medicine, law, the arts, or to be a good servant. Max's gift of humility, courage, and a subtle humor, emphasized by this physical tragedy, makes everyone who comes in contact with him just a little more unselfish and compassionate. Living under the same roof with him is a peculiarly happy thing. It's like living in a fourth dimension. Little things that used to matter are only part of the picture of life, but aren't important in themselves anymore."

When Hertha returned from her vacation, she was rested and ready to resume her duties. Apparently, her absence was good for Max, as well, having demonstrated to him that he could live more independently. As she noted in her manuscript, "I came home to a Max, self-assured and confident. 'We never get excited,' he told me. 'If something goes wrong, we just take it slow and easy.'"

PARTY HEARTY

When Gay Chadeayne and Tom Noonan announced their engagement in the spring 1960, all the Starkloffs went to their engagement party. It was one of the first times that Max attended a social function in his wheelchair, and he felt nervous. Ernie accompanied him, and Hertha kept an eye on him during the party. She noticed that he appeared to be enjoying himself, that there seemed to be a group of friends clustered around him the whole time. She apparently did not notice the stares he received, stares that Max tried to ignore. On the way home, she asked him whether he enjoyed himself.

"That was great," Max replied, "I'm going to more parties. At first it was a little hard to get used to, but then the girls began to look better to me than they ever did. It's good for my business, too." He did not tell her how uncomfortable peoples' stares had made him.

On the subject of business, Hertha asked, "Do some of these referrals know you're paralyzed?" "No, why should they?" was the reply.

Hertha wrote in her manuscript:

> And then came the day when Max could turn his left arm from side to side and with a little help could lift it. Outside a miracle, Max would never walk again. That he ever would use his fingers the doctors seriously doubted. Max knew all this. When it was spring and the world was like a large Easter egg, and young people in sports cars drove lazily or exuberantly through the neighborhood, I was alone with him. He had slipped down in the bed because of the spasms, and I couldn't lift him into a more comfort-

able position. We had to wait for Mike [one of Max's Jesuit friends] to come back. The tears squeezed from his eyelids and I left him for a few minutes. In a little while I came back and said, "I'm so proud of the way you're handling this, Max." And he said, "I cried, though."

"If you didn't, I'd be concerned for your sanity."

"There's still a great deal I have to get adjusted to," he said. "For instance, the length of time it takes to do things. Before if I wanted to go out I just went; but to dress me, get the wheelchair ready, the ramps up, going from bed to lift to chair; I'm still making myself take that without getting impatient. I've still got to get used to being so dependent upon other people. The hardest thing is getting other people to do things I feel I could do better, even to adjusting the TV set."

Shortly after Tom Noonan and Gay Chadeayne's engagement party, Max was invited to another party, this time by his sister. "I'm not going," Max said, and stubbornly resisted when Lecil begged him. It was an annual dance for St. Louis Notre Dame alumni that Lecil was attending with Steve. She felt Max would enjoy seeing a lot of his friends there. When Steve stopped by the house to pick Lecil up for the dance, Max was still reluctant to go. Hertha, going out herself for the evening, had asked Max's friend Mary Britton to stay with Max while she and Lecil were away. Mary arrived at 8 p.m.

"I knew he didn't want to go to the party," Mary recalled forty-five years later. "He had attended Tom and Gay's engagement party and didn't like the stares he received. It made him feel self-conscious." But Mary had a plan. She waited until she was alone with Max, then said sadly, "I feel badly that nobody invited me to the dance."

Max commiserated with her. "He was always a good listener," she recalled. "Then he asked me, 'I suppose you wouldn't want to go to the dance with me.' And, of course, I said yeah!" By then it was 9 p.m. Mary rushed home to put on a dress, and Ernie got Max dressed for the party. It was about 10:30 p.m. when they arrived, and the party was in full swing. Mary remembered entering the dance and seeing Lecil dancing with Steve. "When Ernie pushed Max's wheelchair out, Lecil stopped dead. 'Oh my gosh,' she said, and came running over. Soon everyone noticed, and Max was surrounded. Everyone was glad to see him and glad that he came. Max had a great time, and it was a turning point, a huge relief. Yes, people were staring at him, but this time it was for positive reasons. It took him years to get over being stared at by curious onlookers."

INTENSIVE CARE

The spasms in Max's legs continued to worsen that spring. "Eventually they had to strap me in my chair and tie me to my bed," Max recalled. "The spasms became so intense that if I wasn't belted to the chair, the spasms would throw me out. One time I broke two belt loops." Doctors didn't know what caused the spasms, and as the contractions became more frequent and intense, Max believed even the slightest movement, such as moving his eyes or even taking a breath, could trigger them. He became so exhausted at night that he couldn't sleep.

When he talked to chief neurosurgeon Dr. Smolik, Max was told, "If you continue with these spasms, you'll be dead in one year because of exhaustion." Smolik recommended a procedure known as a selective spinal cordectomy. First performed in the late 1940s,[2] the surgeon removes a section of the spinal cord below the injury. How large a section and where it's located is critical. If the cordectomy is too low, it has no effect. If it is too high, paralysis could be worse. It was a highly risky procedure in 1960, and it has been mostly replaced by drug therapy today.

Max's cordectomy was successfully performed in May 1960 and stopped the spasms. Dr. Smolik removed one inch of his spinal cord. But then new problems arose. While the spasms were killing Max in one way, they were keeping him alive in another. By causing Max's muscles to contract and expand, they had been keeping his muscles working, blood circulating, and body moving. Now with complete inactivity, three of Max's former nemeses returned: urinary dysfunction, respiratory infection, and bedsores.

To prevent bedsores, Max had to go back to being turned every few hours, day and night. He had to be awakened and turned several times in the middle of the night. This, of course, interrupted his sleep, further weakening him and rendering him more susceptible to disease. Hertha noted in her manuscript that he developed bedsores and also contracted a cold. To a healthy person, a cold can be a nuisance. To a quadriplegic, it can be life threatening.

Because Max's diaphragm was weakened by his severed spinal cord, his breathing had become shallow and he was unable to cough. Germs, which would normally be expelled through coughing, could settle deep in his lungs. If not treated with antibiotics, he would contract pneumonia. Hertha, Lecil, Ernie, Max's friends, and the young Jesuit scholastics all became Max's intensive care staff, monitoring his temperature, administering antibiotics, turning him, and irrigating his catheter. Hertha organized the routine.

By October, Max's condition had worsened. According to Hertha's manuscript, Max was running a 102°F–104°F temperature, and his bedsores had become worse. "We could no longer control them," she noted. "He was taken to Desloge." Under the care once again of Dr. Machek, Dr. Cannon, and the familiar Desloge staff, Max's urinary infection disappeared in three days. His bedsores, however, took much longer. After a month in Desloge, Dr. Machek gave Max permission to sit in his wheelchair, taking precautions that nothing press upon the areas in which the sores were located. "But for only a half hour at a time," ordered the doctor. "Typical of Max," recorded Hertha, "he stayed up in his wheelchair all day. Ernie took him up Grand Avenue to get a haircut. They returned to his room about three o'clock because, as Max said, 'I thought I ought to get to bed, but when I saw it, I thought "To hell with it," and visited with the nurses instead.'"

By mid-November, Max was eager to leave Desloge. "I've got to get home," he told his mother. "It's awfully easy to get lazy down here, and I'm losing out on my insurance." He was discharged and moved back into 7217 Lindell. Hertha wrote, "Lecil and I suddenly realized that we never spoke of Max dying anymore. We were taking it for granted that he would live a full life and a relatively long one."

•CHAPTER 5•

MARTY'S DREAM

When Marty came to visit Max one day early in 1961, he could tell immediately something was wrong. "She wouldn't look me in the eye," he recalled. Earlier, she had told him about a recurring dream she had. In her dream, they were married, sitting on a living room sofa. One of them would say, "It's time to go to bed." When they reached the top of the stairs, they would say "good night," then turn in different directions to go into separate bedrooms. The dream haunted her.

Marty's purpose for her visit in early 1961 was to end her relationship with Max. "I have someone else," she told him. "Yeah, well I have things to do, too," said Max, trying to imply that he, too, had lost interest. It was a brief visit. Marty said her good-byes to Max and Hertha, then turned and left.

The split was extremely painful for both Max and Marty. Looking back years later, Max said there were many unresolved issues on both sides of the relationship. "At the time," he said, "we were basically bullshitting each other." He regretted the way it ended.

Max's accident had brought Marty face-to-face with a young woman who couldn't bring herself to marry a quadriplegic. Visiting Max day after day, laughing with him through his ordeal, kissing him on his mother's living room couch, helping to put him in bed, Marty had so desperately wanted to believe that Max's condition was temporary, telling herself that the old Max would return some day; that he would drive up in front of Maryville in his sports car and bound up the college steps to sweep her off her feet. But a year had passed. She had taken a semester off from college to return home to sort out her feelings. She had seen violent leg spasms, leaking catheter bags, and Max's inert body falling out of a lift. Over the months, as the reality of Max's future penetrated her consciousness, Marty knew that her life with Max would be one of caring for someone who could not care for himself. Being Catholic had probably made her decision more heart wrenching, as she had been taught to suffer as Christ had suffered, to put others' needs ahead of her own, to be selfless and loving.

She had sought counsel from her parents and from Hertha, and she had talked to the nuns and priests at Maryville. Quietly, she had prayed for God's will for her and for the strength to do His will. But ultimately, she had to face the truth. While she could have married Max on August 9, 1959, she could not have married him on August 10 after the accident.

To Max, Marty's decision manifested his worst fear: that he was no longer a man, that he could not satisfy a woman. "Will women ever find me attractive?" he wondered. Like an ancient curse, Marty's dream now haunted Max, as well. He found himself waking from bad dreams of his own, swearing, angry and frustrated.

Max stuck to his routine. His mother would wake him in the morning and feed him breakfast. Ernie would come at 9:00 a.m., brush his teeth, comb his hair, and lift him from his bed into his chair. By 10:00 a.m., Max would be at work selling magazine subscriptions or insurance. At noon, Max and Ernie would have lunch, and then Ernie would take Max out for a drive in his little Morris Minor. At around 5:30 p.m., Ernie would put Max in bed, laying him on his side. Ernie would leave around 6:00 p.m., usually after

Hertha returned from work. Max would lie on his side until 10 p.m., at which time two high school–aged friends, Chick Patterson and Joe Mooney, would arrive, turn Max on his back, and give him a snack and water, the remote control, and telephone. Max would lie on his back all night, usually unable to go to sleep until midnight or later. He would watch movies until he fell asleep. On weekends he would usually never leave his bed.

On the days when he would go out with Ernie to visit a doctor or store, Ernie would position Max's wheelchair at an angle to the passenger door, then stand between the car and the chair. He would reach under Max, placing his hands under his bottom, and lift him into the chair. Max noticed that people would often stop to watch. "It took a long time to get used to," Max would say. He and Ernie would lighten the moment with jokes.

"At the time," Max recalled, "I was not even aware of the discrimination issue. But I began to notice when I was out in public in my wheelchair that people would treat me differently. They wouldn't talk about serious issues. They seemed to have low expectations of me, and always talked louder to me as if I were deaf. It was easy to isolate myself because going out was such a big production. If I wanted to go to a bookstore, for example, Ernie would have to carry me in because the aisles were too small for my wheelchair. People would stare at me constantly and ask personal questions like, 'How do you go to the bathroom?' I felt so different from everyone else, and I was always afraid of being labeled a cripple or an invalid."

When Ernie failed to show up for work one morning, Hertha called his wife to learn that he'd been in a car accident. The result was permanent brain damage, which, when Ernie eventually returned, manifested itself in erratic behavior. Once reliable, resourceful, and responsible, Ernie after the accident began to drift off center. He would show up late for work and forget what he was supposed to do. Regretfully, Hertha would have to find another person to attend to Max during the day.

One of Ernie's early replacements showed up for his first day dressed completely in white carrying a black medical bag and wearing a stethoscope around his neck. He introduced himself as Mr. Holiday. "He was a wormy little guy," recalled Max. "He carried himself like a Marine, very stiff. He would sit in a chair and stare straight ahead, never speaking until spoken to." At the end of his first day, Mr. Holiday became Mr. Yesterday. Another attendant nearly set the house on fire. A smoker, he had apparently fallen asleep while smoking upstairs in Max's old bed.

Neighbors like Charlie Grimm helped a lot during those days, as attendants came and went. The job required a willingness to learn, since most people lacked experience. It also required a personality match, someone with whom Max could get along. And, most important, it required a delicate balance between allowing Max his independence and controlling his life. Unfortunately, most of the attendants who drifted through Max's life in those years were looking for "real" full-time jobs elsewhere. They came and they went.

Eventually Hertha found Willie. Willie came recommended to her from the Reverend Charles Dismas Clark, a Jesuit priest, who founded Dismas House in 1959 in St. Louis as a halfway house for ex-convicts. Willie had done time for second-degree murder and, according to Max, hated cops. But Willie liked the job and liked Max. He worked for Max for eight months.

There were many days for Max when nobody was home. Hertha and Lecil were working. His friends were getting on with their lives. And Max would spend his days lying in bed. "People with disabilities face new problems after rehab," Max would later say. "Drugs, suicide, depression, anger, and abuse by others."

Max would again use his mind to fend off the demons. "Hope lasted a long time," Max said. "I would spend hours fantasizing. I would invent characters in my fantasies. Pretty fashion models I saw in magazines would become my girlfriends. Sometimes a fantasy would go on for weeks. In my fantasies I was always walking."

BACK TO THE RACETRACK

Max continued to look for ways to make a living. "I was getting bored selling insurance, and I knew I couldn't support myself selling magazine subscriptions." In 1962 he enlisted the help of Sam Furmin, a young man with whom he worked at National Lead until the time of his accident. Together they started the Maxim Company, a company dedicated to the new rage at the time: slot car racing.

"Max never lost his talent for persuasion," his sister Lecil recalled. "He could usually talk anybody into anything, and they would end up thinking it was all their idea." The slot car racing club was one example, formed when Charlie Grimm and Sam Furmin constructed a miniature racetrack in the basement of the Starkloff home. First they built a large plywood table the size of two rooms, then they laid on top of it interlocking pieces of black rubber "road" about six inches wide and eight inches long. Each piece had several metal slots running lengthwise that provided the electrical current and steered the car. The total length of the track ran about 100 feet, bending around curves and soaring over bridges and through tunnels. The racers would place their miniature cars on the track, fitting a small pin on the undercarriage into one of the metal slots. By turning a dial, they could speed up on the straightaways and slow down for the curves. Races were won and lost on the basis of knowing exactly when to speed up and when to slow down and by how much. Too fast into the turn, and the car would jump the track. Too slow, and your competitor would overtake you.

Clubs and teams were formed, and slot car racers of all kinds would come to Max's house on the weekends to race their cars. "They were people of all types," recalled Max. "Auto mechanics, orthodontists, truck drivers, blue bloods . . . you name it." They would hold three- or four-hour races.

The racetrack consumed hours of Max's time each day, as his friends would take turns driving his car. Max remembered one racer showing up at his house with a three hundred dollar car he had built himself. It had a special motor. "We held a time trial. He launched his car. It wiped out at the fence, hit the wall, and shattered into a million pieces." Max and Sam bought slot car parts from a discount hobby store and sold them. They ran an ad in a miniature hobby magazine. The business lasted eight months.

A DEATH SENTENCE

As hard as Max tried to make a go of it, the harsh reality remained for Hertha. Her real estate job was demanding and required that she work at all hours of the day, including weekends. Unreliable attendants for Max increased her stress and demanded that she find, interview, and hire replacements. Coming home at the end of the day when most people could relax, Hertha would have to cook, clean, do the laundry, and take care of Max. With Lecil gone, Hertha was doing it all. At age fifty-seven, it was grinding her to the breaking point.

In summer 1963, Carl was in his second year of studying theology at St. Mary's Seminary, seventy-five miles west of Kansas City, when he received a call from his mother. "I don't know how long I can keep Max at home," she said. The decision to move Max into a nursing home was a very difficult one for the whole family. Nobody wanted to lose Max to an institution. At the same time, Hertha was killing herself . . . physically and financially. Ironically, the government at the time paid $30,000 per year (approximately $221,000 in today's dollars) to keep people with disabilities in nursing homes. They paid nothing to families who wanted to keep their loved ones at home.

She turned once again to the Catholic Church. A priest and friend, the Reverend Bob Doyle, SJ, put her in touch with a Franciscan brother at St. Joseph's Hill Infirmary, a 130-bed, all-male facility located eight miles outside Eureka, Missouri. Operated by Franciscan monks since 1948, St. Joseph's Hill was a statement of modern thought and action, the embodiment of all that modern society could do for its aging male population, with a reputation as one of the best nursing homes in the country.

On October 11, 1963, Hertha drove Max to St. Joseph's Hill in her Nash Rambler. It was a long forty-five-minute drive during which Max remembered "no words were spoken. It was not like going into the hospital for a few weeks. This was it, the end of the road. I was going to where people go to die."

Even the building's entrance supported Max's worst fear. Incredibly, it was not wheelchair accessible, making it impossible for most of the residents to leave under their own volition. Hertha had been told in advance to drive around to the back where there was an open hydraulic freight platform that would lift Max to the first floor.

St. Joseph's Hill Infirmary, ca. 1963. The fourth floor was added after Max's stay.

Willie, Max's attendant, had followed Hertha in a truck that contained all of Max's possessions. He lifted Max into his wheelchair, and Max entered St. Joseph's for the first time via the freight lift. He was dressed in khakis, a blue shirt, loafers, and a jacket. As Hertha wheeled him into the main lobby, a large circular room in the center of the building, she and Max were greeted at the reception desk by Brother Dismas. Brother Dismas was one of the registered nurses. A small man younger than Max, Brother Dismas wore the traditional uniform of a male nurse: white trousers and a white shirt. He welcomed Max and Hertha in a condescending way that immediately made them both feel uncomfortable. "We have not had many quadriplegics stay with us," he told Hertha, not looking at Max. "We did have one once, and he became our pet," he said. Then, looking at Max and patting him on the head, he added, "But you're not going to become our pet."

From the lobby Max could see several statues of saints. He could look east and west down long corridors at the ends of which were bright, airy solariums. On the walls from the floor to about shoulder height along the hallway, in an effort to brighten an otherwise dreary walk to either of the solariums, someone had glued sheets of small, square, green-and-white bathroom tiles. Steve Saller's first impression was "institutional," "sterile," and "lonely and isolated."

The first floor housed the "ambulatories," the aged men who could still walk. Above were the "bed bound," and above that the "lock-up floor" for psychiatric patients. There were roughly 125 residents when Max arrived, and about fifty staff members, all men. The average age of the residents was eighty-five. And then there was Max, age twenty-six.

While the residents struggled with various health problems and the difficulties of growing old, their caregivers, mostly young men in their late teens and early twenties, struggled with their own issues. Many, like Brother Dismas, were gentle, submissive, and eager to please their superiors. They came into the Franciscan Order from across Missouri, feeling the need to commit to something greater than themselves. For the most part, Max remembered, the brothers were intelligent, likable, hardworking, and professional young men. But some dealt with low self-esteem, guilt, family poverty, abuse, homosexuality, and weak social skills, issues that they chose to address or avoid by cloistering themselves inside a religious order. While their high school friends were going into the workforce, getting married, and starting families, these young men found themselves tending to the needs of 125 institutionalized old and dying men. Max, perhaps feeling his own masculinity threatened by his new situation, often felt uncomfortable when tended to by effeminate or secretly gay men. He would be under the care of these young men for the next twelve years.

Max remembered his mother as being "very nervous and uncomfortable." Hertha had made the decision to place Max in St. Joseph's Hill based on her own conscience, along with the advice and counsel of those she respected. It had been motivated by her finally admitting that she could no longer care for her son and that there were no other alternatives. No doubt she told herself that she and Max had been blessed with this beautiful facility.

Without the help of Catholic organizations such as St. Mary's Hospital, St. Joseph's, and the Jesuits, there's no telling where Max would have ended up. Dr. Henry Betts, past medical director, president, and CEO of the Rehabilitation Institute of Chicago, described many hospitals and rehabilitation institutes in 1963 as struggling: "We were all finding our way." Nursing home options for someone with no insurance and limited financial resources were not good.

In spite of her constant reassurances to herself that St. Joseph's Hill was the best for her son, Hertha still experienced pangs of fear and uncertainty. Believing as she did that Max's mental condition was the key to his survival, she asked herself a thousand times if she was doing the right thing. Would the brothers honor Max's intellect? Would they allow him to be independent? Would he make friends? *Would he find a reason to live?*

Brother Dismas took them to the second floor, which would be Max's floor. Hertha followed as he wheeled Max into a small double room on the north side near the elevator, room 221. Like all the rooms at St. Joseph's Hill Infirmary, room 221 was spartan. It consisted of two beds, two dressers, and one chair, and it looked out at the world through one window.

Brother Dismas introduced Max to his roommate, an aging Catholic monk named Brother Francis. Brother Francis was lying in his bed and did not acknowledge their presence. Max would later learn that Brother Francis had multiple sclerosis, a progressive disease of the central nervous system. This, he thought, explained why Brother Francis rarely spoke to Max or, when he did, expressed only anger and hostility.

For Hertha it was one more early indication that she might have made a mistake. She asked Brother Dismas to step outside the room. "Max is supposed to have a single room," she told him. Brother Dismas no doubt informed her that single rooms were scarce at St. Joseph's Hill and that her son would get one as soon as it became available. There was nothing he could do. Max remembered the moment with a smile. "Here I was basically a welfare patient, and my mother was demanding a single room."

At 4:30 p.m., it was time for dinner, which was brought into Max's room by one of the nurse's aides. The food was institutional and consisted of unrecognizable meat, overcooked vegetables, bread, and milk. It tasted as bland as it looked. Hertha promised to bring Max a home-cooked meal when she came to visit every Thursday, a promise she kept for twelve years. Both tried as hard as they could to put on the Starkloff front: chin up, eyes forward, no looking back. By 4:45 p.m., as it began to get dark, Hertha said good-bye.

Max, feeling that he had reached the end of the line, felt more alone than he had ever felt in his life. He was being passed from one strong and loving woman to fifty seemingly indifferent men in the middle of nowhere. Would his friends visit him out here? How would the brothers treat him? Would he live here until he died? He'd been sentenced to a life term in an institution and his only crime had been to break his neck.

At 6:45 p.m., a nurse's aide arrived, introduced himself, and put Max in bed. The brothers were taught not to get too close to the residents emotionally in order to prevent the possibility of forming attachments. According to Max, there were three nurse's aides at that time, and he preferred all of them to the brothers, as the aides were "more relaxed."

At 9 p.m., his roommate spoke to him for the first time. "It's time to turn the television off," Brother Francis said. "It's 9 p.m." Max, being new and not knowing that St. Joseph's Hill had no such rule, obeyed. At 9 p.m. on a Friday night, twenty-six-year-old Max Starkloff was told to go to bed.

Max described the next day as "chilly and lonely." He sat in his room all day reading magazines and trying to adjust to his new life. He had no desire to meet his fellow residents. Several of the brothers came in and introduced themselves. He remembered Brother Pius, who Max described as "another touchy-feely sort" who seemed to be hovering around in the early days.

Brother Damien introduced himself at some point during the day. He was the head administrator of the nursing home. Brother Damien dressed in the traditional Franciscan brown robe, tied around the waist with a white cotton rope. He was a short man with a rounded belly and, according to the staff, "ruled with an iron fist." He was in charge of managing the day-to-day business of St. Joseph's Hill, which included the food menus and kitchen operation, and he approached all his responsibilities with a strictly by the book attitude.

Brother Damien reported to Brother Bernardo, a stocky, swaggering thirty-year-old Franciscan who patronized the residents and controlled the staff. Brother Bernardo was the Franciscan "superior," in charge of the Franciscan Order. One member of the staff remembered him as being "stern, tough . . . like George C. Scott in *Patton*." On matters pertaining to St. Joseph's Hill Infirmary, Brother Bernardo reported to a board of directors. In a religious order based on vows of obedience, both Brother Bernardo and Brother Damien could expect unquestioning compliance from the Franciscan brothers on all matters.

When the residents were not being tended to, they were on their own to the degree that they could be. Those ambulatory residents who had special skills or hobbies were encouraged to pursue them. Residents who liked to garden, for example, helped the brothers tend to the nursing home gardens. For the majority of residents for whom mobility was a challenge, the nursing home would organize activities such as barbeques, summer picnics, and bus rides into town to see a ball game or a movie. Residents could also watch TV or a movie in the solarium or just sit and stare into space.

Like an auto part entering an assembly line, Max was pulled into the nursing home's routine on his first full day. He was awake when one of the nurses brought him his meds at around 8 a.m. At about the same time, an aide brought him breakfast, which he ate in bed. After breakfast he was left alone for an hour or more, during which he was encouraged to take a nap. At around 9 or 10 a.m., an aide returned to bathe him, brush his teeth, comb his hair, empty his catheter, and lift him into his wheelchair. Rather than take the time and effort to dress him, the aide simply transferred Max in his pajamas and covered him with a blanket. Remembering the quads at Desloge, Max worried that this daily routine meant that he would never wear pants again.

At 11:30 a.m., lunch was served. Max could eat in either of two dining rooms or he could eat in his room. He chose to eat in his room. From lunch until 4:30 p.m. when dinner was served, Max spent his first afternoon at St. Joseph's Hill reading magazines and growing increasingly despondent.

He doesn't remember what his roommate, Brother Francis, said or did that day, but undoubtedly it was an adjustment for both men as nurses and nurse's aides tended to each in the confines of the small room. The fact that Brother Francis was crabby and irritable made it even more unpleasant.

Max's first afternoon was interrupted by Brother Anthony, one of the nurses who Max instinctively liked. He introduced himself and asked about Max's range of movement. Max explained that he had limited movement in his left deltoid, biceps, and triceps.

"Have you ever used these?" Brother Anthony asked, showing Max a rubber knob the size of a tennis ball.

"What for?" asked Max.

"If I attach several of these around the perimeter of the left wheel of your wheelchair, you may be able to move your chair by pushing on them with your wrist."

"I'll try it," said Max. Brother Anthony attached the rubber knobs to Max's left wheel. With great effort he managed to move himself a few inches. It was the first time he was able to move himself since the accident almost five years before. The significance was lost, however, because Max had nowhere to go. He thanked Brother Anthony politely and spent the rest of the day in his room. At 7:45 p.m., Brother Pius appeared to prepare Max for bed. By 9:00 p.m., all lights were out.

Socially, everything changed for Max when he entered St. Joseph's Hill Infirmary. None of the people in Max's "new world" had ever known Max the race car driver, Max the athlete, or Max the Marine. These people had only known him since he had become Max the quadriplegic. To them, he was just 1 of 125 residents.

ISOLATION SETS IN

Unlike living at home, where friends frequently dropped by, few of Max's friends were willing to make the ninety-minute round trip to Eureka. They were all getting on with their lives. "I felt so isolated and lonely," Max recalled. "I desperately needed to talk to someone. I couldn't talk to anyone in my family about it because they were responsible for putting me there and already burdened with guilt. I couldn't talk to friends because I felt embarrassed. I didn't want friends to visit because I didn't want them to see me in a nursing home."

Two of his earliest visitors were Patty Wilkerson and Gay Chadeayne Noonan. Patty, after graduating from Maryville in 1961, had entered the Convent of the Sacred Heart in Albany, New York. Patty and Max both remember frequent and long visits at St. Joseph's Hill during those early years. "I remember sitting on the edge of Max's bed," she recalled. "In my family, feelings were almost irrelevant. Max's desire to express his feelings to me was such a gift. I had no idea at the time that I was important or could have any impact. Max was the first person who ever spoke honestly about what was going on inside of him. And that was so important to me." Forty-five years after the accident, Patty still choked up while telling the story.

Max remembered they "would talk about everything" for hours. Patty wanted to be a nun since the age of twelve. She had just been asked to leave the convent for reasons she didn't understand and was wrestling with many big issues in her life. "Both of us," recalled Max, "were searching for direction."

Between visits, Max learned to rely on the power of his imagination. "I would create a family, give each [person] a name, and imagine how each person looked," he remembered. "Sometimes I would create baseball teams, memorizing imaginary players, their batting statistics, wins and losses. I created a racecourse in my mind and memorized every curve. I would fall asleep while fantasizing and the next day pick up the fantasy where I left off."

·CHAPTER 6·

BROAD AND BRAZEN STROKES

L ate in the afternoon on Monday, October 14, Max met Brother
Matthew. "He saved my life," Max would recall. Using his new
wheelchair knobs installed by Brother Anthony, Max had slowly
pushed himself out into one of the solariums after lunch, where
he sat alone. Brother Matthew, forty, appeared in the solarium
wearing the traditional brown Franciscan robe and an old apron
smeared with oil paints. He sat down next to Max and started
chatting and joking. He was the resident artist, he explained, and
he had his own studio in the monastery next door. Brother Matthew held a degree from the Newark (New Jersey) School of Fine
Arts and a Purple Heart for injuries in World War II.

"Have you ever thought of painting?" he asked Max.

"No," came the reply.

Unknown to Max at the time, Brother Matthew had taught
four other quadriplegics to paint using various creative ways
to hold a brush. He wheeled Max to his studio, located on the
ground floor of the old castlelike monastery. Hanging on the walls
were hundreds of small, colorful paintings of clowns and animals,
which all exuded a cheerful contrast to the hard gray Ozark gran-
ite. Light flooded into the room, and Max inhaled the distinctive
smell of oil paints.

"I sell these to the tourists who visit the Black Madonna
Shrine," Brother Matthew explained, motioning to the colorful

paintings. The Black Madonna Shrine, located about a mile up the road, is a Franciscan monument that attracts hundreds of tourists each year. Brother Matthew's studio was not air-conditioned in the summer. In the winter, it was heated by a small, wood-burning stove. His three-legged cat, Yardstick, was curled up in one of the chairs.

A week later, Max returned. "Let's get going," he said. Brother Matthew cleared a space for him in an accessible corner of his studio. He rigged up an easel from a hospital-bed table and placed it on top of a bench. To the side of Max's wheelchair he attached a shelf on which was rigged a revolving painter's palette. With a touch of his brush, Max could turn the palette to access any color.

Brother Matthew had also taken the caps from hypodermic needles and placed them on the ends of brushes. He positioned Max close to the canvas, squeezed tubes of colors onto the palette, and started teaching him to draw using a brush clenched in his teeth.

At first Max would draw simple things, a tree or a building. Then Brother Matthew would cut pictures out of magazines and ask Max to copy them. Max worked hard, six hours a day, totally captivated by his newfound artistic talent. "It made me feel independent and creative. I could decide what I wanted to paint, pick whatever color I wanted, and create."

It was not easy getting Max into the studio because, like the nursing home itself, it was not wheelchair accessible. Brother Matthew would have to lift Max up three steps in his wheelchair to maneuver him into the entrance. It was a task he performed willingly every day. Within months, Max was showing amazing progress.

While Max was finding new life on the inside of St. Joseph's Hill, Hertha was finding new life on the outside. In a letter to Carl

Brother Matthew wheeling Max from the
art studio.

dated simply "Sunday eve," she wrote, "Oh it is so GOOD to listen to nothing but the down-pour, then to walk and walk and walk and stop and listen. To look at birds, leaves, fuzzy caterpillars. To look at the sunlight making a path through the trees; butterflies thinking they were birds."

On October 22, 1963, Max, using the electric typewriter he brought from home, wrote Carl a letter. He had learned to use a mouth stick, a long fourteen-inch dowel with an eraser on one end, to press each letter on the typewriter keyboard. For each capital letter, he would depress *Caps Lock*, depress the key for the

MAX PAINTING, JANUARY 1964. PHOTO BY ROY COOK. COURTESY OF THE
ST. LOUIS GLOBE-DEMOCRAT.

letter he wanted capitalized, then depress the *Caps Lock* key again
to unlock it, and continue. "Well, I'm finally getting situated out
here and liking it more every day," he wrote. "I actually have a
lot more freedom and am able to do a lot more." His letters were
always positive and upbeat. "They were basically a lie," Max recalled years later. "I just didn't want anyone to know how miserable I was. After all, what could they do?"

His letter to Carl continued, "There is a Bro. Matthew out here
who is an artist. In fact all he does is paint. Anyway, I think he may
TRY and teach me how to paint. I would paint with my mouth by
hooking the canvas on the wheelchair. It will be fun to try."

While Brother Matthew promised a world of creativity and freedom within his small studio, Max still had to spend most of his time in an institution with aging and dying old men. Like Max, each resident was placed in the nursing home because, for one reason or another, his family either couldn't or wouldn't care for him.

Orville Benson was one of Max's neighbors. A small man in his early sixties who walked with a cane, Orville had had a stroke, creating a condition that the nurses called "automatic speech." According to Max, Orville was intelligent and aware of everything going on around him; however, if asked a question, he would always reply, "Yah, yah, yah. I be God damned!" or "Oh, balls!" Orville had no family as far as Max knew, and over the years, Max would invite him to be with his family during the holidays.

ORVILLE BENSON.

Three months after Max's arrival, he was moved across the hall into a single room, room 216. Here he would reside for the next seven years. Room 216 was furnished the same as his old room except it had half as much furniture (one bed) and faced the front of the building, or the south side. It was two doors east of the solarium.

Each morning the nurses would hold their regular staff meetings in the solarium, giving reports on each resident. If Max's door was open, which it usually was, he could hear every word spoken in the meeting. The nurses would cover every intimate detail of every resident's life such as, "John's a little grumpy this morning," or "Bill's constipated." Max learned to turn on his radio to drown out the meetings, but one morning he overheard one of the nurses talking about him. "Max had a bowel movement yesterday," the nurse said. "It was hard and large."

NEIGHBORS

While St. Joseph's residents changed monthly and numbered in the hundreds over the twelve years Max spent at "the Hill," some of them stood out in his mind. On the south side of the building to the west of him in a double room was Roy Rothcoff. Roy was seventy-five to eighty years old, stood five feet nine inches tall, and had thick white hair. He had survived a stroke and, although he often appeared cranky and irritable, Max liked him and saw his mannerisms as his means of survival. Roy kept the brothers and aides on their toes.

East of Max were more single and double rooms, plus several wards. Jack Coleman occupied the room three doors down. He was a huge man in his early seventies and was in the Hill because he had had a stroke and had no family to care for him. He was a professional opera singer and had sold his recording studio to raise the money to enter St. Joseph's Hill. He owned stacks of opera records and loved to play them on his record player at high volume. On Saturday nights, he listened to the Metropolitan Opera broadcast on the radio, taking particular delight in the Texaco Opera Quiz hosted by Edward Downes during the second intermission. The brothers found him an irritant because he preferred playing his records to playing by the book. To keep him in line or to punish him for playing an opera too loudly, they would confiscate his records or radio.

Jack was also a palm reader and amused the nurses and aides by reading their palms. Once Max asked Jack to read his palm. "You have a long, long life line," he told Max. "There is a break in your line when you were younger." Max took that to represent his accident. "And," Jack continued, "there is going to be a woman in your life. She will be tall, have dark hair, and be quite a bit younger than you are." Max couldn't imagine at the time how accurate Jack's prediction would be.

Next door to Jack were several wards containing two to four beds each. In one of the wards lived Jimmy Gallagher. Jimmy had cerebral palsy. With great effort he managed to move himself around on the floor in a wood-and-wicker Roosevelt wheelchair, fully reclined. His speech was slow, muffled, and hard to understand, and for that reason, the brothers considered him mentally retarded. Seeing Max reading one day in the solarium, Jimmy wheeled himself up to him and with great effort asked Max to read to him, which Max did. He was reading Kierkegaard at the time. Jimmy returned every evening for two to three years, and Max read to him for one hour or more each night.

Leo Grace was one of Jimmy Gallagher's ward mates. Leo was a stubborn, pompous, cigar-chewing old man who knew important people. France "Fran" Laux was important in his day, and fortunately for Leo, Fran lived one floor down on the ambulatory floor. Fran had been the Voice of St. Louis Baseball for KMOX radio from 1929 until 1943. He called the Cardinals and St. Louis Browns games live from Sportsman's Park and re-created the games from Western Union telegraph dispatches when the teams went on the road. Fran knew all the star players. A photograph taken in 1930 shows him in his prime, posing with Lou Gehrig and Babe Ruth. Known as a quiet, low-key broadcaster, he was a dour-looking man, articulate, and well educated.

Fran often bragged that he had worked for twenty years without missing a broadcast or arguing with a player or umpire. That was because he hadn't yet met Leo Grace. After Fran entered St. Joseph's Hill, they could be heard arguing baseball out in the hall. Then the subject would change to the brothers and staff. After grousing about them for a period of time, Fran would always end the discussion by saying in his loud baseball announcer voice, "Well, they're not very good Christians!"

Further east toward the end of the hall were three single rooms. Papa Shank occupied one of those. Described by one member of the staff as being "about 104 years old," he had to be "locked" into bed each night with leather restraints. One door down from Papa lived Walter Reed. Walter was the information epicenter at the institution. In constant pain from rheumatoid arthritis, his legs were permanently bent. In order for him to sleep, harnesses had to be employed, which the brothers hung above his bed. Walter could only move about with the aid of a wheelchair, sitting very stiff with his head tilted back.

Walter's room was filled with electronics. On top of his desk sat a microphone, a Morse telegraph key, and a ham radio trans-

MAX, POP LANG, AND FATHER FITZGERALD, WHO ALL LIVED
AT ST. JOSEPH'S HILL.

ceiver. On a table next to his bed were a television and an AM-FM
radio, both of which he would rely upon every day to get national
and local news. He also subscribed to a number of newspapers
and magazines: the *St. Louis Post-Dispatch*, the *St. Louis Globe-
Democrat*, plus *Time* and *Newsweek*. Not only was he informed
on news happening on the outside, he somehow always knew what
was happening on the inside, as well. He knew who was leaving
and who was arriving, and what was happening to each resident
at all times. Walter took an interest in Max, and vice versa. Max
would visit him for the news of the day and found him informa-

tive and entertaining. Next to Walter Reed in the room adjacent to the east solarium lived Father Mel Schneider, a retired Catholic priest suffering from multiple sclerosis. According to one staffer, Father Schneider was in a lot of pain and "yelled a lot."

Early in his tenure at St. Joseph's, Max met Mrs. Abbot, a volunteer social director and one of the few women working there at the time. Mrs. Abbot tried repeatedly to get Max involved in the Hill's social activities, such as bingo and other games, movies in the solarium, or trips to St. Louis and nearby attractions. Max would have nothing to do with any of these and heard later that Mrs. Abbot once referred to him as "angry and bitter."

The tours inside St. Joseph's Hill did nothing to improve Max's attitude. Busloads of women tourists visiting the Black Madonna Shrine and Grottos nearby would continue their pilgrimage to St. Joseph's Hill Infirmary, where they would visit Brother Matthew's studio to buy his cute and colorful paintings, perhaps say a prayer in the chapel, and get a tour of the nursing facility.

Brother Patrick, a short, heavy, dark-haired, unpleasant man Max remembered as "a real jerk," would be their tour guide. Without knocking, he would enter Max's room while Max was lying down and invite all the women into the small room to see his paintings. Tousling Max's hair like one would an obedient dog, he would exclaim, "Isn't it amazing that he can paint a straight line? He actually holds the brush in his teeth!" The women would cluck and marvel. "Considering how he paints, I think Max is pretty good," he'd beam. Departing, several of the women would pause, gaze at Max and say, "Isn't it nice that you have something to occupy your time?"

Max recalled, "I felt like a monkey in a cage. I started closing my door when I heard him coming, but he would barge in anyway. Then I would play possum and pretend to be asleep. None of it made any difference to Brother Patrick. When he finally left, he would always leave the door open."

Every so often, one of the residents would die in his sleep. When this happened, and it was usually discovered by one of the nurses or nurse's aides early in the morning, St. Joseph's policy called for assuring that all the residents were in their rooms with their doors closed before removing the corpse to the morgue in the basement. Once removed, the doors were opened and the residents could resume whatever they were doing. Of course, the procedure itself was notification to every resident that one of their fellows had expired and all anyone had to do was visit Walter Reed to learn the name and room number of the deceased.

One day, while wheeling himself into one of the solariums, Max saw a man in a chair who appeared to be asleep. As he got closer, he noticed that the man appeared to have a hot dog hanging out of his mouth. Curious, Max pushed himself closer to see to his horror that the hot dog was the man's tongue. The man had died.

FAMILY TIES

Hertha was a frequent visitor to the Hill, as she came every Thursday and always brought a home-cooked meal for Max, which the two of them would often eat together in his small room. She also made sure Max came home for Thanksgiving, Christmas, Easter, and other occasions. She would drive her Nash Rambler up to the back of the freight lift, and a couple of nurse's aides would wheel Max down on the lift and up to the car, lift him in, and tie him to the front seat with sheets. When she got Max home, Hertha would enlist the help of neighbors and would often ask the Jesuits to help her. Because Max's hospital bed, lift, and other things had been moved to St. Joseph's Hill, he would only stay for the day. Then someone would drive him back to the Hill later in the day.

Max's first visit home was on November 28, Thanksgiving Day. Upon arriving, he saw for the first time that Hertha had reconverted her first floor back to its original layout. The dining room was back to being the dining room. He knew also that his slot car racing track in the basement had been dismantled and given to Sam Furmin when the Maxim Company was disbanded. Max remembered no melancholy on his first trip home, just gladness to be there and to see his friends and family.

Lecil and Steve arrived and introduced Max to his nephew, Christian Saller, who was only twenty-one days old. Little Gretchen, one year and eight months old, gave her Uncle Max a kiss. They had brought so much child-care equipment! Lecil and Steve were now a young family. They, like many of Max's friends, had gone on with their lives, marrying and having children, while Max felt he was stalled on the highway of life. He allowed himself a brief pang of sadness, but—taught by his mother—it was never his habit to dwell on negative emotions. "I never lost hope," he later recalled. "It would make me sad when my friends would come out to visit me at the Hill and they would bring their spouses and children, and I would envy them so much. But I always felt that somehow I would leave St. Joseph's and have a family of my own someday. I didn't know how or when, but I never lost hope."

A PAINTER NAMED STARKLOFF

By winter 1964, a reporter from the *St. Louis Globe-Democrat*, Nell Gross, had heard of the young quadriplegic painter cloistered in a Franciscan infirmary. She wrote in the paper's Sunday magazine,

With the jaunty air of a Continental clenching a cigarette holder, the handsome young man grips his brush. Then with bold, broad strokes he sweeps the canvas with a blaze of powerful color."

Plunging into art with the same dauntless courage he developed during the troubled last four years, Max now dashes off paintings at the rate of two a week. His first seven, recently displayed at Kenrick Seminary, sold at $25 each. From a later exhibition at Fusz Memorial, 3700 West Pine Blvd., six more were sold at $35 apiece.

Between work sessions, he lives and dreams painting and studies history of art. Ideas for new paintings come faster than he can paint them; his mind rushes with pictures demanding expression.

Next to the photograph of Max holding a brush in his mouth is the headline "How a Courageous Former Marine, Paralyzed from the Neck Down in Auto Crash, Found a New Interest in Life—in Painting."[1] Only four months after meeting Brother Matthew, Max had already sold thirteen paintings.

Max also read voraciously. Carl had introduced him to his favorite existential philosophers, Albert Camus and Søren Kierkegaard, one an atheist and the other a Christian. Both philosophers believed in the absurd, that is, that humans exist in a meaningless, irrational universe wherein people's lives have no purpose or meaning. Camus had died, ironically, in a sports car accident in January 1960 of a broken neck. "His death," wrote the Parisian newspaper Le Monde, "confirmed in a macabre way his vision of an absurd, inexplicable and incomprehensible world."[2]

PHOTO FROM A NEWSPAPER ARTICLE TITLED "A PAINTER NAMED STARKLOFF." COURTESY OF THE *ST. LOUIS GLOBE-DEMOCRAT.*

Max was most intrigued with *The Myth of Sisyphus*, a long essay on the absurd that Camus wrote in 1942. According to Greek mythology, Sisyphus was sentenced by the gods to roll a boulder up to the top of a mountain, let it roll back down, then repeat the task forever. Camus saw Sisyphus as a happy champion of the absurd, since he was aware of his fate. This awareness, according to Camus, transformed his torment into victory. Max was so taken with this idea that one of his later paintings was of a man pushing a boulder uphill, a painting that reflects Max's state of mind at the time, as it exudes all of the torment of Sisyphus but little of the transformation to victory.

THE PAINTING *MAN AND HIS ROCK*
BY MAX STARKLOFF.

Søren Kierkegaard was a Danish philosopher and self-styled "religious poet" writing in the early to mid-nineteenth century. Rebelling against schools and society in general, which, in Kierkegaard's opinion, were producing legions of nonindividuals, he maintained that each person should take responsibility for defining his or her own self. To do so involved going through a progression of stages: "aesthetic," or immersion in sensuous or pleasurable experience; "ethical," in which one makes a choice of and commitment to a life path; and "religious." One must passionately and repeatedly renew his or her beliefs in a higher power, Kierkegaard maintained, which can never be rationally understood but only believed in. One's *beliefs* ultimately determined one's *true self*.

The teachings of both philosophers resonated with Max on many levels. While he may not have felt the victory of Sisyphus at the time of his painting, Camus's essay kindled a hope that victory could be attained—even in spite of the most desperate of "life sentences." And Kierkegaard's rebellion against normalizing institutions also must have struck a chord. Indeed, both philosophers in their own ways supported rebelliousness and offered Max road maps through the absurd world in which he lived.

Watching the news one night in Walter Reed's room, Max realized he wasn't the only one rebelling. Racial violence had erupted in many cities across the United States. The press was calling the summer of 1964 "the long, hot summer." President Lyndon Johnson, campaigning on the promise of the Great Society, had signed into law on July 2 the Civil Rights Act of 1964:

> To enforce the constitutional right to vote, to confer jurisdiction upon the district courts of the United States to provide injunctive relief against discrimination in public accommodations, to authorize the Attorney General to institute suits to protect constitutional rights in public facilities and public education, to extend the Commission on Civil Rights, to prevent discrimination in federally assisted programs, to establish a Commission on Equal Employment Opportunity, and for other purposes.

At the time, nobody could absorb its full impact. No doubt Max and Walter discussed the news of the day, as the race riots of the summer of 1964 exploded in Harlem, Philadelphia, St. Augustine, Florida, and other cities. To many of the older residents in the all-white institution, it must have seemed like all-out anarchy.

•CHAPTER 7•

WHAT ARE YOU DOING IN A NURSING HOME?

The dawn of the New Year, 1965, saw more civil rights actions and anti–Vietnam War demonstrations. Dr. Martin Luther King Jr., having just been awarded the Nobel Peace Prize, had been called upon by black leaders in Selma, Alabama, to help them get black people registered to vote. During January and February, no doubt Walter Reed, Max, and the other residents at the Hill saw on the evening news Dr. King and others being roughed up and thrown in jail. The following month, three men gunned down Malcolm X at Manhattan's Audubon Ballroom. And on March 7, state troopers beat King's voting rights marchers on the Edmund Pettus Bridge in Selma, a day that now lives in infamy as "Bloody Sunday."

Max's world at the Hill, however, continued as it always had, with Max focused on his own mission: becoming the best artist he could be. In a letter to Carl dated April 12, 1965, Max wrote,

> My show is less than two weeks away and I'm better pre-pared for it than expected. There will be about 14 paintings for sale, and a few others on display, including your train station.

> Did I tell you that Mother, Brother Matthew, and myself went out and took pictures? Anyway, the pictures turned

out fine and should keep me busy for a long time. I am just finishing up an old deserted house that is about 5 miles from here in Allenton, Missouri. There is so much to paint around here that a person doesn't know where to start. When you are here maybe we could take a ride and you can see this country.

Keep praying for that exhibit. Not that I make a lot of money, but that somebody thinks that my paintings are good enough for a gallery.

On June 2, 1964, after thirteen years "in formation," Carl Starkloff was ordained into the priesthood in a ceremony in St. Marys, Kansas. Hertha and Lecil attended, but it was deemed too far for Max to go. Max was able to attend Carl's first Mass, however, at St. Joseph's Church in Clayton, Missouri, a few weeks later.

At about that time, Carl delivered more good news: Father Sebastian, the chaplain at St. Joseph's Hill, would be taking a three-week sabbatical that summer, and he, now *Father* Carl, had agreed to conduct the daily Masses. He would be able to see Max almost every day for three weeks. Max was delighted not only to have Carl with him at the Hill, but also to have an ally, as he continued to resent the brothers' unceasing efforts to control every aspect of his life.

"I remember the food was awful," Max recalled. "They had a tendency to overserve you stewed tomatoes. Too many times a week! We'd have these stewed tomatoes with all the juice sloshing around the meat and the mashed potatoes, so much that it all looked like it was going to float off the plate. So I put it on a tray and brought it downstairs and showed it to Brother Damien, who was the administrator. I wanted to make the point that the meal was ruined because it was not being served properly. "He said, 'How dare you come down here and complain—after we've treated you so nicely.' That really upset me. I went back up to my room and cried. I was so mad."

During the summer, Carl would make the forty-five-minute drive every morning from his room at Saint Louis University to St. Joseph's Hill to conduct Mass. During the afternoons or evenings, Max and Carl would go out in Carl's car. One night in the summer of 1965, Carl brought Max back to the Hill and went inside to get someone to help him lift Max out of the car. Walking into the building, he found several nurses who claimed to be too busy to help. Finally he asked the head nurse on duty that night, Brother Patrick, Max's tour-guide nemesis, who said he would come right down. Carl returned to Max and they waited, but Brother Patrick never appeared. Finally, Carl's patience began to run out. He went in again and within minutes Brother Patrick came hustling out to help. "What did you say to him?" Max asked his older brother later. "I told him to get his fat ass downstairs right now."

By 1966, Max had moved his paints and canvases from Brother Matthew's studio to his room. This was made possible by the gift of a custom-made electric easel designed and built by Hertha's friend, Tom Drennan, president and CEO of the Sioux City and New Orleans Barge Lines. "It was big," recalled Max, "and made out of steel posts. They electrified the easel so it would go back and forth horizontally and also go up and down vertically. That way I could paint on larger canvases and move them around." As his room was very small, the easel and whatever was on it dominated the room. Max's neighbor, Roy Rothkopf, would clean his brushes for him every day.

AVOIDING THE TRAP

By 1967 Max had been living in the nursing home for a little more than three years. "I never lost hope," Max said, although hope ebbed and flowed. "A major article in *Time* promised a cure for quadriplegia. It was about a Canadian neurosurgeon who worked on quads in Russia and got them to walk. There were pictures of quads walking." Max wrote a letter to the doctor via *Time*. He never received a response, as the whole thing was later revealed to be a hoax. "That sort of thing happens all the time," he would say later.

He also found articles about Vietnam veteran quads who were moving to Mexico, where they could hire personal attendants for extremely low wages. Without telling his family, Max explored living in Guadalajara. With attendants, he believed, he could live independently as the vets were doing. He pictured himself living on the beach in Mexico. He sent for brochures but eventually abandoned the idea because he didn't want to hurt his mother's feelings. And he was fearful of placing his critical daily living needs in the hands of strangers.

Max said years later about life in a nursing home, "It was easy to fall into a trap of complacency, of having all your needs met every day. If you could get rid of your pride and self-worth," said Max, "you'd be fine." "The hallways were completely deserted at 6 p.m.," Max recalled. "All you could hear were the TV sets. All the residents had to look forward to every night was to check their *TV Guide*. That scared the hell out of me. I wanted to avoid getting caught in that trap." He avoided the nursing home's dining room, as well as its mindless social and recreational activities, and tried to focus on staying mentally active.

After looking back, Max said that it was long periods of isolation and loneliness that, surprisingly, helped him the most.

"Those early years, 1963–1970, were very critical years. Critical psychologically and emotionally. I didn't know what I was getting into in 1963. Would I die at the Hill? Would I have friends? Would I be chronically lonely? There were no [interstate] highways in those days, so it was quite a long drive for my friends. I was really frightened."

Max started painting out of curiosity and because he desperately wanted to keep his mind active. As he explored the world of art, he became interested in many painters, particularly the German expressionists. "A lot of expressionist work was very angry," Max said. "As was my own work. I identified with the way they expressed their feelings in their work. Expressionism really intrigued me." To get ideas for his paintings, he read a lot. And he thought a lot.

"I went to bed at 6:45 every night," said Max. "So I was alone from 6:45 until about 11:00 every night. There [were] only a table lamp and two small windows, so there was nothing to distract me. I would lie in bed and listen to classical music, and images would run through my head as I listened. The images inspired paintings. St. Joseph's gave me time to think."

Max's thinking did not go unnoticed at St. Joseph's Hill. "I was the only liberal in a very conservative establishment," he recalled. "I was constantly getting into debates and arguments with the staff and residents. I supported Martin Luther King and the whole civil rights movement. I supported antiwar demonstrators. Many people took offense at my liberal views. A few people called me a Communist."

Max continued to express himself in his paintings. "One of my paintings showed an angry black man," Max said. "Another was a portrait of a hippie with angry eyes."

The monks talked about his work to each other and to Max. Upon seeing Max's feelings expressed on canvas, some of the monks asked Max, "Why are you doing this? It's not right." "So I started painting nudes just to shock them," Max recalled with a grin. "And it worked, of course."

Max continued to worry about the future. "I had little college; no degree. I had no business experience. I felt stuck. The time by myself forced me to begin thinking about what I could create that would enable me to be financially independent."

THE PAINTING *FOR THE MONKS* BY
MAX STARKLOFF.

During the day, Max's daydreams were effective in warding off boredom and despair. Alone for hours at a time during the days, he would often fantasize about meeting a beautiful girl. In his fantasies, he was always upright on his feet when he met the girl, gorgeous, of course, with a perfect body, smooth skin, and silky blond hair. He envisioned himself a successful artist, and she would happen upon him painting. Curious, she would initiate the conversation. Max would create the witty dialogue that would eventually win her heart. His daydream scenarios would often continue for weeks as he and his fantasy girlfriend embarked on adventures together.

In 1967, another event captured Max's attention. For the first time ever, young women were being hired to work at the Hill. With names like Wilma, Hazel, Thelma, and Dora, they began to make the rounds. Most were farm girls, a little on the stocky side, plain looking, hardworking, well meaning, and simple. Not exactly what the residents might have been fantasizing about but a lot more exciting than watching the monks or, worse, each other.

Max remembered meeting one nurse's aide on what must have been her first day on the job. She was plain looking and had two teeth missing. "She was very sweet and caring," Max recalled, "but one step above the brain of a squirrel." Her black hair was pulled back in a knot behind her head. On this particular morning, she was giving Max a sponge bath while he lay on his back. As she worked her way from his neck to his feet, she finally stopped in the middle and said as casually as she could in a Missouri twang, "Do ya want me ta wash your scruples?" According to interviews with four St. Joseph's Hill staffers, she was a housekeeper, not a nurse's aide. Perhaps she thought cleaning the rooms also involved cleaning the residents.

Max also remembered nurse's aides like Terry Goggins and Donna Oberkramer, who were highly professional, dedicated, and became good friends. When a new aide named Bobbie arrived, however, in 1968, the testosterone level, such as it was, went way up. The news probably came from Walter Reed: single, nineteen to twenty years old, and sex-ee! "Have you seen Bobbie?" some of the old men asked Max. "You've gotta meet her! She's foxy."

Max, knowing that Bobbie would come to Walter Reed's room first on her bed-making rounds, positioned himself in the doorway of Walter's room. Sure enough, along she came. "I remember thinking, 'They're right,'" Max recalled. When she entered the room, she introduced herself to Max. He liked the way she looked him in the eye, and especially the way she asked him for his room number.

"That evening when she got off at 4:30," Max recalled, "she came in to say 'hi' to me. She said, 'Can I sit down and visit?' 'Sure,' I said. So she sat down on the edge of the bed and we talked. She asked a lot of questions, such as where I was from and who my family was, casual conversation. Then she got up to leave and she looked at me and said, 'Can I give you a kiss?' 'Hell, yes,' I thought, and she gave me a kiss on the mouth, tongue and all!" It was Max's daydream come true. "That was the beginning of my realization that maybe I'm not asexual," Max said, "that maybe I could be attractive to a pretty woman."

Max and Bobbie became an item and went on dates for a while, a situation that created a lot of controversy at the Hill. No doubt, with its all-male history and population of celibate Franciscan monks and aged men, the management had not had a lot of experience with the issue of a female staff member dating and being intimate with a resident. "One evening we were going out for dinner," Max recalled. "I was dressed in a coat and tie, and Bobbie was dressed up as well, looking very fine. Seeing both of us, one of the monks, Brother Mark, a sheepish little man, started quizzing me. 'Who's your guardian?' he asked.

"'I am,' I told him. I was thirty years old at the time.

"'Well,' stammered Brother Mark, 'You have to get permission to go out.'"

"This was new," Max recalled, "since I had never had to get permission before. So I asked him why. He looked embarrassed. 'Well,' he stammered, 'we're just not sure if this is appropriate.'" Max told him to get out of his room and leave them alone, and nothing more was said. Word did get to the head nurse, Brother Patrick, however, who decided to handle it a different way. "Brother Patrick staked himself outside my room one evening, when he knew my mother would be arriving. When he saw her, he said, 'Mrs. Starkloff, may I have a word with you?' When he had taken her aside, he explained in a very concerned tone that I had been seeing one of the young nurses.

"'Oh, yes,' my mother exclaimed. 'Isn't that wonderful!' Brother Patrick was totally taken aback by my mother's response. When she reached my room that evening, she was giggling. 'I think I just upset Brother Patrick,' she said."

MIKE'S MARK

Early in 1968, Alabama governor George Wallace and Robert Kennedy announced their candidacies for the Democratic presidential nomination, and President Lyndon Johnson announced he would not run. Four days after Johnson's announcement, Dr. Martin Luther King Jr. was assassinated.

Seven days after that, President Johnson signed the Civil Rights Act of 1968,[1] making it illegal to discriminate in the sale, rental, and financing of housing based on race, religion, and national origin. Discrimination against people with disabilities who wished to buy, rent, or finance the purchase of a home would continue for another twenty years.

At St. Joseph's Hill Infirmary that year, a new nurse's aide named Mike Dahl arrived. Mike had been a Trappist monk for ten years before coming to St. Joseph's Hill. Max took an instant liking to Mike and vice versa. "There was nobody like Mike on this earth," Max said. "Mike was my age, about six feet two inches tall, with light-colored hair. He was a big man, but not overweight, and a poet at heart; a dreamer, and a philosopher." Mike was also a talented painter and a sculptor and spent hours in Max's room talking and listening to Simon and Garfunkel records. "He had a big imagination and even bigger dreams," Max said. "He was always looking for the ideal world." To Max, who felt shut in and powerless, Mike provided intellectual fresh air.

Unfortunately for Max, Mike was employed at the Hill for only about a year. He continued to stay involved in Max's life, however, in various ways. Whether it was his conversations with Mike, reading philosophers, his success as a young artist, or seeing the success of people struggling against the war and racial discrimination, Max began to gain more self-confidence. "I began to realize about then," Max said, "that the real problem wasn't my disability. It was society's limiting attitudes about disability, my own attitude included!"

Spring 1969 brought warm breezes, budding flowers, and Gay Chadeayne Noonan to St. Joseph's Hill Infirmary. Gay, along with Lecil, Steve, and their children, organized a visit one sunny weekend and brought with them Gay's guitar and a picnic lunch. There was a lot of discussion about art. Inspired by Max Beckmann,

Max had switched to a German expressionist style two years earlier. Gay told Max she had visited a friend recently who collected art and she noticed one of Max's paintings hanging on her wall. "That's a Starkloff!" Gay exclaimed to her friend, excitedly. "I just love the painting," remarked her friend. "It has a power in it that I've never seen anywhere else."

An entry dated March 31, 1970, in a diary that Max kept for only a few weeks gives a glimpse of what Max was feeling at this time:

> What plays an important role in my painting is my being paralyzed. Losing my sense of touch and the ability to move adds a burden to understanding the anatomy along with feeling textures. But the other senses become more alert.

> Something I have learned from the German expressionists is how to live in a hostile environment. These men intentionally stayed in these areas using them to their advantage. I believe much of this is the same with me here. As far as artistic encouragement goes there is absolutely none....

> This is a big problem for me wanting to have an intelligent conversation and not being able to dig one up. When Mike Dahl was working here there was always a penetrating subject brought up. We were interested in much the same things and willing to discuss them. I miss this very much and sometimes find it very difficult to keep my mind from being wasted....

> There must be encouragement from some direction because I believe as Eric Hoffer says "the artist is chronically

insecure." A person can paint for months at a time and never have public encouragement. The painter needs recognition, not for the money because he could popularize himself with the public by doing what is "avant-garde" or doing whatever will sell. He needs recognition of his honest work to instill confidence and to let him know that what he is doing is worthwhile.

By the end of 1969, Max received encouragement from a totally unforeseen direction. A letter arrived from a woman in Chagrin Falls, Ohio, who he had never met, Gini Laurie. "What are you doing in a nursing home?" she wrote. Max later learned that Laurie had heard about Max "through the grapevine" and decided to write him.

An early advocate of independent living, Laurie is regarded by many as being the "grande dame" of the Independent Living Movement.[2] Laurie was adamantly against nursing homes and often ended her presentations with the message "[Quadriplegics] need a pair of hands that they can direct. They do not need to be buried alive in a nursing home. They need to continue to live their lives as they choose."[3] No doubt, some words to this effect were conveyed in her letter to Max, providing possibly the first encouragement Max received to leave the nursing home and begin living independently.

Max continued to pour himself into painting, however, working hard to complete enough new paintings for a one-man show at Maryville College in December 1969. He presented thirty paintings, a huge number for someone with only six years' experience. "I worked hard," Max recalled. But it would be his last year as a serious artist. "After that show was over, I didn't feel that excited about painting." Something inside him had changed.

GINI LAURIE, GRAND DAME OF THE
INDEPENDENT LIVING MOVEMENT.

The year 1969 seemed to have unlimited possibilities, as Neil Armstrong and Buzz Aldrin demonstrated on July 20 when they walked on the moon. If man could walk on the moon, why couldn't a quad live independently outside a nursing home?

NURSING HOMES IN LIFE

Other people were beginning to ask the same questions as Gini Laurie. In 1963, Max was among the few under sixty years old in a nursing home. By 1970 thousands of young men with Vietnam War injuries, many with paralytic conditions, found themselves institutionalized at Veterans Administration (VA) hospitals. Conceivably, these men could have futures, but not with the care they were getting.

That same year, *Life* magazine produced a groundbreaking piece on the treatment of wounded vets. Reporter Charles Childs reported that

> one out of every seven U.S. servicemen wounded in Vietnam is fated to pass into the bleak backwaters of our Veterans Administration hospitals.

> With 166 separate institutions, the VA hospital system is the biggest in the world. The 800,000 patients it treats in a year, mainly men wounded in earlier wars, range from cardiac to psychiatric cases. It is disgracefully understaffed, with standards far below those of an average community hospital. Many wards remain closed for want of personnel and the rest are strained with overcrowding. Facilities for long-term treatment and rehabilitation, indispensable for the kind of paralytic injuries especially common in this war of land mines and boobytraps, are generally inferior. At Miami's VA hospital, while sophisticated new equipment sits idle for lack of trained personnel, patients may wait hours for needed blood transfusions. At the VA's showplace hospital in Washington, D.C., a single registered nurse may minister to as many as 80 patients at a time. At the Wadsworth VA Hospital in Los Angeles, doctors who work there describe ward conditions as "medieval" and "filthy." [4]

The article followed a Marine lance corporal, Mark Dumpert, who was sitting in the front passenger seat when his military truck was hit by a six-foot rocket. It took seventy-five minutes to transfer him to a hospital ship, then four days later medevac surgeons fused his broken neck and told him the good and bad news: He would survive, but he would be paralyzed from the neck down for the rest of his life. Eventually he ended up in the Bronx VA Hospital.

"Here in this ward," he said in the interview, "living with the misery of six neglected guys who can't wash themselves, can't even get a glass of water for themselves, who are left unattended for hours . . . it's sickening.

"Nobody should have to live in these conditions," Dumpert insisted. "We're all hooked up to urine bags, and without enough attendants to empty them, they spill over the floor." The article featured a two-page photograph of Dumpert dripping wet in a shower stall waiting helplessly in his wheelchair for an attendant to dry him.

"The rats were the worst. I had been sleeping on my stomach," Dumpert recalled. "It wasn't 11 o'clock, but I had closed my eyes. I suddenly awoke to find a rat on my hand. I can't move my hand, so I tried to jerk my shoulders. I screamed and the rat jumped slowly off my bed."

Many nursing homes combined the neglect of the VA with abuse. In his book *No Pity: People with Disabilities Forging a New Civil Rights Movement*, Joseph Shapiro wrote about a young man with cerebral palsy, Jeff Gunderson, whose struggling single mother had run out of options for her son's care. He was sent to two nursing homes in Wisconsin from age eighteen to twenty-seven: At both nursing homes, Gunderson says, the staff tried to break him. Sometimes aides tied him to his bed. They would drag him into cold showers as punishment. To make him use the bathroom on a schedule convenient for the nurses, they would put ice cubes down his pants. It was a form of torture for Gunderson, because the cold set off his spastic muscles. On several occasions,

Gunderson says he was given a suppository before sleep and, since he could not move by himself, he would spend the night lying in his own feces.[5]

Such reports led to a move by many to shut down the worst institutions—*deinstitutionalization* it was called. Oddly, it was often the family members of those in the institutions who fought to keep them open. Critics said those families did not want to face having to bring their loved ones home to care for them.

Max remembered the article in *Life* magazine and had heard and read about similar nursing home abuses. While he considered himself lucky compared to others confined to institutions, he still felt morally outraged that otherwise healthy people like him were being subjected to neglect and abuse for no reason other than the fact that they were disabled.

"Once you were institutionalized," wrote Mary Johnson in her book *Make Them Go Away*, "you were at the mercy of staff. Incarcerated for no crime other than disability, people considered severely disabled or 'feeble-minded' were historically segregated into special institutions, usually run by the states. They were not able to leave, no matter how much they wanted to. No other non-criminal group in America, not even slaves, had been so confined."[6]

THE DREAM

Max's dream occurred in May 1970. "I dreamed of an apartment complex built for people with disabilities in which they could live and work. It was accessible; there were environmental controls—lights, phone, doors, etc.—attendants. It was a utopian environment for people with disabilities where they could also be entrepreneurs. And it wouldn't just house people with disabilities. Anyone could live there."

Max fell asleep again assuming that the idea would probably sound ridiculous in the morning. But then morning came, and the idea still excited him. He told Brother Anthony of his dream that morning, and instead of telling Max it sounded ridiculous, Brother Anthony responded encouragingly, "I don't know why that wouldn't work."

Max called Gay Chadeayne Noonan. "He said, 'I have this crazy idea.' He laid out the idea, and then asked me what I thought. I remember thinking that it was a great idea, but that it would never work."[7] Next he called his mother, who was enthusiastic. "Call Ted Bakewell," she suggested. Bakewell was her boss at the real estate company that bore his name. He was also a family friend. After hearing Max's idea, Bakewell asked some questions, then reacted positively. "It could work," he told Max. As a first step, Bakewell suggested that Max put together a board of directors. To do that, Max felt he would need a more professional way to present his idea.

With help from the nurses, he typed a rationale for why he felt such an apartment was necessary and assembled photos from magazines, which he pasted in a binder. He also collected letters from rehab nurses and disabled people talking about the perils of life in a nursing home and pasted them in the binder. "Max seemed different after he came up with his apartment idea," Gay recalled. "He was more positive, goal oriented."

In early June, Max held a meeting at his mother's house. In attendance were Steve Saller, his brother-in-law, and Father Bob Doyle, a Jesuit priest who was finance chief at Jesuit Provincial House. Moved by Max's idea and brochure, both men were supportive and enthusiastic, but neither had the resources nor the expertise to get it off the ground. They suggested he seek legal advice.

Max then called a friend and attorney, John Boyce. According to Max, "Boyce got things rolling." Like Ted Bakewell, Boyce felt a board of directors would be a good first step. Being an attorney and knowing Max would need to raise money, he recommended that Max apply to the IRS for 501(c)(3) status, exempting him and future donors from federal income tax.

Max asked his doctor, Dr. Elizabeth Stoddard, associate director of rehabilitation at Jewish Hospital, to serve on his board, and she accepted. Hertha recommended her friend Tom Drennan of Sioux City and New Orleans Barge Lines. He accepted. Another family friend, Marjorie Eddy, also agreed to serve. Max had his board.

Soon thereafter, Drennan called Max at the nursing home and offered to get an audience with U.S. Rep. Jim Symington, newly elected to Congress from Missouri's Second District. Drennan suggested that they write a proposal outlining Max's idea for the apartment with the hope of possibly receiving government funds. They decided to name it the Para-Quad Project, short for paraplegics-quadriplegics. The proposal, written July 10, 1970, from St. Joseph's Hill in Eureka, Missouri, under Drennan's signature as temporary chair of the Para-Quad Committee, spelled out the ambitious extent of the project:

> A facility designed as a residential and commercial complex has been conceived that would enable physically disabled and handicapped individuals, primarily paraplegics, quadriplegics and amputees, [to] render a service to the local community and contribute to the economy of the country. Of prime importance is the fact that, upon becoming a reality, the complex would allow these people to become self-supporting through participation in private enterprise.

In the preliminary planning stages, a complex consisting of 250 dwelling units and 50 to 60 commercial units incorporated into one connected structure is envisioned as the pilot unit. The overall project and planning is under the direction of Mr. Max Starkloff, a quadriplegic, who has enlisted the help of several civic, religious and business leaders, all volunteers, who will help formulate plans to obtain the necessary funding for feasibility studies, location surveys, architectural assistance, etc.

In addition to his administrative responsibilities, Mr. Starkloff is responsible for the technical design features which would enable the inhabitants to work and reside within the complex with a minimum of effort and a minimum of dependence upon aides. (Technical designs include such projects as ramps, door widths, and placement of wall plugs, bathroom fixtures and other details to facilitate the highest degree of physical independence.)

The livelihood of the inhabitants of the complex would be derived from ownership and/or employment in the commercial stores and shops of the complex. In addition to individual proprietorship, national and regional companies would be solicited as tenants whose responsibility it would be to hire and train the physically handicapped who reside in the complex.[8]

Max, Drennan, and the committee sent the proposal to Symington's office with high hopes, but no money was forthcoming.

Max's friend Mike Dahl, in the meantime, had been telling everyone he knew about "Max's project." One of the recipients of this news was a Catholic priest, the Reverend Jerry Wilkerson, who suggested that Max see an architect-friend, Laurent J. Torno. Laurent had graduated from the Washington University in St. Louis School of Architecture in 1962 and helped start the architecture firm Berger, Field, Torno, Hurley, Architects. The firm employed sixteen people and did a lot of work for Southwestern Bell, as well as a lot of housing work specializing in renovating and readapting historical buildings. Rev. Wilkerson suggested to Dahl that Torno might know of an existing building that could be readapted to accommodate people with disabilities.

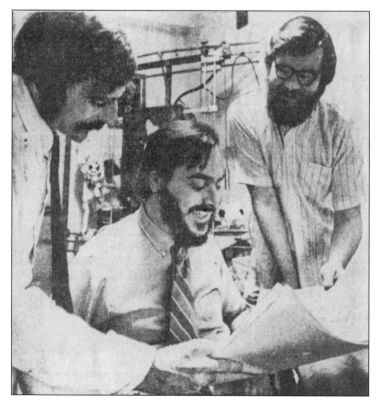

LAURENT TORNO, MAX, AND MIKE DAHL REVIEW PLANS FOR A NEW APARTMENT COMPLEX. PHOTO COURTESY OF THE *ST. LOUIS POST-DISPATCH*.

Dahl drove Max into St. Louis and visited Torno in his office. Max presented his apartment idea using his homemade brochure. He talked about his concept for the apartment, his board of trustees, and his appeal to Symington. Torno remembered Max's first visit. "His initial idea was to create a vertically integrated complex in which one lived, worked, and played. It was a very naive sort of concept, which before long Max realized was predicated on the notion that somehow or other people who are disabled didn't have all the dissimilarities that everybody else does. But Max was determined to build a building that would facilitate independent living." Torno recalled, "The concept of a building that would facilitate independent living interested me. But what really interested me was Max. He had an extraordinary outlook on life."[9]

Torno would make countless eighty-mile round trips to the nursing home to continue discussions with Max, and he would later devote thousands of professional hours to Max's project. He never charged Max a cent. When asked why he donated so much professional time to Max's project, Torno said, "I judge people a lot by their faces. There was not one ounce of self-pity. This is the hand he was dealt, so he's gonna play it. And he's gonna use absolutely everything he's got to play that hand. It's very easy not to realize how disabled he really is because his whole personality just completely overcomes this extremely high level of disability. Then you start spending time with Max and you quickly realize there aren't a lot of people like that in the world."[10]

During his early discussions with Max, Torno felt that market research would be essential—not only for determining the size, scope, and capabilities of the project, but also for justifying it to investors. "If we're going to build housing," he told Max, "we have to find out what the need is." He suggested that he and Max work with a group of urban planners and designers who called themselves Team Four.

Team Four had started just two years earlier in the summer of 1968, formed by four recent master's program graduates from Washington University in St. Louis: three urban planners and one with a degree in urban law. The name, Team Four, had been inspired by Team Ten, a group of ten influential architects who came together to help rebuild Europe after World War II.

Torno introduced Max to Richard Ward,[11] the managing partner of Team Four. Like Torno, Ward was also impressed by Max and his vision and believed that further research was necessary. He and his partners had no experience with anything like Max's project, and he felt they needed an accurate assessment of the demand for disabled housing, as well as whether such a project could support fifty to sixty commercial units. He and his partners would be willing, he said, to donate their time and services initially to get it going. However, the market research and needs assessment would cost $20,000 in out-of-pocket expenses. It sounded like $20 million to Max.

A few days later, John Boyce called to say he was unable to gain 501(c)(3) status for Para-Quad. "It's too new," he told Max. "You have no bylaws, no structure, no funding." Max asked him, "If I open a chapter of an existing foundation, the National Paraplegia Foundation (NPF),[12] could I put the Para-Quad Project under its not-for-profit wing and thereby gain 501(c)(3) status?" Boyce thought for a minute. "It's a bit unorthodox," he said, "but I think it would work."

By July 24, the secretary of the State of Missouri certified and declared Paraquad (Max's new styling of the word) a corporation. Anyone wishing to visit the new corporation would find its headquarters in room 216 at St. Joseph's Hill Infirmary and President Max Starkloff working at his desk, a door laid across two pieces of furniture.

The news of Max's project began to spread. Bob Huskey, a quad, first heard about Max's project when taking painting lessons from Brother Matthew at St. Joseph's Hill. Huskey was not a resident of St. Joseph's. "Brother Matthew brought the subject [of Max's apartment complex] up one day," Huskey recalled. "He asked me if I thought Max's idea was crazy. Did I think he was being realistic? He asked me if I would talk to him."[13]

When Huskey visited Max at the Hill, they became instant friends. "When I met Bob, I met my first role model," Max said. "Here he was, a quad like me, and successful on the outside. He was married, had two kids, exuded confidence, and was content with his life." Huskey had broken his neck at the age of twenty-one while bodysurfing. At the age of twenty-four, he fought his way into Southern Illinois University in Carbondale, Illinois, a campus with limited accessibility at the time and little or no experience with severely disabled students.[14] He was thirty-three years old when he met Max. He had earned a Ph.D. from Saint Louis University and was in charge of a staff of twenty speech pathologists and audiologists at St. Louis Special School District. He was also president of the board of the Easter Seal Society of Missouri and on the board of the Missouri Speech and Hearing Association. He later went on to become associate superintendent of St. Louis Special School District, responsible for all the special education programs in St. Louis County.

Huskey was an early advocate of independent living. "Max's idea seemed huge. There was nothing like it at the time, and no guidance in any way about anything. I thought Max's idea made a lot of sense," Huskey said, but then added, "I remember him telling me he needed to raise twenty thousand dollars, a figure that seemed impossible."[15]

Specially designed homes for the disabled were not unprecedented. In 1959, the year of Max's accident, James Rosati and Sons, developers of a fourteen hundred–unit retirement village in St. Petersburg, Florida, built "a specially designed home for physically disabled, cardiac and elderly persons," that they called Horizon Home. The home's amenities, which included ramped doorways, accessible light switches, wider hallways and doors, and a specially designed kitchen, were based upon the recommendations of Dr. Howard Rusk and his staff at the Institute of Physical Medicine and Rehabilitation at New York University Bellevue Medical Center and their book, *A Functional Home For Easier Living.* Horizon Home was a pioneering effort lauded by Dr. Rusk in his weekly health column in the *New York Times.*[16] There are no records, however, of anyone ever designing an apartment building to meet the special living and working needs of disabled people while also accommodating nondisabled people.

Max also told his friend Patty Wilkerson about the project. She had moved to San Francisco in fall 1968, after graduating from Saint Louis University with a master's degree in social work, where she was working in a psychiatric hospital. After hearing about Max's apartment idea, she asked, "Have you heard about Ed Roberts?" Max hadn't. By the time Wilkerson finished describing Roberts and what he was doing, Max wanted to meet him immediately. It was the first time Max had heard of other people with disabilities advocating for independence, the first inkling of a "movement." Roberts lived in Berkeley, California.

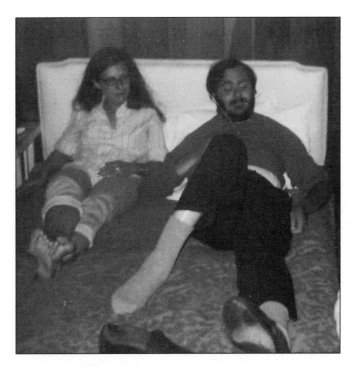

PATTY WILKERSON AND MAX IN A MOTEL ROOM
IN MENDOCINO, CALIFORNIA.

SAN FRANCISCO

Max, accompanied by one of the monks from St. Joseph's Hill who
was flying to San Francisco to see his sister, visited Wilkerson and
Roberts late that summer.[17] Mike Dahl, who had moved earlier to
San Francisco to pursue Wilkerson, met Max and offered to drive
him to see Roberts. It was Max's first visit to Berkeley. After seven
years in a nursing home in Eureka, Missouri, it was, in Max's
words, "quite a culture shock." The University of California–
Berkeley campus was an epicenter of countercultural activities.
Berkeley students in the 1960s saw themselves as the generation

MIKE DAHL, MAX, AND PATTY WILKERSON'S BOYFRIEND,
JIM LOVE, IN CALIFORNIA.

that would save the world . . . through free love, feminism, antiwar protests, gay rights activism, civil rights demonstrations, organic farming, and other revolutionary ideas.

Max and Dahl felt the excitement. It was unlike any place they had ever seen. People talked differently. They dressed in self-made, brightly colored tie-dyed T-shirts, bell-bottom pants, head scarves, and beaded necklaces. The men wore their hair long or in Afros. The women wore thin peasant blouses with no bras underneath. There were VW buses painted with peace symbols and Peter Max–style psychedelic graphics.

Dahl drove Max to the address Roberts had given him, 2532 Durant Avenue. Had Max ventured a few blocks over to Telegraph, he would have seen the first accessible street in the nation, as wheelchair ramps had just been installed in 1968 or 1969.[18] Roberts's apartment and office was located in a second-floor apartment above a Mexican restaurant in a neighborhood that looked more like Mexico than California. The apartment was accessible by a long, steep, jerry-built wooden ramp at the back of the building.

Dahl pushed Max in his folding wheelchair up the ramp into the back of the apartment. Inside Max saw a number of people, some in wheelchairs, all talking animatedly. A radio played the new Rolling Stones hit, "Gimme Shelter." The apartment's living and dining rooms had been converted into an office. The floors were bare, dusty wood. The place was sparsely furnished with Goodwill furniture and cheap desks. There were no books, no pictures on the wall. Open windows were framed by old, dusty curtains left behind by a previous tenant.

A large, heavyset man noticed them and came over. He had a black, bushy beard, a lot of wild-looking hair, and was dressed in overalls with no shirt. Max told him he had come to see Roberts. Without speaking, the large man crossed the room to a group of four or five people surrounding a man in a wheelchair. He spoke to the man, nodded, then returned to Max. "He'll be with you in a minute, man," said the giant. Then, holding up two fingers in a V, he said, "Peace, brother," and disappeared.

Roberts was seated at a forty-five-degree angle in a power wheelchair controlled by a joystick at his left hand. A plastic tube ran from his mouth to his respirator, attached to the back of the chair. He gulped air every few words when he talked. He had a broad, strong face with long, unkempt hair and a moustache and beard that exaggerated the fact that his head was out of proportion to his body. As Max drew closer, he was greeted by a warm smile and penetrating eyes. Max, dressed in his usual khakis, button-down cotton shirt, and Bass Weejun loafers, felt out of place. "I was embarrassed, excited, and intimidated all at once," Max recalled. "The whole free-spirit thing was something new. And I wasn't used to seeing a busy quad with a respirator."

Roberts spoke between inhalations, so his sentences were succinct and direct. While he could intimidate people with his focused nature and penetrating eyes, he could just as easily melt them with his heartwarming smile and sense of humor.

As a healthy, active fourteen-year-old, Roberts had contracted polio in 1953. "I had a serious fever," he said "and within twenty-four hours, I was paralyzed and in an iron lung."[19] When Roberts's mother asked his doctor whether he would live or die, the doctor told her to hope for his death. "If he lives," said the doctor, "he'll be no more than a vegetable for the rest of his life."

ED ROBERTS, DATE UNKNOWN.

Roberts decided he wanted to die. He stopped eating. In spite of the hospital's intravenous feeding, he lost fifty-four pounds. The nursing staff gave up on him. "My last special duty nurse left, and the next day I decided I wanted to live. You see, that was a big turning point. Up until then, these nurses were available and doing things for me around the clock—I didn't have to make any decisions for myself because they were always there. When they all finally left, that's when I realized that I could have a life, despite what everyone was saying. I could make choices, and that is freedom. I started to eat again."

After about a year in the hospital, Roberts moved back home to a small suburban town on the San Francisco peninsula. An eight hundred–pound iron lung moved back with him. Roberts's mother, Zona, was a feisty labor organizer who believed that if

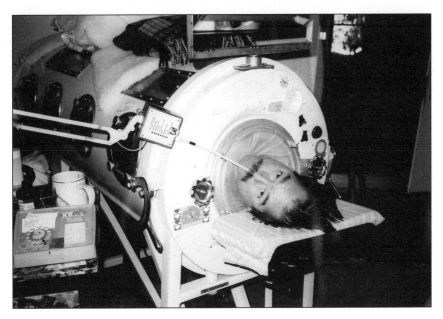

ED ROBERTS IN AN IRON LUNG, 1986.

you asked a person a question and received a no answer, then you were either asking the wrong question or the wrong person.[20] She got her son excited about education, "education from the neck up." For three years, Roberts attended high school by telephone. "During my senior year," Roberts recalled, "my social worker and my mother got together and kicked me in the ass. They told me that if I didn't get out of the house now, I would never get out. So I went to school for the first time. I had taught myself glosso-pharyngeal breathing, where you swallow air into your lungs, so I had been spending time out of the iron lung before. But I was scared to go out and be seen by people.

"I remember the day very clearly. I arrived during lunchtime. My brother lowered me out of the back of the station wagon, and it was like a tennis match—everyone turned to look at me. I looked at someone, right in the eyes, and they turned and looked away. That was when I realized that maybe it wasn't my problem; maybe it was their problem. I checked myself out, and I realized two things. First, their looking at me didn't hurt, physically, and secondly I realized, hey, this is kind of like being a star . . . and I've been a star ever since." During his senior year, Roberts could spend one day a week in the classroom. He could go six hours without his iron lung.[21]

"It was the end of my senior year when they told me that I couldn't graduate—because I hadn't taken P.E. and driver train-ing. My mother was so pissed off. 'He can sit on my lap and I'll hold the damned wheel for heaven's sake!' she told them. The vice principal came over to my house and told me, 'Now, Eddie, you wouldn't want a cheap diploma now, would you?' We kicked him out of our house. My mother took it to the school board. This was my first real fight, and she was the one who showed me the ropes.

We told the board, and they thought it was absurd."[22] Roberts received his high school diploma.

After high school, Roberts attended the nearby College of San Mateo, hoping to become a sportswriter.[23] In 1962 his adviser convinced him to apply to the University of California in Berkeley. Before doing so, however, he applied to the California Department of Rehabilitation for financial assistance. He was turned down, told by the counselor that he was too disabled to ever work. Roberts's mother and others took action. They went to the press. Out of embarrassment, the Department of Rehabilitation granted him financing. He applied to UC Berkeley and was accepted. The application form contained no questions about disability.[24] When the school found out he was disabled, however, it refused him admission on the grounds that the campus wasn't accessible. "When I first began talking with the administration, they told me, 'We tried cripples, and they don't work,'"[25] he recalled.

But Roberts was adamant. He found routes around the campus that would enable him to attend classes. He reapplied and then was told that the school had no dorms that would accommodate an eight hundred–pound iron lung. Determined, Roberts got permission to stay on campus at the university's Cowell Hospital, arguing that the hospital floors would support the weight of the iron lung. He won his admittance, ironically, the same time as another rights activist. "The same semester James Meredith, an African-American, was escorted into an all white classroom [in Mississippi], I was rolling into a Berkeley classroom,"[26] Roberts remembered.

As word of Roberts's success spread, the university cautiously admitted five more quads, then one year later admitted nine more.[27] Ed Roberts and the other quads began to share their experiences and frustrations in late-night rap sessions, taking over the third floor in Cowell Hospital. They discussed their ideas passionately, challenging authority, discarding accepted beliefs and practices, drawing up radical philosophies of independence, and refusing to accept powerlessness and lack of control over their own lives. By 1967 they were calling themselves the Rolling Quads and had become a political force to be reckoned with on campus.[28]

By 1968, Berkeley had accepted enough students with disabilities to the point where it needed more space. Roberts petitioned the university for a place where students with disabilities could gather to take advantage of peer learning. He learned about the Student Special Services Program at the U.S. Office of Education, wrote a proposal, and was awarded a grant to begin a new program called the Physically Disabled Students' Program (PDSP). PDSP was so successful, disabled people in the community began to use its resources.[29] Eric Dibner was a participant in the early establishment of the PDSP: "We would help people find attendants and help them with housing services . . . transportation—because back in 1970–71 you couldn't ride a bus if you used a wheelchair. [We helped] people with the peer counseling issues, which were really important for just knowing how to do something and feeling that you can do it. And [we helped] people with benefits counseling: how to use the system and make the system work. And [helped] with equipment, assistive technology—like wheelchair repair."[30]

When Max came to Berkeley in 1970, Ed Roberts was working to expand the PDSP program off campus, creating what he called the Center for Independent Living, which opened in 1972. Like PDSP, it would provide services designed to help people with severe disabilities live independently in the community, outside hospitals and institutions. It would be managed and staffed *by* people with disabilities *for* people with disabilities, he told Max.

The old medical model, which for centuries had held disabled people hostage under the yoke of "sick patient," was being thrown out in favor of a new self-care movement.

Under the old model, the physician was the expert and principal decision maker. The patient was sick and best "cured" through the use of surgery, drug therapy, and other ministrations applied in hospitals and other institutions by "trained professionals." Under the new model, once the disabled person is medically stabilized, he is encouraged to be in charge of his own care and treatment. "The sick role," wrote Nancy Crewe and Irving Zola in their book, *Independent Living for Physically Disabled People*, "is intended to be a temporary one. But for the long-term or permanently disabled person, there is no possibility of immediate recovery, in the sense of being restored to one's original physical condition. Because disability is often an irrevocable part of their existence, disabled people, as a result of the sick role, begin to accept not only their condition but also their very personhood as 'aberrant' and 'undesirable.' Moreover, they begin to accept the dependency prescribed under the sick role as normative for the duration of the disability."[31] The disabled person gradually slips into a kind of second-class citizenship. How Max agreed with that!

The student program Roberts started was radical. He redefined independence as the control disabled people have over their lives. "Independence was measured not by the tasks one could perform without assistance but by the quality of one's life with help," wrote Joseph Shapiro in his book, *No Pity*. "The health care system offered only custodial help. Roberts rejected this in favor of innovative self-help and group organizing."[32]

The Independent Living Movement advocated living on one's own resourcefulness, encouraging even the severely disabled to acquire whatever services they needed in order to participate fully in society. Based on his experience living and learning with the Rolling Quads, Roberts and others felt that the best people to counsel disabled people were not nondisabled doctors, nurses, and therapists, but rather ordinary disabled people just like himself. They were the ones who knew how to meet the challenges—mental, physical, and spiritual. Or if they didn't know, they were sure as hell going to learn.

The Center for Independent Living "was a revolutionary concept at the time," Roberts recalled. "Most people never thought of independence as a possibility. But we knew what we wanted, and we set up the center to provide the vision and resources to get people out into the community. The [center] was also revolutionary as a model for advocacy based organizations: no longer would we tolerate being spoken for. Our laws said that at least 51 percent of the staff and board had to be people with disabilities,[33] or it would be the same old oppression. We also saw [the center] as a model for joining all the splintered factions of different disability organizations."[34] It was the start of a nationwide self-help movement that would forever change how people with disabilities saw themselves.

Max told Roberts about his idea: an apartment built especially for people with disabilities—that would also be available to nondisabled people—to serve as both an office and living quarters, and as an environment for entrepreneurialism. He talked for a long time. Roberts listened patiently without interrupting or asking questions. When Max finished, there was a long pause. "It felt like twenty minutes," Max recalled, "but I'm sure it was only a few seconds." When Roberts finally spoke, his first words were, "That's not the way we do it here." Max's confident smile faded. He was puzzled. He even felt offended.

Roberts was opposed to special living centers no matter how well designed or integrated. He believed disabled people should live wherever they wanted. Their "struggle for independence was not a medical or functional issue, but rather a sociological, political, and civil rights struggle."[35] Nondisabled people relied on a wide variety of services, such as auto mechanics, grass mowers, carpenters, plumbers, pharmacies, and grocery stores, to live independently. Why couldn't disabled people live just as independently with a wide range of services available to them? In spite of the fact that Max described an apartment for *everyone*, not just disabled people, Roberts was against it.

Now it was Max's turn to listen. "Ed talked mostly about advocacy, about how we need to change the system. Building a building doesn't change society. It just helps a few people," Max remembered Roberts saying. Roberts championed the right for the disabled to participate fully in society and to change whatever laws necessary to make that happen. "The more he talked, the more sense he made," Max said. "I'd never thought about laws or how to change them."

Roberts probably mentioned two recently passed laws that gave hope to the disabled. The Architectural Barriers Act of 1968, generally considered to be the first federal disability rights legislation, mandated that federally constructed buildings and facilities be accessible to people with physical disabilities.[36] Another law, the Urban Mass Transportation Assistance Act of 1970, declared it a "national policy that elderly and handicapped persons have the same right as other persons to utilize mass transportation facilities and services."[37] Passage of these laws had little impact at the time. The Urban Mass Transportation Assistance Act contained no provision for enforcement. While the newly opened (1972)

San Francisco Bay Area Rapid Transit (BART) system was being touted as a model of accessibility, most local mass transit systems aggressively resisted modifying their systems to make them accessible. The Washington, D.C., subway system, for example, under construction in 1970, refused to approve installation of elevators until a court order required it to do so.[38]

The Architectural Barriers Act required that all *new* federal and federally assisted facilities designed for public use be readily accessible. However, there was no provision for modifying existing structures. State statutes addressing the problem of architectural barriers also generally ignored the need for modifications of existing buildings.[39] If people with a disability wanted to present a grievance or complain about this to their public officials, they would be unable to gain access to the public building.[40]

"Advocacy, advocacy, advocacy," Roberts liked to say. "I encourage everyone to go out and get arrested" he proclaimed in a speech. "Not just for anything, but for the cause. Getting arrested for what you believe in can really change your perspective; it can strengthen your resolve. . . . John Hessler and I used to roll right up to the front of the demonstrations and stare down the police. What could they do? When they threatened to arrest us, we just asked them, "How are you going to get us there? Do you have an iron lung in your prison?"[41]

"By the time Roberts was finished talking," Max recalled, "I was so excited, I couldn't wait to get back to St. Louis." He had been to the mountaintop. "The most important thing I learned from the trip," Max would say in a speech sixteen years later, "was that there was a good future, not only for me, but for other disabled people as well. I was committed to sharing this with other people in St. Louis and to work to bring independent living to St.

Louis and be a part of this progressive movement."[42] Ed Roberts
opened the first independent living center two years after Max's
visit in 1972. It would become a model for hundreds of centers
across the United States.

•CHAPTER 8•

GATHERING STEAM

Fired by his desire to live independently and build his project, Max began talking to his mother about how he might get a car. He believed he could modify a van of some kind and felt he would have no problem getting someone to drive him. Hertha appealed to her brother, Gus Beck. A wealthy oil and gas exporter who lived in Canada, Uncle Gus had always been extremely generous to Hertha and her children. He gave Max fifteen hundred dollars toward a car. Max used the money to buy a used Volkswagen Microbus and had ramps built to enable him to be wheeled in and out of it. Once he had the van, he soon found that the young nurses and nurse's aides would gladly drive him for nothing more than a cheeseburger and chocolate milk shake from Steak 'n Shake.

Sometime that summer, buoyed by his life's new direction, Max took his father to a baseball game. But Max was nervous. He told one of the Franciscan brothers, Joe, who accompanied him, "My father is an alcoholic and is capable of anything." His prediction was correct. At one point during the game, his father excused himself to go to the bathroom. When he didn't return, Max and Joe went to find him. They found him passed out. "He had wet himself, and the bottle he had was broken." It was an image of his father Max never forgot. Joe picked Carl up and carried him out to the car. In March 1971, Carl Starkloff was dead from pneumonia. Max had visited him in the hospital and held out his hand. Without opening his eyes, his father grasped it and held on for a few minutes. It was the only physical contact Max had had with his father in over a decade.

Max continued working to make his project a reality. "It had gathered so much steam at that point," recalled Max, "that I felt I had to go through with it, even though I agreed with Ed Roberts that it wasn't the right solution." A lot of people had gotten behind "Max's Paraquad project," and he didn't want to let them down.

Accumulating enough hard data on people with disabilities in and around St. Louis to justify a complex with 250 apartments and 50–60 commercial units was not going to be easy. Data on a national scale was sparse. Locally, it was nonexistent. One reason was the difficulty in defining *disability*. For instance, an epileptic person might be able to use public transportation but could be severely limited in securing and working at a job, according to Ann Gailis and Keith Susman, writing in the *Georgetown Law Journal* in 1973. "Similarly, an individual with a spinal cord injury may be able to obtain employment but incapable of utilizing public transportation in order to seek and maintain employment."[1]

Frank Bowe in his book *Equal Rights for Americans with Disabilities*, published in 1992, observed, "No one knows precisely how many Americans have disabilities. In part, this is a problem of definitions. What do we mean by 'disability'"?[2] The best definition, crafted for the purpose of passing Section 504 of the Rehabilitation Act of 1973 and, later, the Americans with Disabilities Act (ADA), "worked well for the purposes of civil rights issues, and we as a nation have almost a generation of case law to help us to interpret it. This definition does not, however, lend itself readily to demography: it is hard to count people using this definition."[3] Bowe said population surveys, such as those conducted by Louis Harris and

Associates, used a "self-report definition." People are only counted as having a disability if they say they have a disability.[4]

Max—and anyone in a wheelchair in 1970—would no doubt say that almost 100 percent of the homes and commercial buildings in St. Louis were inaccessible. In 1990, even after passage of the Architectural Barriers Act (1968), the Rehabilitation Act (1973), and the Americans with Disabilities Act (1990), *all* of which dealt specifically with removing barriers, experts estimated that accessible housing amounted to 1 percent of the nation's total.[5]

Architect Laurent Torno, who knew one of U.S. senator Tom Eagleton's aides, arranged for Max to meet with Eagleton to discuss the project and ask for funding. Max remembered Eagleton as being very supportive. However, the only tangible result of the meeting was a form letter from the senator opening, "Dear Max; It was great to see you again. [This had been their first meeting.] And please give my best to your family." Max left the letter out on his dresser. It was spotted by one of the staff, who viewed it as a personal letter, and word quickly spread throughout the nursing home that Max and Eagleton were close friends. Max remembered that his treatment immediately improved.

One day soon after, Brother Dismas decided that some books that Max had placed on his bedroom windowsill made the building look unkempt from the outside, so he moved them without Max's permission. Max had a friend move them back. "Do you think you can do that just because you know a senator?" fumed Brother Dismas. "Yes," answered Max, assuredly. Brother Dismas, who had patted Max on the head on his first day at St. Joseph's Hill and assured him that he would never "become our pet," never bothered Max again.

ON A ROLL

Max received his first motorized wheelchair in 1971. It was manufactured by Everest and Jennings, a company that invented the lightweight, folding, manual wheelchair in 1933, essentially the same design seen in hospitals today. Everest and Jennings introduced the first mass-market, power wheelchair in 1956 and sold it without competition until the U.S. Justice Department filed an antitrust suit against the company in 1977.

Max described his first motorized wheelchair as very rudimentary compared to the one he would use decades later. It looked like the manual version, only it had large wet-cell batteries located beneath the seat between the large rear spoke wheels. It was controlled by a lever on the armrest and moved very slowly, about two to three miles per hour. To stop it, one had to use the manual brakes, located above each of the rear wheels. For a quad, that meant there were no brakes, so Max had to make sure he only operated the chair on a level surface.

The batteries that powered Max's wheelchair lasted only a day before they needed to be recharged, and they had to be replaced every six months. But to Max at the time, "it was freedom. I felt excited when I first got it. I wheeled out into the hall, and it felt like I was going really fast. It allowed me to be more independent."

While other manufacturers sprang up in the late 1970s and early 1980s with high-performance, ultralight manual wheelchairs,[6] there was little progress or innovation in the design and manufacturing of motorized wheelchairs until 2000. They had been slow and flimsy. In 1997, Max suffered an injury to the head when the right front wheel of his Everest and Jennings motorized wheelchair snapped on the lip of a curb cut, spilling him on to the sidewalk.

In 1971, however, Max's power chair not only gave him increased mobility and freedom, but also more clout. Max told a story of waiting for Brother Pius to put him in bed. "Every evening at quarter to seven was my time to go to bed. This was their schedule. It wasn't my selection. So at quarter to seven I went to my room and waited."

He waited ten minutes, and then, thinking that he had been forgotten, went to the nursing station on his floor. Nobody was there. Finally, he took the elevator down to the main kitchen in the basement. There he found Brother Pius. "They were just having a Coke and chatting," Max recalled.

Irritated, Max said, "Brother, it's almost seven and I thought you were going to throw me in bed at quarter to seven."

Brother Pius said, "Get up there, and I'll come when I'm ready."

Max said, "I just took my chair and rammed the stool he was on. I just really rammed it. It was one of those stools on wheels and the impact almost knocked the stool out from under him. And I said, 'You get your fuckin' ass up there right now!' And he beat me to the room."

The combination of a motorized wheelchair and his new van gave Max a great deal of mobility and enabled him to pursue his Paraquad dream with even more vigor. A friend of Hertha's, Adelaide Cherbonnier, suggested that Max meet with Morton D. "Buster" May. May was the chair of May Department Stores, a huge national retailing company his family had founded in Leadville, Colorado, in 1877 and moved to St. Louis in 1905. By 1970, May Department Stores was generating well over $1 billion in annual sales. Buster May was well known in St. Louis as a generous philanthropist and supporter of local causes.

To prepare for the meeting, Max wrote a proposal for Paraquad. He painstakingly typed it on his ancient electric typewriter, which was missing the letter *k*. It took weeks to complete the document, then he had to go back over it and insert the letter *k* using a small felt-tip pen, which he held in his mouth.

When the big day finally arrived, Max and Hertha went to May's office. "It was a big office," Max recalled, "and there was a huge marlin on the wall, thirteen feet long. It was a record catch. I read him my proposal, and he said, 'I'll do you a favor. I'm not going to say no. Rewrite it, and come back in two weeks.'" When Max returned, May gave him $5,000 (roughly a $23,000 gift in today's dollars), his first major gift for Paraquad. More important, he told Max he could use his name to open doors, which it did.

Max had noticed that May wasn't using his right arm. Later he learned that May was paralyzed on one side because of a stroke. The two men became close friends, and May continued to support Paraquad for many years. The experience built Max's confidence in many ways. Not only did it start him on what would become a very successful fund-raising career, but it also was a turning point in how he regarded his disability. "My pride wanted me to try to conceal my disability," Max said. "Buster encouraged me to get out and let it show." Max took this advice to heart, as that year he gave lectures at Maryville College School of Nursing and the Saint Louis University School of Physical Therapy, and he also helped lead a spinal injury workshop at Washington University in St. Louis.

In October 1971, Max chaired the second meeting of the St. Louis chapter of the National Paraplegia Foundation (NPF). He had been working for months to establish a chapter in St. Louis, and in August he had hosted a small initial membership meeting in which an executive board of five officers and five executive members was elected. Max was elected president.

The NPF's mission was identical to his own: to improve the quality of life for people with spinal cord injuries. It did this through public educational outreach programs, which advocated civil rights and equal opportunities for people with disabilities; by campaigning for and financing research in spinal cord regeneration; and by promoting the building of local rehabilitation programs and facilities.[7] By establishing a St. Louis chapter of the NPF, Max could further his agenda for people with spinal cord injuries, learn more about what was going on within the newly emerging disability rights community, and, most important, gain opportunities to network with people who might help him with his Paraquad project.

The meeting was held at St. Louis Community College–Forest Park. Thirty-five people attended, including Laurent Torno and Max's friend from St. Joseph's Hill Infirmary, Mike Dahl, both of whom were elected to the NPF executive board. Also in attendance would have been the members of Max's Paraquad board of directors and Gini Laurie, publisher of the *Rehabilitation Gazette*, who had just moved back to St. Louis from Ohio, with her husband, Joe. The purpose of the meeting was to educate the public about spinal cord injury and to recruit members to the NPF. To help draw an audience, they invited a young genitourinary surgeon, Dr. Saul Boyarsky. Boyarsky was new to St. Louis, having arrived in July 1970. He had been a professor of urology at Duke University and was hired by Washington University Medical Center to head up its Genitourinary Section.

Dr. Boyarsky brought with him some new ideas for the rehabilitation of people with spinal cord injuries through the formation of interdisciplinary teams. He called for the formation of independent, specialized one hundred–bed units called spinal cord injury (SCI) centers that would treat, rehabilitate, and train para- and quadriplegics.

In his speech that day, he predicted, "Medicine of the '70's will bring many changes: to emphasize patient care, increasing self-care, increasing economies in hospital facilities, emphasis on out-patient care, and specifically directed research rather than basic research. Doctors and patients will readjust their roles toward each other. I think that the paraplegic will teach the whole medical profession a good deal for the benefit of all other patients. The paraplegic must be his own physician, and use the doctor, nurse, social worker and psychologist as consultants."[8]

Boyarsky was focused on returning rehabilitated spinal cord injury patients back into society. "It is possible for spinal cord injured patients to aspire to re-enter the mainstream of society, to lead a full life," he said. "Enough students have resumed classes and enough physicians have returned to take care of their patients, and enough paraplegics and quadriplegics have left spinal cord injury centers and rehabilitation institutes to justify this hope."[9]

Max followed Dr. Boyarsky to the podium. He called for "employment opportunities and employment services; private, independent living facilities; transportation systems which virtually do not exist for [people with spinal cord injuries]; and the elimination of architectural barriers in public buildings."[10] Max continued, "We can begin working on these problems "by throwing our full support behind any project that is dedicated to bringing the SCI person out of isolation, back into society." As examples, he gave Dr. Boyarsky's spinal cord research center project, Paraquad, and the "St. Louis Easter Seal Society's idea of workshops."

"Once a person leaves the SCI Center eager to get back into the swing of things, there would be waiting for him such things as workshops, opportunities for college, training programs, and facilities for adjusting to an environment that is now different and more difficult because of [his or her] disability." In other words, all the things that weren't waiting for Max when he was ready to "get back into the swing of things."

Max went on to outline the challenges facing people with spinal cord injuries. "Presently there is no way for the SCI person to get from one place to another, except by cab or private transportation. So what we must do is look into the possibility of integrating into the [St. Louis mass] transit system facilities for SCI persons."

He encouraged people with SCIs to insist on employment services, as well as employment opportunities through Social Security and vocational rehabilitation agencies. "The kind of work the SCI can do is endless," said Max, "from professional and executive to clerical. Also, many different trades are possible."

He enlightened the audience about the obstacles between the SCI person and full integration into society. "Steps, the lack of ramps, too narrow doorways, doorsills, poor restroom facilities, etc. can prevent an SCI person from getting a job, finding a place to live or just enjoying oneself. This can be changed by first impressing on architects and contractors the importance of our needs."

He called for greater legislative vigilance. "By checking legislation," he said, "we make sure there are laws meeting the requirements for barrier free structures. If the laws are favorable we make sure they are being complied with. If the laws are not favorable we begin a lobbying force.

"As of right now," Max continued, "the SCIs have no nucleus, but right here we have all the ingredients of putting one together.

In all of the areas just mentioned, we can serve in advisory and consulting positions, health care fields, business, and professional and civic matters to offer our talents and knowledge that we have acquired. Also, I believe we have something to prove.

"There are approximately 40,000 to 50,000 disabled persons in the greater St. Louis area, and we really do not know where most of these people are. Why? Partly because of the obstacles just mentioned. It all becomes a vicious circle. Because of architectural barriers one cannot work, if one cannot work, one cannot have proper housing. If one does not have proper health care facilities, one does not have the health to carry out his hopes and dreams. Because of these things the SCI person stays isolated, away from what is happening. This is not only tragic and an economic waste of human resources, it is ridiculous. We are here right now to change this, so let's see what we can do about it. Thank you."[11]

On October 13, 1971, in front of thirty-five people, Max painted a different picture from those he painted with a brush clenched in his teeth at the Hill. It was a picture of a mountain of impossible dimensions: inadequate health care and rehabilitation; no transportation; architectural barriers; lack of employment opportunities, education, and housing. And all among a segment of society that was isolated and difficult to reach.

In the audience that day was a young paraplegic, Jim Tuscher, who would join Max to fight for disability rights for the rest of his life. Tuscher became disabled because of a spinal cord tumor. He was twenty-three and just out of the Marine Corps. One of the lucky SCIs, he went through a six-month rehabilitation program in New York at the Rusk Institute of Rehabilitation Medicine. After leaving Rusk in June 1965, he pursued his education, earning a B.S. degree from the State University of New York at Brockport in 1966, a master's in education in counseling and guidance at the University of Missouri–Columbia in 1968, and a specialist degree in counseling and student personnel services at the University of Missouri in 1969. On the day of Max's speech, he was one year into a job counseling "students with problems" at St. Louis Community College. Max's sister, Lecil, met Tuscher at the community college, where she was taking some accounting courses. "She told me her brother had this concept for people with disabilities where they would live upstairs and then work in some kind of strip mall downstairs," Tuscher recalled. "I found it repulsive."[12]

Tuscher had turned his life around and was making his way nicely in the world, counseling people with more problems than he had. "I had a lot of privileges when I became disabled," he recalled. "Rusk Rehabilitation in New York, the best insurance, three years of higher education. I came from an environment that valued education. I was married. I had resources that other people didn't have. I had nothing to do with the disability community at that point."[13]

But a few days before the NPF meeting, Tuscher received a puzzling letter from the organization announcing that he had been elected to the board of directors. "What kind of organization would elect a board member, sight unseen?"[14] he laughed. It was enough to pique his interest and entice him to attend the meeting. "I remember meeting Max, Laurent Torno, Gini Laurie. It was kind of neat."

Max's call for advocacy and the removal of architectural barriers must have resonated with Tuscher, as he and Gary C. Fox had just published a four-page, two thousand–word article in the September/October issue of the *Journal of Rehabilitation* titled "Does the Open Door Include the Physically Handicapped?"[15] As

JIM TUSCHER JOINED PARAQUAD IN
1979.

a student in a wheelchair, Tuscher was frustrated at the lack of accommodations for people in wheelchairs at the two universities he had attended and the community college where he worked. Knowing how impossible the job of changing every educational institution in the United States would be, he decided to appeal to the community colleges. His case: "The open-door admission policy has been one of the proudest claims of the community college in America. Any institution where barriers to handicapped people remain unmodified has no right to this claim. When the door is closed for any reason other than the student's inability to profit from the programs offered, the open-door policy is not in effect."[16] He called for "not merely modifying existing community junior colleges but also . . . establishing new institutions which are accessible to the handicapped students. The goal, of course, is eventually to have comprehensive community junior college districts covering all areas of the country, with all facilities modified."[17]

Many years later Tuscher admitted, "It took me years to get the Independent Living philosophy from here" [pointing to his head] "to here" [heart]. Like most people with disabilities, he had had to make a major paradigm shift. Centuries of neglect had effectively "taught" disabled people that living independently was simply not an option for them. Tuscher could not conceive of a world where people with disabilities could live in the mainstream because no one had considered modifying or building *every* educational institution, public and private building, street corner, bus, and train in the country with them in mind. His vision of modifying just the community colleges was grand for its time, but it was nowhere close to the concept of Independent Living that was emerging in the 1970s.

Tuscher joined the Paraquad staff in 1979 and ultimately became responsible for Paraquad's public policy efforts. As Paraquad's liaison to the Missouri General Assembly, he lobbied successfully for state policies that enabled people with disabilities to live independent, productive lives, and in 1989 and 1990 he was among those who successfully lobbied the U.S. Congress for passage of the Americans with Disabilities Act.

"A DREAMER WHO REFUSED TO QUIT"

Max continued to raise money for his project by writing and visiting foundations and government agencies. Two staffers at the *St. Louis Post-Dispatch*, reporter Patricia Rice and columnist Jake McCarthy, caught wind of Max's bold plan. Rice outlined the $15 million dream: 250 apartments for disabled and nondisabled residents with 30,000 to 100,000 square feet of shopping and office space. "The complex could include a health club for the non-disabled and physical therapy for the disabled. Housekeeping and catering services would be available for all residents. Apartments from efficiency to three-bedroom size would include architectural modifications for the disabled. All kitchen facilities could be reached from a wheelchair. There would be no doorsills, narrow halls or steps. Cost estimates for such a center have reached $15,000,000." [18] Rice's article included a photograph of Max reviewing plans with Laurent Torno and Mike Dahl.

McCarthy's column appeared on January 31, 1972, and was headlined "A Dreamer Who Refused to Quit." "When Max Starkloff speaks, you can hear the power in his voice and his strength shows in his eyes," McCarthy wrote. "He is a big and ruggedly handsome man of 33." He continued:

> [Max's] new dream is to build a St. Louis housing development for the disabled—something that's never been done in America.
>
> Working with Max Starkloff on his project is a team of experts who believe in its possibilities. "There have been no less than 30 attempts around the country to develop this kind of thing," architect Laurent Torno says, "But they've never really materialized—maybe because nobody ever went about it in the right way."
>
> Max himself talks about how the disabled disappear from society. "You'll see an item in the paper that says an accident victim is in critical condition. If it's a spinal injury, the world never hears of him again.

"We want to find the disabled who want to live a human life without self-pity or the pity of others, or the doting of well-meaning relatives, or the loneliness and desperation of being out of the mainstream."

That's the kind of dream Max Starkloff never lost.[19]

The articles must have touched upon the dreams of other people with disabilities, as Max's phone at St. Joseph's Hill began to ring incessantly. "A lot of vets in Jefferson Barracks . . . were asking for help," Max said. "They would say, 'I'm stuck here [in a nursing home]. How can I get out?' And here I was stuck in an institution as well." In addition to learning about housing problems, Max also heard complaints about other barriers to independence, such as curbs, buses, and jobs. And he heard from individuals who found fault with his ideas. A well-meaning physician wrote, "You should be ashamed. You're making promises to people that you can't fill. You're going to hurt people."

In February 1972, Max succeeded in gaining 501(c)(3) status for Paraquad by making it a subsidiary of the National Paraplegia Foundation of St. Louis. He also authored *Para-Quad Concept and Program*, a thirty-five-page, spiral-bound "conceptual prospectus" that spelled out the entire plan. One section dealt with architectural considerations and was authored by Laurent Torno.

Torno dove into the challenges facing designers, for instance: "The wheelchair is itself a piece of multi-purpose mobile furniture. In a home gathering of people who use wheelchairs most ordinary furniture would be totally redundant and consume large amounts of space preventing the 'conversational grouping of several wheelchairs.'" In another example, he considers that "most able bodied persons can accommodate unforeseen storage needs by piling higher, deeper, under, over, etc. The restricted range of motion possible for a paraplegic or quadriplegic deprives him/her of those options. How do we provide for unforeseen storage/furnishing needs of residents?"[20]

Torno suggested defining the physical actions required to produce motion in the wheelchair—forward, backward, sideways, rotation—and to measure or establish the relative difficulty required to perform these actions within differing space constraints and for differing categories of specific disabilities. "For instance," he wrote, "a person weaker in the left side motor control may have extreme difficulty in performing right turning motion, and may be forced to perform a 90-degree right turn by going 270 degrees to the left. The frequency of this disability would dictate the extent to which space must be allotted."[21] Torno estimated the cost of the 200-unit development, including the "Prototype Unit Research Program," to be approximately $5.5 million.[22]

As part of the research into the Paraquad idea, Max, Torno, and Richard Ward held a meeting at Barnes Hospital to discuss the needs of people in wheelchairs. They weren't expecting more than about five people to attend the meeting and were surprised when about twenty-five showed up, all in wheelchairs. For Max it was an important moment: "For the first time I was in a room filled with people the same height as me. We were making eye-to-eye contact. At first it was intimidating, but as I talked to them, I realized what other problems were out there."[23]

In July, Max undoubtedly noted with pleasure the publication of a letter he wrote earlier in the year to the *American Journal of Nursing*, which read:

I am a C-4 quadriplegic who feeds himself, pushes his own wheelchair, writes, and can use a typewriter. I am director of Para-Quad, Inc., president of the Greater St. Louis Chapter of the National Paraplegia Foundation, and am involved in many other activities that give me a full and productive life.

However, I have just finished reading "Independence is Possible in Quadriplegia" (December 1970) and once again I find myself categorized as not capable of functioning as a productive human being. The author, Dr. Lucien Trigiano, states that the C-4 quadriplegic cannot feed himself, cannot maneuver himself in a wheelchair, etcetera. . . .

With his charts and categorizing, Dr. Trigiano has placed limitations on people who need to see a positive approach to the problem. We should quit placing people into slots to make it more convenient for those who do not wish to look at the real problems that are preventing so many from being productive. The problem is not what classes of people can do, but what the individual can do.

Dr. Trigiano is approaching the problem negatively. We know that the C-4 quadriplegic needs physical assistance, but where Dr. Trigiano gets the idea that the C-4 quadriplegic cannot be financially independent is beyond me. Of course there is more work involved, but this is where the real problem exists. I wonder if we are ready to handle it.[24]

One evening in 1972, KMOX-TV news anchor Julius Hunter interviewed Max at the west end of Busch Stadium. The news?

St. Louis's first curb cut,[25] a ramp built into the new sidewalk to accommodate people in wheelchairs. While people in wheelchairs couldn't enter most public buildings, offices, schools, universities, or stores—if they wanted to watch the St. Louis Cardinals, they could do so. "While I'm happy to be able to attend a Cardinals game," Max told Hunter, "people need these kind of curb cuts everywhere so they can get out of their homes, go to work, and live independent lives."

·CHAPTER 9·

"MY SISTER'S A DAMNED FOOL"

On a nice fall day in October 1973, a physical therapist, Colleen Kelly, age twenty-three, started her job as the new head of the physical therapy department of St. Joseph's Hill. She was fresh out of Saint Louis University and came to the Hill with radically new ideas. "Up to the point I arrived," Colleen explained, "St. Joe's program was a maintenance program, where they pretty much gave people range of motion exercises and kept them occupied. I wanted to start a true rehabilitation program. I wanted these people to go home."[1]

On Colleen's first day, her predecessor, Roger Noeff, was taking her around to introduce her to the staff and the residents. As they were walking along the first floor, a young man in a motorized wheelchair came along. He was dressed in a denim shirt and dark blue pants, and he had long, slicked-back hair. "Hello, Roger," the young man said.

"Hello, Max," Noeff said.

After Max had passed, Colleen asked Noeff, "Was that Max Starkloff?"

"Yes," he replied. "Do you know him?"

"I've heard about him but never met him," said Colleen. She first learned about Max in 1972 through her sister, Mary, who started working at St. Joseph's Hill that year.

Colleen was then a junior in the physical therapy program at Saint Louis University. Mary told her about Max and how handsome and charming he was. Colleen expressed interest because she'd never seen a quad outside of a health care environment. Mary confided in Colleen that Max had asked her out, but she had not wanted to go. "Why not?" asked Colleen.

"Because he's disabled," replied Mary.

"So?"

"What if he falls for me?"

"What if he does?" asked Colleen.

"Then I'd have to let him down."

Colleen pressed her sister: "Why?"

"Because he's disabled!"

Colleen never forgot that conversation, wondering still years later how her sister could be so snobbish and closed minded.

Mary continued to tell Colleen about Max, and the more she did, the more Colleen thought Max sounded like a nice guy. One day Mary told Colleen that St. Joseph's Hill was starting a physical therapy department. Colleen met with Brother Damien, who was impressed with Colleen's credentials. Noeff, the current head of the Hill's physical therapy unit, was able to work only part-time. They needed a full-time therapist. Brother Damien asked Colleen to accept a full-time position, once she had graduated from Saint Louis University, and she agreed to take the job.

When she finally saw Max in person on her first day at St. Joseph's Hill, she only saw him from the back and remembered wondering about him. "His hair was slicked back," she recalled. "I thought he might be a 'greaser.'" Later, after Colleen had established herself in her new department, Max—for some reason in a manual wheelchair—had pushed himself up to the physical therapy department in search of someone to drive him in his VW van into St. Louis to have lunch with his mother and Sister Helen Marie Holzum. He asked Jan York, one of Colleen's assistants, who said she couldn't do it. Jan introduced Max to Colleen. Now Colleen saw his face for the first time. Her thought was, "My sister's a damned fool. This man is drop-dead handsome." "I'll drive you," Colleen volunteered, trying not to look too eager. "I know Sister Helen from when she was my teacher in PT school." Max and Colleen started talking and never stopped.

Colleen was tall and thin with long brown hair. "A string bean," was how one staffer described her, "but a sweet lady. A take-charge lady." A onetime beauty pageant contestant, Colleen had a lovely face with bright eyes and a megawatt smile.

Twelve years younger than Max, Colleen was born on December 24, 1949, the oldest of twelve children. Her mother, Johanne Molini Kelly, was Italian and had immigrated to the United States when she was two years old. Her father, Robert Leach Kelly, sold Youngstown storm windows when Colleen was growing up, but later became a successful financial planner. Her parents were married in 1948 and moved into a small house in south St. Louis.

"We were a very Catholic family," said Colleen. "In our parish, every family had a lot of kids. It was not unusual to see families with eight to ten children." Colleen's sister Mary was eighteen months younger, and together they would help their mother take care of their ten younger siblings. At age sixteen, Colleen started working one to two nights during the week and all day Saturday as a bookkeeper at the Franciscan Province of the Sacred Heart.

When it was time to go to college, Colleen's parents told her they could not afford college tuition. They suggested she go to Saint Louis University and get a job there, which she did. "This was my first venture from a sheltered life into the real world," she recalled, "which turned out not to be a very protective environment." She enrolled in night school. The struggle to earn her tuition during the day and get a degree at night turned out to be too much. "Seeing me struggling," recalled Colleen, "one of the Franciscan priests encouraged me to attend Quincy College," a hundred miles north in Quincy, Illinois. It was run by the Franciscans, and they offered a lot of financial aid. She enrolled for the spring semester in January 1970. Colleen remembered her grandmother and mother altering all her clothes to bring them more into the fashion of the times. She had just turned nineteen, and it was her first trip away from home.

When Colleen arrived at Quincy, she soon learned it was "one big party." She was introduced to panty raids, food fights, parties, and love—and that was just in her first semester. "I fell in love and was going to marry, and then fell out of love," Colleen recalled. She entered a beauty competition and ran for Miss Quincy, a precursor to the Miss Illinois pageant, but, ultimately, did not win. She had so much fun, she flunked out.

"The promised 'abundant' financial aid turned out to be nothing more than student loans," Colleen recalled. She applied for student aid at Saint Louis University and took out more loans. "It was a very stressful period," Colleen said. She entered Saint Louis University in fall 1970 and made Spanish her major.

To help pay off her student loans, Colleen got a job as a clerk with the Loehr Employment Service (later B. Loehr Staffing), a job placement agency. Occasionally, she would help as a receptionist. One day when Colleen was working at the front desk, a man came in to apply for job placement. While filling out the forms, he and Colleen chatted. "What do you want to do?" he asked her.

"Help people," replied Colleen.

"Then you ought to do what my wife does," he told her. "She's a physical therapist." That was the first time Colleen had heard the words *physical therapist*. "By the time he had finished explaining what a physical therapist did," Colleen recalled, "I had decided that that would be my major."

She went to see Sister Mary Imelda Pingel, the nun in charge of Saint Louis University's physical therapy program. Sister Imelda reviewed Colleen's grades and shook her head. "I don't think you can handle our program," she told Colleen. "To get into the program, you have to take human gross anatomy [human dissection]. It's a very tough class. With your grades, I don't think you could pass it."

Colleen was devastated. She went to the chapel to pray—and cry. When she came out, eyes filled with tears, she walked right into the Reverend Paul C. Reinert, president of Saint Louis University, who she knew was a friend of her parents. "Why are you crying?" Rev. Reinert asked. When Colleen explained, he said, "Praying was the right thing. Don't give up." Colleen went back to Sister Imelda and pleaded to be allowed to enroll in gross anatomy. "If Dr. John Shea [the instructor] will accept you, you may take the course," she was told.

Colleen begged Dr. Shea to allow her to take his class, and to her surprise, he said, "Sure. I'm a hard teacher, but if you can cut it, you can take it." She registered immediately to take it that summer and never worked so hard in her life. The room where they dissected the cadavers was not air-conditioned. The smell of the dead bodies and formaldehyde was overpowering. She and her classmates helped each other through the course, and Colleen got an A.

Colleen had always heard the words, "If you really want something, you have to work for it," but now she had come to truly understand the last half of that statement.

Colleen finished her training as a physical therapist in 1973. She passed her boards, which she described as "grueling and hard," on her first try.

Shortly after meeting Max, and about one week into her new job at the Hill, Colleen organized a get-to-know-you staff lunch in a gazebo outside the main building and invited Max. "It was a beautiful sunny day in late October," Colleen remembered. "The maple trees were a beautiful golden yellow. We just chatted about who are you and where are you from, that kind of thing." That evening around 5 p.m. and many evenings thereafter, Colleen would go downstairs from her office to visit Max in his room on the second floor. "We would just sit and talk," Colleen recalled. "We didn't watch TV. We talked." It didn't take Max long to ask Colleen out on a date.

Joann Bright, a nurse's aide, had asked Max if he wanted to join her and her husband at their house for dinner and games. He decided to bring Colleen along. Colleen drove Max in his van to the Brights' house where, after dinner, they played a game called Blacks and Whites. "It was one of those educational games put out at the time by *Psychology Today*, supposed to educate people about racial issues," recalled Colleen.

"Blacks started the game with $10,000," Max said, "and whites got $1 million. It was supposed to show how the rich got richer and the poor got poorer." "Max ended up with all the money," Colleen recalled. "And of course I was flirting like crazy."

After that, Colleen began to spend more time with Max in his room every evening. Max had a red popcorn popper in his room, which Colleen started using on these evenings to cook corn on the cob, chili, soup, hot dogs, and other simple dishes for herself and Max. Though dinner was served at the Hill promptly at 4:15 every afternoon, Max and Colleen relished the simple meals she prepared in the popper.

By 7:30 p.m., a staff member would arrive to transfer Max from his chair to his bed, during which time Colleen would step out of the room. Then she would return and continue talking into the evening. "It was in those conversations," Colleen explained, "that I began to learn about people with disabilities being institutionalized. Until that time, I had only seen the rehabilitation side of disabilities, the side where we help them to get out into the community. Now I was seeing that there was this whole other side . . . from the perspective of the disabled people. And I was absolutely fascinated by it and by the fact that Max really wanted to do something about it. And I wanted to help him do something about it. What he was telling me struck me as grossly unfair. I guess you might say my social conscience was awakened by what Max was telling me about what happens to people with disabilities, and I began to pay attention to how politicians voted and how programs were funded and who was more sensitive than others. And over a period of time, I began to move from a conservative Republican point of view to a more liberal Democratic point of view, because when I talked to people with a Republican point of view, they didn't seem to share my angst about people with disabilities.

"I began to learn about transportation that was not accessible and housing that wasn't accessible, and why were people with disabilities in nursing homes . . . those things hadn't occurred to me before. My view of the world was that people with disabilities could go to the hospital or to some place with a rehabilitation program and come out and live a better life, but I really hadn't gone any further to think about what that life might look like or how would you do it or how would family members cope. So I began to enter a world that I knew little about, but that I found fascinating. And I was taking this journey with Max."

Colleen offered to drive Max to his National Paraplegia Foundation meeting, where she met other people with disabilities, like Jim Tuscher and Speed Davis. "And I met Gini Laurie, and my life began to take on a dimension outside of work that was actually quite fascinating. I was beginning to learn about the need for change and also strategies for changing public policies that didn't work well." Colleen also became interested in the independent living facility Max was developing with Laurent Torno and others, the concept that he called Paraquad.

As Max and Colleen's relationship began to get serious, some of the brothers became concerned. Brother William, the director of nursing who Colleen described as "a sweet man, and very 'by-the-book,'" asked her one day if she felt her romantic relationship with Max was professional. She replied simply, "He's not my patient. And what I do after hours is my business." That was the end of it. However, Brother Damien, the head administrator, chose to look the other way. He had respect for Colleen. She was bringing Medicare patients into St. Joseph's Hill, and this was generating additional income.

In addition, Colleen worked hard to keep everything on a professional level. She would see Max on her own time and not when she was working. When she arrived in the morning, she would go to his room and give him a kiss. After work, she would go to his room, where they would cook with the popcorn popper and snuggle until about 11 p.m.

MAX AND COLLEEN AT HERTHA'S HOUSE, SUMMER 1975.

"And we would talk," Colleen recalled. "I had dated a lot of young men, but none of them seemed to have a sense of purpose. Max did. That was what really attracted me to him." Max talked passionately about Paraquad, Ed Roberts, independent living, the emerging Disability Rights Movement, and pending legislation. They talked about the Rehabilitation Act of 1973, which that year was rewritten, resubmitted, and passed again by Congress. This compromised version of the law contained changes President Richard Nixon approved. It eliminated independent living and client advocacy programs because they were deemed too expensive and an administrative nightmare, but it kept Section 504, lauded by disability rights advocates as "the linchpin of change,"[2] which barred programs receiving federal aid from discriminating against people with disabilities and ensured equal access to education.

As president of the new St. Louis chapter of the National Paraplegic Foundation, Max had the responsibility to mobilize the
disabled community to take political action. While Congress had
passed the Rehabilitation Act, Section 504 became bogged down
in the Nixon bureaucracy. The Department of Health, Education,
and Welfare continued to express concerns about cost and administration and eventually simply refused to issue regulations to implement the law.

Max, from his "office" at St. Joseph's Hill, got on the phone
and began networking with disability rights leaders in other cities.
What were they going to do? What actions should they take? In
addition, other legislation was being passed, which was quickly
redefining independence for people in wheelchairs, such as the
Federal-Aid Highway Act of 1973. For the first time, it required
states and planning organizations to give pedestrians, including
the disabled, consideration for curb cuts and wheelchair ramps.
How would they get this money? Who should Max talk to? How
would it all work? And what about the new law just introduced in
Washington mandating special "handicapped parking"?

As if all of this wasn't enough, as president of Paraquad, Max
also had an apartment complex to build . . . and a lot of money
to raise. "Max would write the letters," Colleen recalled, "and I
would type and edit them, acting as Max's assistant. We got so
we were doing that every night." Max continued to spend hours
on the phone each day networking and raising money for Paraquad. Sitting for long periods on a foam cushion in his motorized wheelchair caused him to get frequent pressure sores, which
meant frequent trips to the hospital and long periods in bed to
ward off a potentially life-threatening infection.

During one of these bouts, Max went to visit his plastic surgeon, Dr. Bill Stoneman, who recommended he try a new device
called a ROHO cushion, invented by two brothers, Bob and Bill
Graebe. When Max mentioned this to Colleen, she said, "I know
those guys!" As a physical therapy student doing an internship
at St. John's Hospital, Colleen had met the Graebe brothers in
one of her classes when they came one day to demonstrate their
cushion for the PTs. It was unlike anything the therapists had
ever seen. Made of neoprene rubber and air filled, it had many
balloons that the person would sit on. She remembered that the
brothers dropped a set of car keys into the cushion and asked each
therapist to sit in it. They were all surprised that they could not
feel the keys.

MAX SEATED ON A ROHO CUSHION, 1987.

Colleen called Bob Graebe to get a cushion for Max, and he invited her to his home in Belleville, Illinois, where he made the cushions in his garage. A biomedical engineer, Graebe was disturbed by the people he saw in nursing homes suffering from pressure sores. He went to work to invent a cushion that could help prevent such sores and created what he called Dry Floatation technology, because the cushion mimics the properties of water in a dry, air-fluid environment. On the day Colleen came to visit, he gave her a ROHO for no charge. "That cushion saved my life," Max said. "Without it, I simply could not do the things I do." That began a lifelong friendship with the Graebe family, and today the ROHO Group, still headquartered in Belleville, sells products in over seventy countries.

By the end of 1973, Max and Colleen were an item at St. Joseph's Hill. "The men who lived there delighted in our evolving relationship," Colleen reminisced. "They liked Max, and they liked me. There was nothing going on. And to have two young people in a burgeoning relationship—they delighted in that. We were the talk of the building." Max added with a wink, "The employees were always speculating about what happened behind my closed door." Colleen continued, "But we were also really busy. Our lives began to fill up with NPF meetings, or Max had been asked to come in and speak to a group of therapists in St. Louis, or we came into St. Louis to meet with his doctor, Betty Stoddard, who was on the board of Paraquad. We talked a lot about ideas, and I made myself available to drive Max wherever he wanted to go."

Max and Colleen brought in the New Year 1974 in a memorable way. Patty Wilkerson's mother, Dorothy, had for years hosted an annual New Year's Eve chili party at her St. Louis apartment, to which the Starkloffs were always invited. Dorothy died that year, but Patty's sister, Joanne, decided to continue the tradition one more year before moving the furniture out. Max's sister and brother-in-law, Lecil and Steve, were there, along with Max's mother. "There was a huge snowstorm that night," Colleen remembered, "and Max's VW van did not do well in snow. So we decided Max should spend the night."

Later that night, after the last guests had left, Colleen called her mother to say she would be spending the night in a friend's apartment. "There was a huge canopy bed, and I lifted Max into the bed. Then he invited me in, too," Colleen laughed. "We got very intimate. It was the first time." Max was thirty-five. Colleen was twenty-three.

The following morning Hertha returned. Thinking Max would be alone, she let herself into the apartment and began preparing breakfast for herself and Max. Colleen remembered walking out into the kitchen that morning—wearing a bathrobe. "And there was Hertha! I thought I would die, but she didn't seem to mind," Colleen said. "She was actually quite tickled."

NETWORKING

Max began to network and form strong relationships with other disability rights leaders in St. Louis, as well as in New York, Houston, Chicago, Boston, Berkeley, and other cities. Gini and Joe Laurie hosted large meetings at their home at 4502 Maryland Avenue in St. Louis's historical Central West End. These frequent meetings were catalysts for connecting people with disabilities. Max and Colleen attended many of those gatherings. Once, Max recalled, the ambassador from England, Sir Peter Ramsbotham, and Lady Ramsbotham were the guests of honor. They had a daughter, Mary, who was quadriplegic, so Gini Laurie introduced them to paras and quads in St. Louis who were leading the way toward a new lifestyle for disabled people. Subsequently, the Lauries and Max and Colleen were invited to visit the ambassador in Washington, D.C.

Gini Laurie was a huge influence upon Max. While she did not have a disability herself, she came from a St. Louis family of polio survivors . . . and nonsurvivors. During a polio epidemic in 1912, the year before she was born, four of her siblings contracted polio. Two sisters, Virginia, three, and Grace, nine, died during the epidemic. One brother became severely disabled at six years old. And her oldest sister, twelve at the time, was mildly disabled by the disease. Gini, a combination of the names Grace and Virginia, was named for the two sisters who had died.

She spent most of her life working to help polio survivors—and all people with disabilities—live more independently. When her husband's work took them to Cleveland in the late 1940s, she worked as a Red Cross volunteer at the Toomey Pavilion at Cleveland's City Hospital. One of her jobs was to help publish its newsletter, *The Toomeyville Gazette.* As residents left the Toomey Pavilion and the fourteen other similar respiratory centers around the United States, the need to stay in touch and share information became increasingly important. Laurie commented once that it was "apparent [polio survivors] had two vital needs . . . people and information. They wanted to keep [up] with each other . . . and wanted to share information about their lives and equipment."[3]

In 1958, Gini and Joe began hosting annual reunions of former residents of the Toomey Pavilion, and they also started working full-time on their own version of the newsletter, which they called *The Toomeyville Jr. Gazette.* The *Jr. Gazette,* in Gini Laurie's words, "gathered news from patients, staff, volunteers, and

THE *REHABILITATION GAZETTE*
IN 1972.

keyholes."[4] As it evolved, it also included not just personal news, but also a variety of articles about how people with disabilities of all sorts could live more independently. The range of articles covered every conceivable topic, from education to wheelchair repair to kitchen design. When Laurie died on June 28, 1989, her publication—renamed the *Rehabilitation Gazette* in 1970—had a circulation of three thousand.[5] Not only did Laurie edit four issues a year for over thirty years, she and Joe personally paid the cost to print and mail the publication as well.

By 1974, three years after moving back to St. Louis from Ohio, the Lauries had resumed hosting reunions and meetings at their home and advocating for people with disabilities. Max looked forward to the meetings, and he now was accompanied by his girlfriend, Colleen Kelly.

That year, thanks primarily to Buster May and the Joseph H. and Florence A. Roblee Foundation,[6] Max raised twenty thousand dollars, enough to fund the Team Four feasibility study for his project. Max, Colleen, and architect Laurent Torno were busy searching for possible building sites. And Max had begun expanding Paraquad in his own conception to include not just housing but also services similar to those offered by Ed Roberts's new Center for Independent Living in Berkeley.

In 1974 a third independent living center opened in Boston,[7] cofounded by Charlie Carr and Fred Fay. Carr, a quadriplegic because of a diving accident at age fifteen, also founded the Northeast Independent Living Program in Lawrence, Massachusetts, in 1980 and later became commissioner of the Massachusetts Rehabilitation Commission, a position he holds today. Cofounder Fred Fay, a quadriplegic, held a Ph.D. in psychology and viewed nursing home residents as people who were "incarcerated against their will." He claimed that "their only crime was needing attendant care in the morning and at night; otherwise they were pretty much independent for the rest of the day."[8]

Max met Fred Fay and another disability rights activist, Lex Frieden from Texas, at one of the Lauries' gatherings in 1974.[9] While in St. Louis, Frieden shared a hotel room with a blind man, Roger Peterson, and they struck a deal. Frieden would read the day's program to Peterson if Peterson would push Lex's wheelchair. It was the first time Frieden realized that people with different disabilities could help each other. (In 2014, Frieden's full-time attendant for more than twenty-five years, Mac Brodie, was a Vietnam veteran with no short-term memory.)

Typically, at Gini Laurie's meetings, the agendas revolved around the issues of the day. On one occasion, however, the agenda was the need to bring together disability-run organizations across the country to have a more unified voice and to influence national legislation. Max explained the goal in a 1980 keynote address:

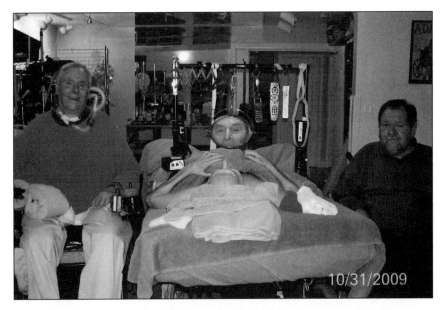

FRED FAY, CENTER, AND CHARLIE CARR, RIGHT, FOUNDERS OF BOSTON
INDEPENDENT LIVING CENTER, WITH MAX AT FRED'S HOUSE IN 2009.

In the course of trying to carry on the functions of their
organizations, [disability-run organizations] ran into so
many environmental and attitudinal barriers that they
began to advocate the elimination of those barriers. They
were experiencing common needs and began to see that
the successful experiences of one person might be useful to
others. Specific groups focused on specific needs: The blind,
the first group to really organize, focused on legislation
and education for the blind; those in wheelchairs worked
on curb-cuts at street corners and ramps into buildings;
the deaf were concerned with communication and socialization; and the developmentally-disabled and those concerned with the mentally disabled were seeking specialized
services.

These groups were, and still are, grassroots organizations manned by volunteer members. After they became organized locally, they began to develop statewide networks according to their needs and interests.

By 1973, a small group of leaders from key points around the country were ready to bring these grassroots organizations together. [We] reasoned that, if all disabled people would work together and speak with one voice, that voice would be heard by our leaders in Washington as well as all across our country.[10]

In June 1974, Max and Colleen, Lex Frieden, Fred Fay, Judy Heumann, Gini Laurie, and other disability rights leaders from around the United States met in Fort Sumner, Maryland, to form the first cross-disability advocacy organization in the United States, the American Coalition of Citizens with Disabilities (ACCD). At this first meeting, Fred Fay was elected president, and Max, Judy Heumann, and Gini Laurie were elected to the board of directors.[11]

Meetings were often contentious. The delegates passionately believed the ACCD should be governed and administered by individuals with disabilities. Resolutions were introduced, and seriously considered, to limit members without disabilities to three-fifths of a vote. Delegates ordered the staff to work on a wide swath of issues, ranging from transportation to housing to education and civil rights, blithely ignoring time and budgetary constraints on carrying them out.[12] "I felt completely intimidated at these early meetings," Max recalled. "The people were arrogant and militant. I didn't understand all the legal and political jargon. At one point, [then ACCD president] Eunice Fiorito turned to me and said, 'You're awfully quiet, Max. What do you think?'[13] I told her I was just learning, to which she said, 'Good; then why don't you sit up here next to the teacher?' I felt humiliated."

The ACCD grew quickly. Initially funded by a grant from the federal Rehabilitation Services Administration, its budget grew from $50,000 in 1976 to $2 million four years later. In one year, 1976–1977, individual membership grew 500 percent.[14]

According to Frank Bowe in *Equal Rights for Americans with Disabilities*, the ACCD was considered a crucial organization because it brought people with a variety of disabilities together from across the nation. "Between 1975 and 1981, it led the movement for greatly expanded civil rights in education, transportation, housing, and other areas of daily life."[15]

Max remembered meeting Judy Heumann for the first time in a hotel in Washington, D.C., where both had come to attend an ACCD meeting. Heumann, at the age of twenty-two, had just founded her own disability rights organization, Disabled in Action, in New York City.[16] "She smoked like a fiend and was very aggressive," Max recalled at an interview at his home. "I thought she was a real jerk." But Max and Colleen eventually came to regard Heumann as a member of their family. Heumann, like Ed Roberts, was against the idea of Max's project. "The objective of transforming communities was to fix the community, not build separate housing," she said.[17]

Quadriplegic like Max, Heumann had contracted polio when she was just eighteen months old. A doctor told her parents, German Jewish immigrants, to place their daughter in an institution. Relatives told them that Heumann's condition could only be attributed to the sins of the parents. Luckily for Heumann, her parents bought into none of this. Her mother, a fighter by nature, fought successfully to get her out of a special elementary school for disabled children and into a regular elementary school, fought successfully to get her into a regular high school, and fought—again successfully—to get her into Long Island University.

Armed with her mother's tenacity and lessons in self-advocacy, Heumann took up her own battles in college, fighting to live in a dormitory, organizing other disabled students to fight for ramped buildings, and even participating in protests against the Vietnam War. When the New York State Board of Education refused to give her a teaching certificate because a physician questioned whether she could get to the bathroom by herself or help children out of the building in an emergency, Heumann sued. Then she went to the press with a David versus Goliath story of a young qualified teacher with a disability pitched in a battle against a coldhearted state bureaucracy. "You Can Be President, Not Teacher, with Polio," ran the headline in the *New York Daily News.*[18] The Board of Education, reeling from the negative press, settled out of court. Heumann received her teaching certificate and, eventually, a job teaching at an elementary school (as well as the honor of being the first person in a wheelchair to teach in the New York City schools).[19]

In 1970, Heumann started Disabled in Action (DIA), a disability rights political action group with a mission to disrupt the status quo. In October 1972, she and members of the DIA organized what many consider to be the earliest '60s-style disability rights protests.[20] President Nixon, running for reelection, had vetoed the Rehabilitation Act of 1972, part of which contained a bill to fund independent living programs. Heumann led DIA and other groups on a march to the Lincoln Memorial in Washington, D.C., and later, four days before the election, to Nixon's reelection headquarters on Madison Avenue in New York, where she and about fifty protestors sat down in an intersection blocking midtown traf-

Judy Heumann in 1987.

fic for an hour. Heumann would go on to help organize more than fifty demonstrations all over the United States—and get arrested in three of them—in order to disrupt people, traffic, and the status quo in the name of disability rights.[21]

Max and Heumann worked with the ACCD in its early meetings to push for the passage and later the enforcement of the Rehabilitation Act of 1973, what many in the Disability Rights Movement consider to be its greatest achievement.

The Rehabilitation Act of 1973 was designed to revamp the federal vocational rehabilitation program. Added to the bill at the last minute almost as an afterthought was a small section, 504, that made it illegal for "any program or activity receiving Federal financial assistance" to discriminate against an "otherwise qualified handicapped individual."[22] It was the first such federal law in U.S. history.[23] Unfortunately, Section 504 contained no enforcement procedures. Without these, the law could simply fade into obscurity, one of many passed by Congress each year that state good intentions but are never enforced.

Responsibility for implementing the act fell to Caspar Weinberger, newly appointed secretary of the Department of Health, Education, and Welfare (HEW), but it ultimately was delegated to one of HEW's agencies, the Office for Civil Rights (OCR). When it came to legally established rights, the OCR took a hardball approach. Since its founding in the mid-1960s, the OCR had tackled many discrimination barriers, including desegregating public school systems and dealing with uncooperative or hostile public officials and community leaders. Hard bitten and trial tested, OCR staff members worked to establish formal and strict legal protections, as well as the administrative and legal mechanisms to enforce them. Within HEW, the OCR was also known for something else: Upholding the law always came first; costs second.[24]

Peter Holmes, OCR director, assigned responsibility for Section 504's implementation to Martin Gerry, his new deputy, who assigned it to a staff attorney, John Wodatch, and his staff. Their first order of business was to define the term *handicapped individual*. The definition in the 1973 act dealt primarily with employment, since the act itself was originally designed to deal with vocational rehabilitation. It defined a handicapped individual as any individual whose disability "results in a substantial handicap to employment."[25]

Unfortunately, when it came to "discrimination under any program or activity receiving Federal financial assistance,"[26] this definition was inadequate. It ignored those with disabilities so severe they were incapable of being employed, including children and the elderly. It failed to take into account those with disabilities who might need to use federally subsidized public transportation. And it omitted those who employers frequently discriminate against based on a past disability that had since been successfully treated, such as a nervous breakdown or heart condition.

A new definition of handicapped individual was drafted and attached as an amendment in December 1974, defining a handicapped individual as any person whose disability "substantially limits one or more of such person's major life activities."[27] In subsequent reports from the OCR staff, the meaning of this broader definition was fleshed out to include drug and alcohol addictions as disabilities, since medical and legal authorities had concluded these were diseases, and as such the OCR felt people with these conditions should be protected from discrimination.

Next the OCR needed to determine what constituted *discrimination*. Here they drew heavily on their civil rights experience, aware of how the subtle but powerful barriers of stigma and attitude could prevent women and people of color from full participation in society. The OCR identified two broad barriers to people with disabilities that prevent them from full participation: attitudinal barriers and physical barriers. For people with disabilities, however, discerning discrimination would be even more difficult. Unlike the outright hostility that often faced women and blacks in the workforce, for example, people with disabilities were almost always treated with "kindness," even though it was frequently only a mask for pity, fear, and condescension. In most cases, a prospective employer couldn't deny that a woman or black person could perform a given job. However, in many cases—without evidence—an employer could assume, and often did, that a disabled person was unsuited for the task just because of the disability.

One way to enforce integration in the workplace was through affirmative action, that is, asking employers to treat all job applicants equally and to be blind to sex, race, and national origin.

Equal treatment does not work, however, when it comes to employing people with disabilities, as some people can perform a job only with special accommodations.

Physical barriers were easier to discern, but not always. In a January 18, 1975, memorandum to Peter Holmes, John Wodatch wrote:

> Many barriers are scarcely noticeable to non-handicapped persons. Obviously, an office building which may only be entered by first climbing a flight of stairs is inaccessible to a person in a wheelchair who seeks employment there. But so too is the building where a ramp to the entrance has been constructed, but there are no restroom cubicles wide enough to accommodate a wheelchair. Hallways which have low hanging signs or light fixtures which those with sight can avoid are barriers to the blind; and deaf persons cannot readily negotiate in a building where, when audial warning devices are used, there are no corresponding visual indicators.[28]

The Architectural Barriers Act of 1968 prohibited barriers such as these in new buildings receiving federal financial assistance. However, Section 504 applied to "any program or activity receiving Federal financial assistance." This broadened accessibility to include airports, colleges and universities, public libraries, museums in many thousands of communities across the United States—any organization receiving federal financial assistance, directly or indirectly.

Many recipients of federal funds, universities and public school systems in particular, inhabit old structures with architectural barriers that would be prohibitively costly if not impossible to remove. Requiring total accessibility in these cases seemed unreasonable, and yet allowing exemptions would weaken the law.

The OCR staff recommended a compromise approach, *program accessibility*, which said that "as long as disabled people could participate in all parts of any given program, they did not need to have access to every room or even every building housing the program."[29] Stricter standards were proposed for all new construction, and no waivers or exceptions would be granted. All recipients of federal financing would be given three years from the effective date of the regulation to comply—or lose their financing.

The OCR believed that the economic benefits of providing full access to disabled people would more than outweigh the costs. Eliminating forced dependency on government and public charity and allowing disabled people to educate themselves and obtain training and jobs would ultimately decrease welfare costs and increase tax revenues.

In drafting the regulation, OCR staffers consulted relatively few people outside HEW, except when it came to better understanding discrimination because of handicap. Here they frequently consulted disabled individuals on an informal basis through a loose network of personal relationships, as well as established disability organizations, such as ACCD, the American Council of the Blind, and the National Association of the Deaf.[30] Judy Heumann was one of the people consulted by OCR staffers. Gradually, through people like Heumann, the OCR was able to solicit Max and Colleen, Ed Roberts, Lex Frieden, Fred Fay, Gini Laurie, and other disability rights leaders. It would take three years of political maneuvering, demonstrations, analyses, petitions, letters, and another presidential administration before the regulations would be implemented.

Meanwhile, Max had succeeded in raising the twenty thousand dollars needed to fund a market research study for the Paraquad building. In October 1974, he awarded the contract to Team Four. Max also engaged the services of two other prominent St. Louis organizations, Washington University and D'Arcy MacManus Masius, an international advertising agency headquartered in St. Louis, both of which agreed to provide their services to Max at no charge.

Martin Bell, professor of marketing at the School of Business Administration at Washington University in St. Louis, and his graduate students developed a questionnaire designed to gather statistical information on the housing, transportation, and employment needs of the disabled in the St. Louis region. It was mailed to some five thousand disabled people within a 120-mile radius of St. Louis.[31] Pat Hough, Associate Research Director at D'Arcy, developed a public information campaign, which would use the press and public service announcements to inform the disability community of the Paraquad project.

"DO YOU KNOW WHAT YOU ARE DOING?"

That fall, 1974, Max and Colleen were seeing a lot of each other. Their discussions about disability rights issues had grown more passionate and intense. "I remember we were driving in the country somewhere," Colleen recalled, "and it was a fall time of year, and when I drove the Volkswagen, I could see him in the rearview mirror such that we could talk, and we did that constantly while we were in the van. And he said to me one time, 'You know, you have a very strong future in disability rights.'

"And I said, 'I do? Why do you say that?'

"And he said, 'because you're so interested and you're smart and you take things on and you get 'em done and you care and you're passionate about this issue.' And he said, 'In five years, you'll be a leader in this movement.'

"And I thought, 'How does he know that?' And I remember smiling and thinking, 'Well, I hope so.' It would really be exciting to play a leadership role in something as exciting as this is . . . whatever this was . . . I mean, I don't think I really knew . . . I knew there was a need for a change and I knew that we were gonna work on it together. That was never a question.

"As a matter of fact, friends of mine who were physical therapists would say, 'I heard you are dating this handicapped guy,' and I would say, 'Well, yeah.' And they would ask, 'Why are you doing that?' And I would say, 'Because I love him.'

"'Don't you think that that's sort of risky?' And I would take them on right away and ask, 'Well, why is it risky? What's risky about it? Come on, I'm in love with him.'

"'But he's handicapped. How will you have kids?' Because we all went through physiology class and knew that for spinal cord injured people to have children naturally was a pretty tough deal. It didn't happen very often back then.

"And I said, 'Then we'll adopt kids. What's the big deal here?' And I would say, 'This is not a cause, guys, this is a relationship. I am in love with him. I love him. This is not a patient that I'm enamored with. Besides, he never was in my department anyway.'

"And one of my friends who I really cared a lot about said, 'Do you know what you're doing?'

"And I said, 'Yeah, I'm falling in love with a guy. That's what I'm doing.'

"She said, 'Well, I sure hope you do. What about pressure sores? What about bladder infections?' And I said, 'What about strokes? And heart attacks? And car accidents? And all these other things that happen to people as a part of life. I said, 'Gail, you don't know what's going to happen in your life. You can't predict. I can't either.'

"She said, 'But you're taking a risk.' And I said, 'I don't think I am. I'm falling in love like anybody else would.'

"She at the time was dating a medical student. And she was pretty excited that she was dating a medical student. And after she got out of PT school, she got a job. She put him through med school. They had a child. Then after he got out of medical school, he divorced her. And I never said a word. But it later struck me as strange that she was so preoccupied and worried about whether or not I could have a happy and satisfying marriage to a man with a disability, when there are other factors that tear marriages apart. And, sadly, that happened to her. She never remarried."

A SENSITIVE PLAN

By July 1975, Max had the findings from the survey conducted by D'Arcy and Team Four. Four hundred twenty-nine surveys were returned, a modest response rate of 11.3 percent. It was quite possibly the first of its kind. The survey conclusion reads:

> . . . there is considerable active interest among the disabled population of the St. Louis region in the possibility of living in the proposed complex . . . one half of the respondents, or 214 people, expressed a high level of interest. Only 16% were clearly uninterested.

> Although 62% of these 214 people are unemployed, they have a substantial amount of training and education. Half of those who are unemployed (about 75 people) would like to work, suggesting substantial employment potential in a range of job capacities.

> The majority of the 214 people interested in Paraquad are under 35 years of age. 21% are paras and quads and 25%

have MS. Although 15% are satisfied with their present housing in every way, they are still interested in moving to Paraquad. The two most cited reasons for wanting to move are a desire to get out into the community more and a desire to become more independent of families and friends.

Not only is the number of people interested in Paraquad high, but these people appear to have a lot to offer Paraquad . . . this survey clearly indicates the existence of a potential market.[32]

Given that the respondents had only seen a written description of the complex—an idea—and did not know the location or costs, the researchers admitted that the level of interest, while high, should still be regarded as "tenuous." Nevertheless, "a strong element of support has been identified which should only grow in size as the project becomes more concrete." And they were planning a follow up with a phase two study in a few months. Max finally had begun to build the foundation that he knew he would need in order to begin raising the millions of dollars it would take to make his dream come true.

Team Four also completed a site analysis that summer for the complex. The study considered twelve sites in St. Louis and identified six as having "significant potential." Sixteen listed project objectives, gleaned from interviews with Max and the Paraquad board of directors, gives an indication of Paraquad's ambitions:[33]

Functional integration of residential and commercial components.

Ease of movement for productive activity for physically handicapped.

Maximum of private [*sic*] for residents.

Maximum of independence for residents (minimization of need for assistance.)

Integration of disabled with non-disabled.

Fully open to any race, creed, color or family situation.

A range of community facilities easily available to residents.

Viable commercial and business facilities capable of being operated by disabled.

Attractive, contemporary, non-institutional design.

Assistance services available at all times.

Rents comparable to similar apartments in same area.

Reasonable rents within the ability of most potential residents to pay.

A reasonable income as well as internal "profit" to offset losses accrued in achievement of wider aims.

Integral physical therapy facilities.

Housekeeping services available.

A range of optimal dining facilities available to disabled residents.

The site Max and his board would eventually select, located at 4545 Forest Park Boulevard, had been known as the Boulevard Apartments and was located in an area of St. Louis known as the Central West End. A historical and highly eclectic neighborhood, it lies within the city's central corridor and contains streets that were platted in the early to mid-nineteenth century. Home to millionaires and paupers, the area contains large, single-family homes on private streets, as well as apartments, flats, and rooming houses. Over the years, the Central West End has been vulnerable to economic downturns, its population shifting from prosperity to privation during difficult times.

The 1960s and 1970s had been a particularly low period in the history of the Central West End, with many of the unique stores, antique shops, art galleries, and restaurants giving way to hippie "head shops," tattoo parlors, saloons, nightclubs, and crime. The drug culture moved into many communities across the United States during the 1960s and 1970s, and the Central West End, with its artsy, eclectic, and bohemian reputation, proved to be a magnet for hippies, drug addicts, prostitutes, and other marginal citizens.

At about this time, a Washington University board chair, James S. McDonnell (founder, McDonnell Aircraft Corporation, later McDonnell Douglas), and the chairman of Barnes Hospital, Edgar M. Queeny (former CEO of Monsanto Corporation and noted conservationist), led the formation of an organization called the Washington University Medical School and Associated Hospitals (WUMSAH). WUMSAH consisted of the Washington University Medical School, Barnes Hospital, Children's Hospital, Jewish Hospital, and Central Institute for the Deaf.

In the early 1970s, businesses, institutions, and a sizable portion of the St. Louis population began moving west to the outer suburbs. Among these were several of the area's largest hospitals: St. John's, Missouri Baptist, St. Luke's, and DePaul. Meetings of the WUMSAH Board were called to decide on the future location of the WUMSAH institutions. Ray Wittcoff, a representative of the Jewish Hospital, had a vision for redeveloping the area around the medical center. After much discussion and study the group felt that it would be in the best interests of both the medical institutions and the city to "face the issue and rehab the area."[34] They decided to stay, a decision largely credited with saving St. Louis's historic Central West End and helping to restore it to what it is today.

WUMSAH carved out an area of about one hundred square blocks bordered by Lindell Boulevard on the north, Kingshighway on the west, Boyle Avenue on the east, and Interstate 64 on the south and formed a new corporation, the Washington University Medical Center Redevelopment Corporation (WUMCRC), under which all subsequent studies of the area and any development would fall.

WUMCRC engaged a large and respected architectural and engineering firm, Hellmuth, Obata + Kassabaum (HOK) to create a plan for the area. HOK, formed in 1955, had by 1975 established a reputation as one of the country's most innovative firms capable of handling large-scale projects.[35] HOK created a plan but also a lot of controversy.

According to Jerry King, a young international land developer later hired to be executive director of WUMCRC, "It just created this huge furor in the neighborhood, and it was exactly the wrong kind of plan."[36] HOK had recommended a demolition and reconstruction plan to a group whose goal was to rehabilitate and restabilize the neighborhood while maintaining its historical appearance. It was not the sort of job suited to a large firm that prided itself on large-scale innovative design.

WUMCRC then brought in an experienced land developer, Richard Roloff, recommended by Washington University board member George Capps. Roloff walked the streets and talked with people until he had a good understanding of the neighborhood and neighbors, and he convinced the city to grant eminent domain power in their defined 185-acre area. According to Dr. Danforth, "he and Ray Wittcoff are the real heroes of the redevelopment."[37]

Shortly thereafter WUMCRC engaged a smaller firm, one with more of a history of renovation, and one known to Max Starkloff: Team Four. "They came in with a much more sensitive plan," King said.[38]

Danforth, armed with new Team Four plans for the area, met with Civic Progress, an organization of CEOs and top executives from St. Louis's largest private sector employers with a mission "to improve the quality of community and business life in the St. Louis region."[39] Danforth proposed that they purchase bonds to fund development of the area, which they did.[40]

King remembered visits from Max and Colleen during the early stages of the WUMCRC redevelopment. "Max said, 'This is what I want to do. Do you have any properties that might work for us?' We mentioned the Boulevard." King described the Boulevard as looking "like a California motel was uprooted by a tornado and dropped down" in the Central West End.[41] Built in 1962[42] by a California developer, it consisted of seven three-story buildings in a figure-eight configuration surrounding two courtyards, each with a pool. Each building had five rooms to a floor, an elevator, and exterior balconies on one side, which provided the only means of access. There were 120 rooms.[43] "It was awful in terms of its design," King remembered, "particularly for this climate. Inadequate insulation. Inadequate thought given to the kind of winters that we have . . . snow and ice . . . all of that. And over the course of the years, it didn't hold up very well. By 1975 it was being rented [as apartments], and it was a mess."

While it may have been a mess in many respects, it looked great according to the objective measurement criteria established by Team Four. On a list of twenty-one attributes, the Boulevard Apartments tied with two other units with a score of 57 out of a possible 63. According to the report:

> . . . this site appears to possess the characteristics necessary to fulfill the criteria of the Paraquad Program except providing on-site employment opportunities. However, the 9000+ jobs in the barrier-free medical center, and the 1500 jobs at the new Blue Cross facility, the Bell Telephone Facility and other local employers offsets that deficiency.[44]

The report also noted three additional benefits of the Boulevard's proximity to the medical center: supplemental minibus service throughout the area, supplemental police protection by Medical Center security, and expanded commercial facilities within a half block of the site. Max and Team Four recommended the Boulevard Apartments, adapting and reusing the site, a decision Danforth, Roloff, King, and the WUMCRC applauded and supported. It would cost Max and Paraquad $400,000, as is.

ADVOCATE AND EDUCATE

The Boulevard initiative wasn't the only thing keeping Max busy in 1975. "As we went along, we realized that you cannot just develop housing," Max said. "The needs of a disabled person are so interrelated that we found we had to work on all of the issues simultaneously. We also realized that to get people to understand what we were trying to do was something that called for advocacy. In this sense, our advocacy was an educational process. We had to educate the community at large, funding sources, political and civic leaders, institutions, etc., on what we mean by integrating disabled people into the community.

"We got into the need for statewide architectural barriers laws, a need for curb-cut legislation, and a need for better transportation."[45] Max and his supporters quickly persuaded the St. Louis Board of Aldermen to pass curb cut legislation. "Following that," said Max, "the city example spread to the county municipalities."

A much more protracted battle involved the city's aging fleet of buses, 157 of which needed to be replaced. The Urban Mass Transportation Assistance Act stated that cities must provide equal transportation service for people with disabilities. However, the interpretation of this was gray. Bi-State Development Agency, owner of the St. Louis metropolitan region's public transportation system,[46] reasoned that the solution lay in providing separate buses or vans with lifts, which they named Call-A-Ride service. Any person with a disability could call in advance and ask to be picked up, delivered, and returned. Max opposed this. "We advocated integrating the disabled into the existing system instead of allowing the stereotype of separate, special services to persist. So we began negotiations with Bi-State regarding the purchase of accessible buses."[47]

Bi-State made the argument that lifts on any of its buses would be a waste of public tax dollars, since disabled people never used public transportation. It argued for providing a few lift-equipped vans that disabled people could simply call in advance. Why waste money, it asked, on equipping 900 or even just 157 of their buses with lifts that nobody would use anyway? "We argued," Colleen recalled, "that the reason Bi-State never saw any disabled people on buses was because it was impossible for disabled people to ride the buses. No lifts—no riders!"

St. Louis became a national flash point as one of the first cities in the country to test the new Urban Mass Transportation Assistance Act. It was the beginning of Paraquad's two-year advocacy effort, which would gain Max and his organization a national reputation as strong advocates for people with disabilities.

"The federal government was providing 80 percent of the funding" for Bi-State, recalled Bob Baer, then executive director of the organization, "and each time we were going to apply for a grant, we had to have it approved by the board, and we had to have public hearings. Max and the people he knew were more effective than any of the local politicians. In my view, the politicians kind of ran for cover, because at the public hearings a lot of handicapped people would show up to testify and, of course, no public official wants to take on a handicapped person in public. . . . So we felt pressure that we had to do this . . . from the local groups like Max's, from the federal government, and frankly from the politicians who didn't do anything to help us.[48]

"Because we were first in the country to face the issue of bus lifts, we were somewhat flying blind," Baer continued, "but, you know, you've got to start somewhere. "There were maintenance issues with the lifts. Some of the riders were complaining that the lifts took time to lower and for the [disabled] person to get on or off the bus. I think the cycle time was four to five minutes. We got a lot of calls and a lot of letters." If the lift didn't work, which was

MAX AND FELLOW PROTESTORS CALL FOR LIFTS ON
ALL BI-STATE BUSES.

more the norm than the exception, Bi-State would have to bring in a bus with a working lift and ask all the riders to transfer to the bus with the working lift. Delay: thirty to forty minutes. It promised to be a logistical nightmare.

"We did some financial models that showed that the Call-A-Ride vans would have been more cost effective," Baer said. Purchasing 157 lift-equipped buses would have cost almost $4 million more than purchasing the same number of conventional buses.[49] Since federal aid paid 80 percent, Bi-State was looking at an extra cost of $785,000. Bi-State could purchase a fleet of lift-equipped vans with drivers and keep the change.

The American Public Transit Association (APTA) opposed lift-equipped buses, insisting that a separate system of special lift-equipped minivans called "paratransit" could not only do the job more economically but also offer "special service" to those in need. "First," recalled Baer, "[the vans] would have been more personalized. Secondly, I think it would have been superior service. It would have been a more sensitive way to give a handicapped person a ride. Frankly, I don't know how those people got to the bus stops. I mean, the bus didn't make any special arrangements for pickups or drop-offs."

But many advocates for disabled people considered paratransit second rate. Mary Johnson, in her book *Make Them Go Away*, explained:

> Paratransit was never intended to be a complete service for all the disabled people in a community, but only for those who had been allowed to "sign up." In this way it was a benefit, no longer a true public service. It was a subscription service; and like most things associated with the public management of disabled people's lives, it was medicalized. In most cases it required a doctor's OK.
>
> The transit system designed for the general public was available to anyone. Its operators didn't care where you went, when you went or how long you stayed.
>
> Not so with paratransit, whose riders' trips must be approved by the system operator. In many communities, only people who worked, or who used the service for medical needs, were allowed to use the paratransit system.[50]

Johnson concluded, "The reason paratransit was considered a cheaper alternative to public transit was because, in truth, it didn't transport very many people."[51]

APTA (and Bi-State) argued that most disabled people actually preferred paratransit. If all buses, trains, and subways were made accessible, APTA argued, "90 percent of the transportation handicapped would still have the inability to get to and from transit stops, the inability to wait out-of-doors, the inability to travel alone or in crowds and the inability to ride while standing."[52]

Max and his group organized a transportation task force of disabled individuals, as well as organizations serving disabled individuals, to take people to the public hearings. Baer used two words to describe the experience: *emotional* and *powerful*. The hearings were held in the County Council chambers in Clayton. At one end of the room was a crescent-shaped table at which sat seven County Council members. They faced a podium where members of the public testified and, behind it, several hundred chairs. Chairs had to be moved out of the room to accommodate the wheelchairs.

As more people with disabilities filled the room, more accommodations had to be made. Blind people with dog guides. Deaf people with interpreters. People with mental disabilities. People on respirators. Attendants. Family members. And, of course, members of the press.

The seven County Council members, accustomed to sparsely attended hearings, were experiencing something they'd never seen before. Most of the disabled participants had never attended a public hearing. Many of them had never had the opportunity to be heard. They never believed anyone would listen. Now they had been brought together by Max and his colleagues to advocate, to make the world accessible for the first time in history.[53] They had been told, probably for the first time in their lives, that their presence would make a difference.

But before Max and other disability rights leaders could convince the authorities, they had to persuade many of their own constituency. In her book, Mary Johnson wrote:

> Disabled people have been conditioned to special services.
> Most accept them, even though they are far less satisfac-

tory, and are not at all equal, or even equivalent, to services that the nondisabled public enjoys. But many disabled people believe that "special" services are better for them, and are their right.

Paratransit offers protection from the hustle and bustle; the waiting at the bus stop. It's noncompetitive, easy. That you have to decide a week in advance where you want to go is a tradeoff many people are willing to make. What most of us would regard as an insufferable infringement on our "right to be abroad in the land" may not bother someone whose whole life has been a lesson in being a "'patient."[54]

But paratransit was no limo service. After being picked up for transportation, which was arranged at least one week in advance, a person in a wheelchair was loaded into a van with as many as a dozen other people in their wheelchairs. Often the last one to board would wait while fellow passengers were unloaded at their destinations. Arriving on time for an appointment was a crapshoot, depending on the driver's schedule, attitude, and the locomotion of the passengers. There could be no changes in plans, no "Gee, I think I'll go visit Sally" or "Oh, I better stop by the pharmacy and get some toothpaste." The passenger was delivered to the prearranged destination and would be picked up at the prearranged destination.

Getting home was the same routine, as the passenger often waited hours for the van to arrive and was shuttled from neighborhood to neighborhood, watching fellow passengers off-load. A forty-minute round-trip for the nondisabled could easily take three to six hours via paratransit.

Special? Hardly, by most people's definition of the word. "Providing a 'special solution for the handicapped' has been the typical response to disability in modern U.S. society—to segregate it, separate it, us from them, to make them go away and leave us alone," wrote Mary Johnson.[55] Special buses. Special Olympics. Special education. It is always very clear that *special* means *segregated*. Special solutions isolate disabled people from society. But few seemed to think it should be upsetting.

So Max took his case to the authorities, to the press, and to the people. The debate was not about whether people with disabilities would have public transportation made available to them. It was over "special accommodations" versus public accommodations. The right to go where one wanted when one wanted as expeditiously as possible should be available to *all* people. Forcing some members of society to accept a different form of transportation was segregation, plain and simple—just as discriminatory as forcing African Americans into segregated schools. The bus lift issue was a civil rights matter. It was a matter of dignity.

A Gift, a Wedding

In June 1975, Buster May surprised Max with an unexpected phone call. It began with questions about Max's apartment complex. How was it going? Buster asked about Max's personal plans, about Colleen, and about how he was doing personally. And finally he asked Max, "Do you need more money?" Max, caught off guard, remembered telling him that Colleen was making around $10,600 a year as a physical therapist.

"I'll send you a check for $25,000," said May, "as my wedding gift to you."

Max was floored. "And I hadn't even told him my intentions!" Max thanked May enthusiastically, then called Colleen.

"Buster May is going to give us a gift of $25,000," he told her excitedly. "Will you marry me?"[56]

"Of course, I said yes right away," Colleen recalled.

But when Colleen told her parents about it, their reaction was less than she had hoped for. "It wasn't totally unexpected," Colleen recalled. "About a year earlier when Max and I were dating and things were getting serious, I asked my dad, 'What would you think if I were to marry Max?' and he said, 'Your mother and I think you're cracked.'

"A year later, I sat down with them at our farm at Catawissa, Missouri. We went into the living room, a large paneled room that always felt very formal, and I said, 'Mom and Dad, Max has asked me to marry him.' There was a long period of silence. My mother's brow furrowed, and I could tell she was worried. "My dad finally said, 'Well, I guess we knew this was coming.'

"My mother just looked at me and said, 'You don't marry somebody to be his nurse.' And I said, 'I won't be his nurse, Mom. I love him.'

"Dad wanted to know how we planned to manage, and I told him that Max would hire attendants, people who would help him dress and eat. Then Mom said she didn't think we were being realistic—where would we find the money?

"I told them about the $25,000 gift from Buster May [approximately $110,000 in 2013 dollars] and reminded them that I was making $10,600, so we already had two years' pay in the bank. It was a good income to start with.

"My dad finally said, 'Well you're gonna do it no matter what, and we need to get behind it and help in any way we can.'"

Colleen went back to see Max at the Hill. She remembered it was a weekend, and though it was early in the evening, Max had been having trouble with pressure sores and had gone to bed to protect his skin. She walked in knowing he was looking forward to hearing the outcome. "She was upset," Max recalled. "They thought she was crazy. But of course they thought that. She was marrying a quad in a nursing home on Social Security and welfare."

Colleen's parents, Johanne and Robert Kelly, had always been gracious to Max, and it would have been uncharacteristic of them to go against their daughter's wishes. "I understand," he told Colleen. "They'll need time. But at least we can move forward."

At a spring picnic with her mother's extended family the next weekend, Colleen broke the news and received a much more favorable response. "I'll make your wedding dress," her aunt Betty said enthusiastically. Colleen's mother, seeing the family's positive reactions, began to feel more comfortable with the situation. "And from then on, I was free to be happy and go on with planning the dreamiest wedding I could possibly have," Colleen recalled.

She and her mother immediately went to work planning the wedding. "I wanted a formal wedding at St. Francis Xavier College Church with Carl presiding," Colleen said. "We set the date for October 4, 1975, ordered about two hundred invitations, and began looking at wedding gowns and bridesmaids' dresses."

Before the month was out, however, Max and Colleen had one more important ceremony to perform. Max had proposed to Colleen over the phone, but not in person in the traditional way Colleen had always dreamed about. "We got engaged on Gini and Joe Laurie's sofa," Colleen recalled. "They were out of town, and I think we were dogsitting. I had lifted Max out of his wheelchair and transferred him to one end of the couch. Beauregard, the Lauries' big black-and-tan basset hound, was sitting up on the other end of the couch. And I was in the middle. Max proposed to me and gave me a ring." She laughed. "It was white gold with a beautiful aqua stone, which he got on sale at Famous-Barr. He had no money." To Colleen, however, it was the Hope Diamond.

That spring Max started making plans for another big day, his departure from St. Joseph's Hill Infirmary, which he did on October 3, the day before the wedding. At the age of thirty-eight, Max left St. Joseph's Hill Infirmary for the last time. He had lived there for twelve years. It was a monumental day, full of promise and optimism. "I was completely focused on the wedding," recalled Max. "There was no fear, only excitement."

Gary Brocato and Donna Oberkramer, two nurse's aides who Max had gotten to know and like over the years, arrived early to begin loading Max's few belongings into his van. "I didn't have much," Max recalled, "some clothes, a bookshelf . . . not much for twelve years." Max said good-bye to the Franciscan brothers, to Walter Reed, and to other residents he had befriended. He knew he would never see them again. Without looking back, he wheeled himself out to the back loading ramp, down the lift, and out to his waiting VW van. "I remember feeling like I had beaten them," Max said of the Franciscans. "In spite of what they thought or felt, I was getting out and going to live life on my own terms." Independent at last!

He had a busy two days ahead of him. Brocato and Oberkramer drove him first to St. Francis Xavier College Church on the campus of Saint Louis University, where the ceremony would take place. There he met Colleen; his brother, Carl, who would conduct the ceremony; and his bridal party of some nineteen people, including all ten of Colleen's siblings for the rehearsal.

The rehearsal dinner was held at Hertha's house. "It was a small house for such a large wedding party," Max remembered, "but it didn't feel crowded." His sister, Lecil, was there, as was the young orderly, Ernie Brothers, who took care of Max before he moved into the nursing home. Colleen remembered, "Hertha cooked all the food herself." Max added, "It was beef bourguignon."

After the rehearsal dinner, Brocato and Oberkramer drove Max to his new apartment in the Central West End. "It was completely empty of furniture," Max recalled, "except for two beds." After carrying in Max's clothes and furniture, Brocato and Oberkramer assisted Max into bed, then spent the night themselves at the apartment to help Max get ready for his wedding the following day.

The wedding day was October 4, 1975. "It was a beautiful fall day," Max reminisced, "with temperatures in the 70s." St. Francis Xavier College Church was built in the late 1880s by the Jesuits in the Gothic revival style. It stands fifty feet above street level, majestic and accessible only by climbing many steep stone steps. With permission from the church, Robert Kelly, Colleen's brother and a carpenter, built two temporary ramps that would allow Max access to his own wedding. The first ramp entered the church through the rectory in the back. From there, Max could roll through the sacristy behind the altar, then out next to the altar itself. The second temporary ramp, which extended from the altar area to the church floor, would enable Max and Colleen to leave together after they were married.

The entire Kelly family, except for Colleen, was late. "The Kellys are never on time for anything," Max said. But Colleen arrived two hours early. She had asked the only punctual member of the family, her grandfather Joseph P. Kelly, to drive her to the church.

WEDDING DAY: (L TO R) MIKE DAHL, PETER KELLY, FRANK BLOCK, DAN
KELLY, ROBERT L. KELLY JR., MAX, LAURENT TORNO, COLLEEN, ROBERT L.
KELLY SR., JOHN R BOYCE, JIM TUSCHER, ERNIE BROTHERS, DAN NOLAN.

Max remembered waiting for the rest of the Kellys in the sacristy,
where John Boyce had come prepared with a deck of cards and
some new jokes. Finally, with the Kellys in place, the ceremony
started. Max, seated in his power wheelchair and dressed in a
morning coat, positioned himself at the altar to await his bride. He
had a pressure sore on one foot, so he was wearing one black shoe
and one black sock. To his right stood his brother. To his left stood
his best man, Laurent Torno, along with his five groomsmen, John
Boyce, Ernie Brothers, Frank Block, Dan Nolan, and Jim Tuscher,
all attired in morning dress.

As light streamed into the vaulted sanctuary through ancient
stained glass windows, a small group of young Jesuit friends played
guitars for the four hundred guests. Colleen's sister Mary Kelly,

her maid of honor, entered, followed by sisters Christine, Cathy, and Nina Kelly and best friends Roe Pandolfo and Mary Ann Rohan. They were followed by another sister, Mary Carol Kelly, and a niece of Max's, Gretchen Saller, both in the role of junior bridesmaids. Finally, with the groom and bridal party assembled on the altar, the guitarists struck up the "Bridal Chorus." Two more Kelly sisters, young twins Bridget and Maggie, emerged, sprinkling rose petals in front of the bride as she entered the church escorted by her father.

When Carl pronounced them "man and wife," the church erupted in applause. "When we processed out," Colleen recalled, "it was a triumphant moment. The music was really stirring. Max came down the ramp and I met him, and we walked out and greeted everyone at the entrance of the church."

When the last guest had left, Max had to retrace his path up to the altar, through the sacristy and rectory, under the walkway, through DuBourg Hall, then around to a neighboring historic mansion, Cupples House, for the reception. Mike Dahl had moved the homemade, folding aluminum ramp from Max's van to the steps of Cupples House so Max could enter.

"My family prepared all the food for the reception," said Colleen, "and there were four hundred people. It nearly killed my dad." Both her father and her grandfather loved to cook. Max remembered a small bluegrass band and a lot of people dancing. "Other than that, it was pretty much a blur."

Finally, it was time for the newlyweds to head to their new home, an apartment on the thirteenth floor of a distinguished building known as the Hampden Hall Apartments, located at Newstead and McPherson in the Central West End. "The apartment was enormous," Colleen recalled. "It had a big living room with a lot of windows overlooking downtown St. Louis. There was a nice-size dining room overlooking Forest Park, big kitchen with a butler's pantry, two bedrooms with full baths, even a maid's quarters. All for about two hundred dollars per month."

It was late at night by the time they left for Lecil and Steve Saller's weekend home at Innsbrook, where they would spend their honeymoon. An hour's drive west of St. Louis, the home was located on a beautiful lake nestled in the rolling hills of Warren County, Missouri. "The house looked like a two-story Dutch barn," Colleen recalled, "and it had eighteen steps leading up to the front door." Dahl and three friends had been waiting patiently for the newlyweds to arrive. "They carried Max in his wheelchair up those steps," Colleen said.

That night she lifted Max into bed using a technique she would use all their married life. "As a physical therapist I learned to put a belt around the person's waist in order to lift him into bed," Colleen said. "With Max, though, I thought that was too impersonal, so I put my arms around him in a bear hug and then used body mechanics to lift him into and out of bed."

Exhausted after a long day, Max and Colleen fell asleep instantly their first night as man and wife. "After that, though, it got very romantic," Colleen remembered. "The following morning, we just snuggled in bed talking and reliving the wedding." Max recalled, "We spent four days just enjoying each other."

Lecil and Steve had stocked the kitchen with everything the Starkloffs could possibly want. During the days, they spent time out on the deck enjoying the warm sun. At night, as the temperature dropped, Colleen would light a fire in the fireplace and cuddle with Max. "It was peaceful, relaxing, and wonderful," Colleen recalled, "a great way to start our lives together."

Returning to their apartment, all their wedding gifts were just where they had left them. Thanks to the generosity of Buster May, they had enough money in the bank to meet personal expenses. And thanks to the generosity of several foundations, Max had enough money to pay Paraquad's administrative expenses for the next six months.[57] Most important, they had each other.

Colleen remembered their first Christmas: "We had a tall Christmas tree. It was about ten feet tall. And to decorate it, I stood on the arms of Max's chair while he drove me slowly around the tree." Each night as the sun set, their living room would fill with a beautiful soft, golden light.

·CHAPTER 10·

PROTESTS AND PROGRESS

With the approval of the Paraquad board, Max and Colleen rented their first office space in a building at 14 North Newstead Avenue, down the street from their apartment. It had formerly been the St. Louis Mounted Police Headquarters but now was occupied by two tenants Max and Colleen knew very well: Laurent Torno's architectural firm, Berger, Field, Torno, Hurley, Architects; and Richard Ward's Team Four. The new office space enabled Max to work more closely with Torno. "I was the guy who emptied his leg bag three times a day," Torno recalled. "We ate lunch together. We talked all the time." The Starkloffs credit Torno with challenging them to think through every idea and to begin to work as a business. He became their mentor and a close friend.[1]

In an article published in the *St. Louis Post-Dispatch*, reporter Patricia Degener described how Max conducted business:

> At his desk, he uses a special holder for his telephone because he has no firm grip. Although he has part use of his left arm, he uses a stick made from a fiberglass fishing pole with a mouthpiece at one end and an eraser at the other to dial the phone, to typewrite, to shuffle papers and turn pages.
>
> The bathroom, on the same floor level, has wide doorways and grab bars so he can move about independently.[2]

Early in 1976, Max was working hard to raise the money to both purchase the Boulevard Apartments and renovate them. The apartments themselves, plus the land, would cost $400,000. Renovation, Torno estimated, would cost almost four times that amount, $1.4 million. How would someone like Max, a quadriplegic with no college degree, no business experience, no real estate experience, and no real estate management experience—a man who had just spent the last twelve years of his life in a nursing home—secure a loan for $1.8 million?

Jerry King and the Washington University Medical Center Redevelopment Corporation had been successful in securing U.S. Department of Housing and Urban Development (HUD) loans for

MAX AT WORK; HE PAID ALL
OF THE BILLS.

a number of redevelopment projects within their area. King suggested to Max that he talk to William Danforth to see if Danforth and the WUMCRC board would back his application to HUD. Dr. Danforth and the WUMCRC board of directors agreed to do just that.[3] "If I remember correctly," Torno recalled, "to get that done, Bill Danforth had to convince the Washington University Medical Center Board of Directors to both [back] the loan and, in the process, provide all their financial data, which was just one hell of a lot to ask. "But," he added, "just imagine if you were sitting at HUD in Washington and an application came from that cast of characters in St. Louis . . . it was fairly compelling."[4]

Eight months later, on September 5, 1976, Max received the good news—and the bad. HUD had approved a direct loan of $1.4 million for rehabilitation of an existing structure into no more than sixty-five one- and two-bedroom apartments. The bad news: "The funds allocated are to be used [for] housing to serve the elderly and/or handicapped."[5] HUD was only interested in a housing complex for people with disabilities. To get the loan, Max would have to refuse occupancy to tenants *without* disabilities. Though this ran counter to his own personal beliefs, plus the beliefs of the Independent Living Movement, he felt at the time that it was the only way he would be able to raise that amount of money.

But maybe he could bend the rules. After all, he figured, HUD was a big bureaucratic organization nine hundred miles away. "We were so naive," Max recalled, "we thought we could pull one over on HUD and integrate the Boulevard. We quickly learned that federal regulations are not to be messed with."[6] Max would never be able to integrate the Boulevard and, more important, he, Paraquad, and HUD would learn years later exactly why segregated housing for low-income people with disabilities was a mistake.

In mid-1976, a year following Max's departure from the nursing home, Colleen left her job as chief physical therapist at St. Joseph's Hill Infirmary to become assistant director of Paraquad. Having immersed herself in the Disability Rights Movement, she could no longer work in an institution that housed people with disabilities. Instead, she wanted to dedicate herself to an organization that got people with disabilities *out* of institutions. Together, Colleen and Max threw themselves into the myriad issues facing the disabled.

In 1979, thanks in large part to Paraquad's advocacy efforts, the Bi-State Development Agency purchased 157 lift-equipped buses. But it neglected to test the lifts and train the drivers. "Everyone hated the new lifts," Max recalled. "Because they weren't tested, and because the drivers didn't know how to operate them, they would fail in the open position, which meant that everyone on the bus would have to wait while Bi-State provided another bus. Bi-State claimed that this was proof that the technology didn't work. And, because the lifts were unreliable, people with disabilities were afraid to use them, which Bi-State positioned as further proof that people with disabilities didn't use public transportation."

Again, Max and Colleen went to the press. "In the Bi-State metro area," Max was quoted as saying in one article, "there are about 200,000 disabled persons, about 8,000 of whom are in wheelchairs."[7] The lift technology does work, it just needs to be maintained, he said. Bi-State needs to train the drivers.

It was a battle that Max and Colleen ultimately won, as St. Louis would become the first city in the country to have a fleet of lift-equipped buses. However, their victory was short lived. According to a federal report from the Urban Mass Transportation Association, "in September, 1978, scheduled accessible bus service was cut back by two-thirds due to malfunctions of the lift equip-

MAX BOARDS THE FIRST LIFT-EQUIPPED
BUS FLEET IN THE UNITED STATES.
MISSOURI HISTORY MUSEUM.

ment. Wheelchair user ridership decreased gradually during the first year of service but dropped off markedly during the last ten months of the evaluation period."[8]

Six years after Bi-State purchased its first fleet of lift-equipped buses, Bi-State spokesperson Tom Sturgess was quoted in an article in the *Riverfront Times* saying that buses with lifts "get very little use for a number of reasons. Some people can get on the bus but can't get around because there are no curb cuts. And we still have a problem with the lifts—they'll work at one stop and then they won't move, and everybody is stuck. It has discouraged the handicapped population from using it. And it's a very expensive proposition."[9]

The Starkloffs continued their pressure on the City of St. Louis to install curb cuts. "Without curb cuts," Max said, "people in wheelchairs can't move. They can't leave their homes. They can't gain access to jobs, stores, schools. They can't vote, serve on a jury, attend hearings, or appear in court as a witness. A six-inch curb is a six-foot-high wall to a wheelchair user who is trying to live independently." Though curb cut legislation was introduced in St. Louis as early as 1973,[10] the city had installed curb cuts sporadically as workers repaired or replaced sidewalks. But a handful of curb cuts does not help people with a disability who have to negotiate their wheelchairs in a traffic lane because they are unable to access the sidewalk.

In 1976, with only two exceptions,[11] no city in the United States was installing curb cuts on existing streets in any systematic fashion. State laws in most states stipulated that curb cuts were to be installed during the construction or renovation of most streets, but enforcement of state codes and regulations was sporadic at best. It would take several lawsuits years later, in 1992 and 1994,[12] to get major U.S. cities to begin to take the issue seriously. Until then, Max and Colleen were determined to keep the issue in front of St. Louisans.

In an article in the June 24, 1977, *St. Louis Post-Dispatch*, with a headline "Struggle for Independence in a Hostile Environment," reporter Patricia Degener described some of the mobility challenges Max faced in a typical workday:

> Each morning, Starkloff leaves his West End home for the office, a block and a half away. Using his left hand to operate the controls, he rolls down a ramp to the sidewalk, takes a curb cut in front of the house and crosses the street to get to his office on North Newstead. A garage at one side

of his building has a power lift to raise him about five feet to floor level.

In fact, it was the independence afforded him in the Washington University Medical Center Redevelopment area that led him to choose the site for his home and office. He is fairly mobile in his one-block area—the newly redesigned block of Laclede Avenue, which has curb cuts. There are two restaurants nearby that are at sidewalk level and therefore are accessible to him.

But if he had to take a bus to work, he'd be out of luck, because even though there are power lifts on a few Bi-State buses they are not yet in operation. And many of the buildings in his area look accessible, but they aren't, because there are steps to negotiate, narrow doors, public phones and drinking fountains that are too high and toilets that lack hand bars and wide stall doors.[13]

Degener added this comment from Max: "Most people don't realize what a simple thing like a curb cut means to someone in a wheelchair. It means a whole world to travel in."

A NEW PRESIDENT, A FRESH START

It had been over three years since the Rehabilitation Act of 1973 was passed, and the question of whether Section 504, the regulations for implementation, should be approved had still not been resolved.[14] But a new administration under President Jimmy Carter took office on January 20, 1977. HEW secretary Joseph Califano—after enduring massive protests and sit-ins over his own foot-dragging—finally signed the Section 504 regulation on April

28, 1977. He also signed the regulation for the Education for All Handicapped Children Act, passed two years earlier in 1975, guaranteeing the best possible public education for all disabled children.

The disability community was triumphant. Celebrations were organized all over the United States. Disability rights activist Frank Bowe recalled later:

> This advisor [to Martin Luther King] said, "People think that revolutions begin with injustices. They don't. A revolution begins with hope." If you think about that, if you move back to the spring of 1977, then you will understand that the reason disabled people came together and demonstrated as they did in the spring of that year was because *they had hope.*

> It is a tremendously tragic commentary upon the United States of America that it was only in 1977 that disabled people came to have enough hope to protest. It took two hundred years after this country was formed—*two hundred years*—for these people to begin to have hope. That is what happened. A law had been passed in 1973, the Rehabilitation Act of 1973, and included in it was Section 504, which many people realized was going to become the cornerstone of the civil rights of disabled Americans. . . . For four years we had fought behind the scenes to try to get the law implemented and enforced. And at the beginning of 1977, for the first time, we had some reason to hope that the law was at last going to become effective.[15]

The Section 504 regulation was published in the *Federal Register* on May 4, 1977.[16] It was implemented immediately by the Department of Health, Education, and Welfare. Since it applied to all recipients of federal funds, all federal departments and agencies had to develop, publish, and enforce their own regulations, which had to be at least as stringent as the HEW standards.

The disabled protestors' victory celebrations were short lived, however, as the reality of the new regulations began to sweep across the country. Costs became a major issue. Newspapers attacked the Section 504 regulations as being ridiculous and costly examples of political pandering. Small towns were cited in particular. They had to install at great expense ramps into libraries and public buildings even though no one in the town used a wheelchair. HEW estimated that the cost of implementing the 504 regulations would be $2.4 billion,[17] primarily for education. A spokesperson for the National Association of College and University Business Officers in Washington, D.C., estimated that the cost of altering some of the college buildings to make them accessible to the handicapped would be $1 billion.[18] In an editorial on May 1, the *Washington Post* predicted "a welter of lawsuits and quarrels."[19]

In comparing the Disability Rights Movement to the Civil Rights Movement, historian Edward Berkowitz wrote, "Admitting [black student] James Meredith to the University of Mississippi cost nothing in an economic sense. All of the costs were political . . . but to admit James Meredith's handicapped counterpart to a university would cost money rather than save it. It would mean that the physical plant would need to be expanded or modified, and it would require the university to pay the administrative cost of complying with the federal regulations."[20]

While the larger battles were being waged on the national level, Max and Colleen continued working to enact changes in St. Louis. "We knew that we had to be politically connected at all levels, local, state, and national, in order to influence policy regarding people with disabilities," Colleen said. With a St. Louis mayoral race looming in April, Paraquad, in the role of consumer advocate, contacted the 1977 candidates, advocating the need for an Office on the Disabled within the city administration.

Of the four candidates, James Conway was the most vocal about full inclusion of people with disabilities. On March 31, he issued a two-page press release saying,

> Thousands of disabled men and women live in the City of St. Louis. Fortunately, advancements in medical science and rehabilitation techniques are enabling them to lead increasingly productive lives.

> I firmly believe city government has a useful role to play in contributing to the progress being made by the disabled.

> As Mayor, I will use the full authority of that office to help eliminate the major problems confronting the disabled. Those problems are employment, transportation, education, housing and architectural accessibility.[21]

He proposed establishing a "Mayor's Office of the Handicapped," which would be charged with improving communications between the public and private agencies currently serving the handicapped.

With Paraquad providing the leadership and organization, word went out to the disabled population of St. Louis, estimated at the time to be 10 percent of the overall population, to vote for Conway and, on April 5, 1977, he was elected mayor.

Shortly thereafter, and true to his promise, Conway quickly approved[22] an ordinance establishing the Mayor's Office on the Disabled as a division in the Department of Welfare. The office would consist of a commissioner on the disabled, a staff, and an advisory council. Max was appointed by Conway to the advisory council on May 11, 1978. Conway appropriated forty thousand dollars to be used both for operating expenses for the current fiscal year and for matching funds for federal grants.

In addition to other powers and duties, such as preparing and adopting plans, reports, applications, and grants, the Mayor's Office on the Disabled would "study current patterns and conditions of living of disabled persons" and identify what would sustain "wholesome and meaningful living" for them.[23]

Mayor Conway, in consultation with Max, appointed Deborah Dee, a polio paraplegic, as the first commissioner on the disabled. Dee would serve with mixed success in this position for thirty years. Succeeding her in April 2008 was David Newburger (currently co-director of the Starkloff Disability Institute), who was still in this part-time position in 2014. In 1977 only four other cities, Chicago, Los Angeles, New York, and Philadelphia, had established the office. As of 2014, all cities with fifty or more employees are required by the ADA to name an ADA compliance officer.

President Jimmy Carter was not far behind, hosting in May the White House Conference on Handicapped Individuals at the Sheraton-Park Hotel in Washington, D.C. Organizers spent seventy-five thousand dollars to install ramps, lower public telephones, and widen doorways to accommodate over three thousand disabled people who came to meet with President Carter and cabinet members. Max and Colleen were among them.

Ironically, an incident while Max and Colleen were boarding the airplane to Washington illustrated the huge chasm they had to cross between St. Louis and full inclusion in American society. The plane had been late coming into St. Louis, and the flight attendants were trying to board the Washington-bound passengers as quickly as possible for a fast turnaround. Colleen had wheeled Max to their row and was going through the process of transferring him from the wheelchair to his seat, which she did by squatting next to Max in the cramped aisle, placing his arms around her neck, and grabbing him under his arms in a bear hug. As she lifted him, an exasperated flight attendant, looking at the line of people behind them waiting to get to their seats, exclaimed, "Can't he walk just this one time?!" "No," replied Colleen, moving Max into his seat, "He can't."

That same year, Patricia Harris,[24] secretary of Housing and Urban Development, announced the creation of the Office of Independent Living for the Disabled to advocate and promote the needs of people with disabilities. It was the first time housing concerns for the disabled would be treated separately from those of the elderly.

President Carter appointed triple-amputee Max Cleland to head the U.S. Veterans Administration, making Cleland the first severely disabled person to fill that position. Carter at the time estimated that there were 35 million people with disabilities living in the United States—about 1 in 5 Americans—about half of whom had severe disabilities. In St. Louis, the number of disabled people was estimated to be 200,000, of whom 8,000 were in wheelchairs.[25] Finally, their voices were being heard.

NONE BETTER THAN THE BOULEVARD

Architect Laurent Torno, excited by the prospect of designing a unique barrier-free, residential, commercial, and office complex that would accommodate both disabled and nondisabled occupants, continued his design of a prototype unit, working with architecture students at Washington University in St. Louis School of Architecture. For several years, he, Colleen, and Max had spent hundreds of hours evaluating ideas for the complex and researching books and documents on the subject. In summer 1977, Torno and Max visited existing housing projects for disabled people in Columbus, Ohio; Minneapolis; Fargo, North Dakota; and Houston.[26] In August 1977 they conducted a series of workshops with disabled individuals in St. Louis to learn more about specific disability needs and preferences.

In a document dated around 1977, Torno wrote:

> The average man has been the prime concern of the designers for centuries. [Now] new attitudes toward the physically handicapped and new techniques of therapy and prosthesis have added a new dimension to human life and, thereby, a new unit to challenge the designer—the man in the wheelchair.

> In a wheelchair a person's height is decreased by one-third, his width is doubled, his reach is limited by his inability to get his body into close proximity with objects, because of the way the wheelchair is constructed, he needs more room to carry on normal everyday activities. He cannot climb steps. He can go forward and backwards at will, but cannot move abruptly to either side. To travel in a straight line he needs a path three feet wide and he needs almost five feet of straight travel before he can negotiate a turn. Twenty-seven square feet of clear area are needed to permit him to turn about. This is the new entity to be considered when identifying and solving exterior and interior design problems.[27]

The blind, deaf, and retarded require specific alterations to assist them in functioning in everyday environment, but they nevertheless continue to stand erect, move on two legs, and conform to the standards of form, space, and movement which are intrinsic in the design professions. But the person in a wheelchair does not conform.

. . . The real problem of the handicapped is not curbs, stairs, narrow doors, small elevators and rough sidewalks. It is isolation. Certainly architectural and circulation barriers contribute to this, but their removal is not the long-range goal. The integration of the disabled into society is the overall objective.

The goal of Paraquad . . . is a normal living environment for the physically disabled—a mainstream situation including the activities of working, recreation, shopping, entertaining, etc. in which the disabled are integrated with the non-disabled.

It appears that all existing housing for the physically disabled is essentially no more than conventional dwelling design incorporating minimum modifications. . . .

There has been no comprehensive attempt to design a [dwelling unit] in which the handicapped individual with his different height, width, form, and the restricted movement patterns imposed by the wheelchair and/or select impairment characteristics have been dealt with in the conceptual stages of design.[28]

"Once the Boulevard Apartments was identified," Torno recalled, "I called the architect in California and obtained reproducible copies of the original drawings, and from that started doing remodeling studies."

After all their research, Torno and Max knew they were on to something innovative. "From all I knew at the time," Torno said, "no one in the country had produced an independent living unit this good. Even today when I read articles about universal design, as far as I can tell, nobody has done a better kitchen than this one yet. It was an extremely workable kitchen that could be adjusted and adapted to successive tenants. The countertops and wall cabinets were mounted on adjustable wall brackets. We had full wheelchair-accessible sinks and food preparation areas. We had slide-out boards that you could drop a mixing bowl into, so the board would hold the mixing bowl so all you had to do was stir.

"The bathrooms were terrific," Torno continued. "The entire bathroom was basically a wheel-in shower. We used a curtain and ceiling track of the type that's used [to separate beds] in hospitals to screen off the shower water. But you could literally wheel right into the shower from the bedroom. You could make a transfer to a fold-down chair if you wanted.

"I especially designed the vanity counters, their height, shape, and form. We had a mock-up made, and then had a casting made [of the vanity counter] from the mock-up. The vanity counters were unique to this project. The bowl, for example, was big enough so you could wash your hair in it from a wheelchair. We may have been the first dwelling unit to use the spray fitting that you normally find in a kitchen sink in a bathroom vanity. We had side-mounted [hot and cold water] controls with lever handles."

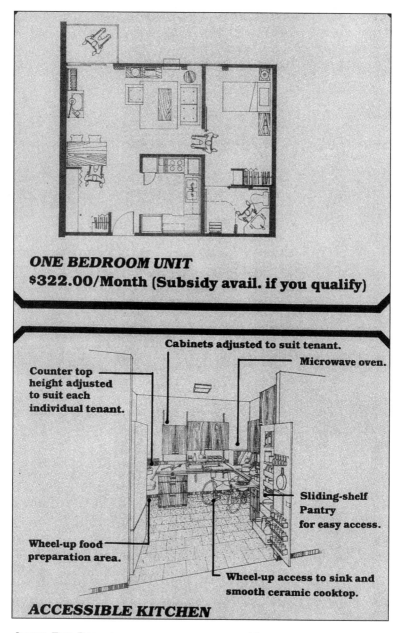

ONE BEDROOM UNIT
$322.00/Month (Subsidy avail. if you qualify)

Cabinets adjusted to suit tenant.

Microwave oven.

Counter top
height adjusted
to suit each
individual tenant.

Sliding-shelf
Pantry
for easy access.

Wheel-up food
preparation area.

Wheel-up access to sink and
smooth ceramic cooktop.

ACCESSIBLE KITCHEN

INSET: THE BOULEVARD SALES BROCHURE. MAIN IMAGE: PAGE FROM
BROCHURE SHOWING ONE-BEDROOM UNIT AND KITCHEN AMENITIES.

All doors were wide enough to accommodate wheelchairs, with sliding doors on the baths and bedrooms. "Security was an issue in the design of the building," Torno recalled, "because disabled people are vulnerable. So we designed the building with automatic locks on the gates and keypad locks." He added, "And we did all this within very tight budget constraints."

The redesigned Boulevard Apartments consisted of eighty-three one- or two-bedroom units with sixteen configured as efficiency apartments. Max's advertising brochure touted location and jobs, as well as accessible living:

> Your apartment is literally across the street from 10,000 jobs at the Washington University Medical Center. It is "down the street" from 1,000 jobs at The Blue Cross Building, which may be the most accessible office building in St. Louis. You will be "around the corner" from Saint Louis University and Forest Park Community College.[29]

The brochure boasted "balconies, patios, exquisitely landscaped courtyards, and a swimming pool." Units could be rented for $253 per month for an efficiency to $383 per month for a two-bedroom unit. For those unable to afford the rent, Paraquad offered "rents adjusted to meet any person's housing budget."

By April 1977, Max had received initial approval of Paraquad's $1.8 million loan from HUD. However, the owners of the Boulevard, now knowing Paraquad's full commitment to purchase the property, began to apply pressure. Paraquad must purchase the building by August 1977, they said, or they would put it back on the market. Quickly, Max had to find $400,000.

"No one believed that Max could raise that amount of money," Colleen recalled. "It was Max's first test of whether or not he could get things done and be perceived as a true leader." He talked to his good friend and Paraquad board member John Wuest, who was a loan officer at St. Louis's largest bank, Mercantile Bank. "He authorized the loan on the spot," Max remembered. "No questions asked. He didn't even ask for any collateral commitments from Paraquad."[30] Max signed a contract to purchase the building on August 27.[31]

But there were a few more hurdles. HUD insisted that Paraquad have full control of the building and an adjoining property before it would close on the loan. To do this, Max would have to raise an additional $73,000. Max reached out to generous friends and raised $80,000 almost immediately, an amazing feat for any fund-raiser.

On October 6, 1977, the *St. Louis Post-Dispatch* heralded the anticipated opening of the Boulevard with a story headlined: "Project Gives Handicapped Housing Hope," in which reporter David Fink wrote about Rod Hanebrink, a young man paralyzed from the chest down in an accident. Before the accident, "he had been living alone, holding down a job and managing his own money. Since the accident, he had had to live with his parents. . . .

"Like thousands of other disabled St. Louisans who've been forced to live with relatives, friends or in institutions, he knows he could make it on his own if St. Louis had apartments with wider doors, accessible bathrooms and other amenities for the handicapped. Now, the prospect of such housing is no longer a daydream."[32]

Independent Living Realized

By 1978, the Independent Living Movement was well under way, with an estimated 450 organizations in the United States either claiming to provide independent living services or calling themselves independent living centers.

Lex Frieden, a disabled young graduate student at the University of Houston, was refused a doctorate in independent living four years earlier because "there wasn't a sufficient base of literature in the field of independent living to get a doctorate degree."[33] Frieden was a quadriplegic as the result of a car accident in 1967 and decided "that if that's the thing preventing me from getting a doctorate, then that's probably in the future going to prevent a lot of people from getting a doctorate, and so maybe I should create some literature." He began to write and publish about independent living.

"And one of the first things I discovered was that there was no definition of *independent living*," Frieden recalled. So he set about creating one. "A lot of people were involved in that process. We tried to use a consensus process for the definition and by do-

LEX FRIEDEN, CENTER, WITH JUSTIN AND YOSHIKO DART, LEFT, AND OSBORNE (OZ) DAY AND MAX, RIGHT, IN 1992.

ing so we brought in people from around the country who were beginning to start little cliques of folks with disabilities to help one another, to provide peer counseling to one another, to share the expenses of housing, attendant care, transportation, and other things. We got people, including Max and Colleen Starkloff, to come to Houston and engage in a round-table discussion about what independent living was. . . ."[34]

They established a minimum set of essential services that must be provided by any independent living center as "housing assistance, attendant care, readers and/or interpreters, peer counseling, financial and legal advocacy, and community awareness and barrier-removal programs."[35]

In 1977, Frieden founded a national organization dedicated to the study and improvement of independent living centers called the Independent Living Research Utilization Project (ILRU) and conducted the first national research on independent living.[36] In 1978, the ILRU polled more than 450 organizations across the United States that claimed to be providing services for independent living and found that only 35 programs met the ILRU's definition of an independent living center. Out of those, only 12 provided the minimum set of essential services.

Paraquad was emerging as one of a handful of effective, comprehensive independent living centers around the United States.[37] Out of its small office at 14 North Newstead, which it shared with Laurent Torno, Max, Colleen, William Bixby "Bill" Sheldon, and Jim Tuscher offered a breadth of capabilities and resources, including peer counseling, workshop development, architectural services, engineering consultation, cost analysis, state legislative and congressional support, and legal consultation. They had worked with (or opposed) a number of federal, state, and city government agencies: National Park Service, U.S. Department of Housing and Urban Development, Missouri Division of Vocational Rehabilitation, Bi-State Development Agency, City of St. Louis Mayor's Office, East-West Gateway Coordinating Council of Governments, St. Louis Board of Aldermen, St. Louis Civil Rights Enforcement Agency, and St. Louis County Housing Authority.

While much of its early work involved housing and advocacy on behalf of people with disabilities, peer counseling and support was and continues to be an important service of Paraquad and other independent living centers. Discovered in the 1950s as an effective way to treat alcoholism, and adopted by Ed Roberts in the late '60s as a powerful aid to the newly disabled, peer counseling was a radically new model for helping people with disabilities. Before peer counseling, Max recalled, people with disabilities were treated by doctors or counseled by psychiatrists or psychologists. These people were certainly accredited and knowledgeable, but they were also ignorant about what it was like living inside a disabled body.

Many disabled people led healthy, active lives before their disability. Paralysis from spinal cord injuries, for example, happens mostly to young people, aged sixteen to thirty, while pursuing sports such as surfing, rock climbing, auto racing, skiing, and football. Imagine waking up in an intensive care unit, and your body can no longer do all the things it used to: getting up and getting dressed in the morning, doing the work you love, dancing, going out for an ice cream cone. How do you go on? "On the inside, you're still you," explained Max, "but suddenly after the accident, you are living in a body that's completely different. Through peer counseling, people who are newly disabled can talk to someone who's gone through a similar experience and come out the other side living a happy, independent life. It's extremely powerful."

Lucy Dolan, a beautiful, lithe athlete, became a quadriplegic after being injured in a rock climbing accident when she was nineteen years old. She recalled at a disability forum in 2006 how she felt before the accident. "I was invincible, in terrific shape. I felt I could do anything."[38]

"I was injured in a small town in Wyoming," Dolan recalled, "and was flown to St. Louis for treatment. My doctor [Harry Hahn] was a pioneer in independent living. After intensive care in a hospital in St. Louis, I did rehab in Denver, and then came back to Paraquad in St. Louis. Max and Colleen were peers. It was an unbelievable experience. It's not the big huge things so much" with being newly disabled, Dolan said. "It's a lot of the little things—not being able to pick up a coffee cup someone left on the floor. Getting from A to B takes planning and time. Getting up in the morning. Going to bed."

In the early days, Max, Colleen, Bill Sheldon, and Jim Tuscher did all the peer counseling, but over time they encouraged other people with disabilities to share their experiences with newly disabled people. They found that peer counseling helps not only the consumers, but the counselors, as well. Everyone in the process gains. The consumers learn coping skills—not just the obvious ones, but the little daily skills that only people with a disability learn from experience. They learn how to manage their own lives, and this gives them self-confidence. Then they reach out to others and become peer counselors themselves.

A Real Community

On September 15, 1979, almost a year from the day construction began, Paraquad held a grand opening for the Boulevard Apartments. In early July, an invitation went out to friends, supporters,

THE GRAND OPENING OF THE BOULEVARD APARTMENTS, 1979.

community leaders, and the media. It read, simply, "The Board of Directors and Staff of Paraquad invite you to share in the realization of a commitment to the disabled community of Saint Louis."[39] For Max, the completion of the first barrier-free development in St. Louis was the culmination of a six-year dream.[40]

The ribbon cutting took place at 1 p.m. on a sunny afternoon as part of an open house from 11 a.m. to 5 p.m. Dr. William H. Danforth, chancellor of Washington University at St. Louis, presided at the ceremony. He introduced speakers St. Louis mayor James Conway; Mark Van Matre, representing Senator Thomas Eagleton; John Heffern, representing Senator Jack Danforth; and, of course, Max himself. In addition to finding eighty-three accessible apartments, visitors also found accessible parking, kitchens with adjustable cabinets and countertops, spacious bathrooms with fixtures designed for people with disabilities, braille letters on elevators and doors, and blinking lights to alert a deaf occupant that someone is at the door. Each unit offered direct access to an outside courtyard and swimming pool or had its own balcony.

What the Boulevard Apartments did not have were institutional services, such as emergency care and twenty-four-hour-a-day supervisor or physical assistance. "Disabled people are not sick," Max said. "They do not need to be pampered. They need to be prepared to meet their own needs, whatever they may be. . . . We're an apartment building and nothing else. We're designed for the individual who cannot find housing to suit their needs."[41]

Max and Colleen moved into a large one-bedroom unit in the Boulevard shortly after it opened. The idea was to live there while the home they had purchased two years earlier at 4446 Laclede Avenue in the Central West End was being restored. Virtually uninhabitable, it was a three-story brick home located within the Washington University Medical Center Redevelopment Corporation (WUMCRC). To encourage redevelopment of the historical houses in the neighborhood, WUMCRC sold them for practically nothing, provided the owners agreed to rehab them. Max and Colleen bought the home on January 3, 1977,[42] for $18,500.[43] Like many of its neighbors, the structure had been used as a boardinghouse after World War II. "It was a wreck," Max recalled. "Right after we bought the house, we would find homeless people sleeping in the doorway. Once we saw a guy standing inside the front door, which he had jimmied. Colleen went after him with a hammer, and he casually walked away—with her purse."[44]

"By 1979," Colleen recalled, "we had managed to put together a financial package [for the new house] that would enable us to take it apart and put it back together again—with all new systems, new plumbing, new heating, everything . . . new walls . . . and we had to have some place to live, so we said, 'Why don't we go live in segregated housing and see what it's like?'" They moved into the Boulevard, apartment 308, and began rehabbing 4446 Laclede, a process that took eight months under the supervision of their architect, Laurent Torno.

By mid-November, the Boulevard had forty occupants. Patricia Degener, reporting for the *St. Louis Post-Dispatch*, interviewed several Boulevard tenants:

> Wanda Johnson, 27, who has been paralyzed from the waist down since birth, has been in her apartment for two months.

> "I lived with my parents," Johnson said, "and they weren't very excited at first about my moving out. I just love it here. It's a real community. Everyone is close. My apartment opens on the courtyard and I can get outside easily.

> "I can do what I want to do. The neighborhood is much more accessible than the South St. Louis neighborhood I lived in before."[45]

To better manage the Boulevard, Max and Colleen relocated their office to an abandoned storefront a few blocks away from the Boulevard at 4397 Laclede. Dan Feinberg, a real estate developer who joined Paraquad in 1981, painted a picture of the office. "It was a dump," he said. "The neighborhood back then was in trouble, and this particular building had been rented by some Saint Louis University students to use as a party house. Picture a one-thousand-square-foot storefront with a tin ceiling, hardwood floors, painted flat black in its entirety. There was some fluorescent strip lighting with black lightbulbs in it. This place was a trip.

DAN FEINBERG.

There was one beat up old toilet with the bare lightbulb hanging on the two wires. Extremely low overhead."[46]

This was where Dr. William H. Danforth, chancellor of Washington University, and Morton D. May, chair of May Department Stores, found Max when they paid a visit to his office earlier that year to inform him that he had been chosen to receive the city's most prestigious award, the St. Louis Award. It was established in 1931 to honor "the resident of Metropolitan St. Louis who has contributed the most outstanding service for its development or . . . shall have performed such services as to bring greatest honor to the community."[47] To say that Max was surprised by the visit and by the honor would be an understatement.

The ceremony was held on November 15, 1979, in the Tucker Theater in the Visitor Center beneath the Gateway Arch. For

Max's mother, Hertha, his brother, Carl (who was unable to attend), and sister, Lecil, it was a triumph. In attendance was a who's who of St. Louis: the members of the award committee, Maurice R. Chambers, chair and chief executive officer of Interco, a global apparel and footwear manufacturer; J. Wesley McAfee, chair, Union Electric Company; Robert Brookings Smith, chair, Mercantile Trust Company; Elliot H. Stein, broker and investment banker; and Charles Allen Thomas, chair of Monsanto. (Buster

MAX RECEIVING THE ST. LOUIS AWARD WITH COLLEEN, PRESENTED BY WILLIAM H. DANFORTH. PHOTO BY THE *ST. LOUIS GLOBE-DEMOCRAT*, 1979, FROM THE COLLECTIONS OF THE ST. LOUIS MERCANTILE LIBRARY AT THE UNIVERSITY OF MISSOURI—ST. LOUIS.

May was also a member of the award committee but could not be present.) Also present were past recipients of the St. Louis Award: Robert Hyland, CBS regional vice president and general manager of radio station KMOX; Charles Knight, chair and CEO of Emerson Electric; the Reverend Paul C. Reinert, president of Saint Louis University; Howard F. Baer, president of Saint Louis Zoo board and board chair of St. Louis Chamber of Commerce; Daniel Schlafly, president of St. Louis Board of Education; and James S. McDonnell, founder of McDonnell Aircraft Corporation, among others. St. Louis mayor James F. Conway and St. Louis County supervisor Gene McNary were also in attendance. Dr. Danforth, who served as secretary of the St. Louis Award Committee, presided. After introducing the St. Louis VIPs in attendance, he asked Max to come forward, introduced Colleen to the audience, and spoke briefly about Max and his accomplishments. Hertha would later say it was one of the proudest moments of her life. And for Max? "After all our struggles, this was a huge step. I had proved my independence. And this had confirmed all [Hertha's] spiritual beliefs."[48]

After the St. Louis Award ceremony, Max was interviewed for an in-depth article, which appeared on the front page of the Features Section in the Sunday, December 8, issue of the *St. Louis Globe-Democrat*. In this article, headlined, "The Newest Minority . . . the Disabled," Max spelled out his plan for the future: "After The Boulevard, the next step for Paraquad is the establishment of an Independent Living Center.

"The idea behind the center," said Max, "is to provide courses for the disabled which include job evaluation, legal rights and related subjects that will improve the opportunities for the disabled to get a job, and to live independently."[49] Max could say this with

PARAQUAD STAFF IN THE EARLY 1980S.

confidence. Not only were he and his associates already providing many of these services out of the Paraquad office, but Paraquad had also received a three-year grant for $200,000 per year from the federal government, making it one of the first ten independent living centers (ILCs) to receive federal funding.[50]

Colleen, whose title was now director of independent living services at Paraquad, printed a flier on new letterhead announcing the center.[51] "The goal of the Center is to enable people with disabilities to live independently as productive and full members of society." She listed twenty services provided.

The Paraquad staff now consisted of Max and Colleen, Jim Tuscher, and Sue Pfeffer, who worked as a part-time secretary, plus Bill Sheldon and a sign language interpreter.

Sheldon was born deaf. When he began falling behind his toddler peers who were learning to speak, Sheldon's parents first assumed that he was intellectually disabled. Once diagnosed, his parents sent him to the Central Institute for the Deaf, where he learned to read lips and communicate by forming words.[52] From a

BILL SHELDON.

prominent St. Louis family, Sheldon had known Max since the age of fifteen, when they would often see each other at local dances. At age nineteen, when Sheldon was working for a physical therapist at St. Louis City Hospital, he remembered his father telling him about Max's car accident and the fact that Max had been paralyzed from the neck down.

It wasn't until 1975, when Sheldon joined the Missouri Governor's Committee on Employment of the Handicapped, that he met Colleen and became a close friend of the Starkloffs. Max and Colleen talked excitedly to Sheldon about something he had never heard of at the time, the Independent Living Movement, and by 1976, Sheldon had joined Max, Colleen, and their movement. He was thirty-eight years old. In 1979, Max and Colleen offered him a job with Paraquad as coordinator of hard of hearing programs. He went on to start the first federally funded deaf services program as part of an independent living center in the United States.[53]

Sheldon knew that many of the battles he would fight to gain rights for the disabled would be a lot like David facing Goliath. People with disabilities frequently found themselves fighting alone for their rights against large and powerful organizations against which they stood a small chance of winning and a larger chance of alienating the organization they were trying to enter. Such was the case when Sheldon entered graduate school at the University of Missouri–St. Louis (UMSL). Upon acceptance he requested an interpreter so that he could participate in class discussions. The university refused, saying it had no money to pay for an interpreter. Sheldon informed UMSL that the law required it provide an interpreter.

What Sheldon knew and perhaps the university administration didn't was that the U.S. Supreme Court in 1979 had ruled in *Southeastern Community College v. Davis* that, under Section 504 of the Rehabilitation Act of 1973, programs receiving federal funds must make "reasonable accommodations" to enable the participation of otherwise qualified disabled individuals. That decision was the Court's first ruling on Section 504, and it established "reasonable modification" as an important principle in disability rights law.

Sheldon went to the president of the university with a letter from the National Association of the Deaf explaining the law, and again met with no success. The university had been providing interpreters for its deaf students, he was told, but could not do the same for their incoming students as it had run out of funding. Sheldon would have to pay for his own interpreter.

Ironically, university officials had approached Max earlier with the idea of awarding him an honorary degree for his work in assisting people with disabilities. They suspended the award, however, when they found out that Sheldon was working with Paraquad. When Sheldon discovered that the university withdrew the award, he was devastated and came to Max to apologize. "Don't be silly," replied Max. "I don't care about the award. You fight them on this. They should give you an interpreter."

Sheldon went on to fight the case and eventually won. Later the university reinstated Max's award and offered to host Max and ten guests at a private dinner with the chancellor. To their surprise, Max brought Sheldon as his guest. "They were shocked," Sheldon recalled. "I later found out that the school had received a $300,000 grant for students with disabilities. They had plenty of money to pay for interpreters."

In working for Paraquad, Sheldon would be asked to fight battles for all people with disabilities, not just deaf people. Early on, he struggled to bring unity to Paraquad's disabled constituency. "At that time I tried to get deaf people and people with disabilities to work together," he recalled. "It took me a long time . . . because deaf people didn't want to be [grouped] with people with disabilities."[54]

Sheldon was able to convince them that they could help each other not only politically, but also in a myriad of other ways. "For example," Sheldon said, "Max helped me with interpreting, and I helped him with his driving." Sheldon's ability to read lips proved essential in communicating with people like Max, who didn't know sign language.

Sheldon used the growing clout of Paraquad and the Disability Rights movement to help bring closed-captioning to movies and TV stations in St. Louis. Closed-captioning, cited as "the most important development in this century for bringing deaf and hard of hearing people into the mainstream" by the National Captioning Institute (NCI),[55] emerged in the early 1980s. The technology to send "invisible" digitally encoded signals as part of a television signal was originally developed by the National Bureau of Standards in 1970 to send precise time information. When that project failed, the ABC Television network suggested that it might be possible to send captions instead to make its TV programs accessible to deaf and hard-of-hearing people. Working with NCI, the network developed closed-captioned decoders which, when attached to a television, decoded the invisible signal to produce captions below the picture.

It wasn't until March 16, 1980, that closed-captioning made its national debut when NCI arranged to get the first generation of closed-caption decoders into deaf households across America and broadcast entertainment with closed-captioning for the first time on three networks, ABC, NBC, and PBS. For Sheldon and the rest of the deaf community, it was a triumph. For the first time ever, here was technology that made it possible for deaf and hard of hearing people to enjoy any TV program.

It was slow to take hold, however, and Sheldon worked with Paraquad to put pressure on the local media, who were not using the technology. ABC and NBC were already using it, but CBS was not adopting the technology. Max invited Allan Cohen, president and general manager of Channel 4 in St. Louis, the CBS affiliate station, to come to Paraquad to learn what the organization was doing for the disabled. When Cohen arrived, he found Bill Sheldon waiting for him with an encoder for closed-captioning and a lot of reasons to begin transmitting closed-captioning on the local news. Shortly thereafter, all three local network affiliates were using closed-captioning.

Sheldon also appealed to Max, who was frequently being interviewed on television regarding bus lifts, not to agree to an interview unless the station consented to caption the broadcast. Max agreed, and the stations complied.

PILGRIMAGE TO MECCA

In early November 1979, Max, Colleen, Jim Tuscher, and Bill Sheldon prepared to visit the Center for Independent Living in Berkeley, California, and the man who created it, Ed Roberts. They wanted to know the methods used for the selection of participants, what forms were used, what information was being gathered, and how the process was evaluated. What programs and services did the center offer, and who offered them? How were they conducted? Small groups? One-on-one? Did they consist of people with different disabilities?

Tuscher called the visit a "pilgrimage to the Mecca of independent living in Berkeley." He continued, "Judy Heumann was there, and the office looked like a used car dealership. There was a bull pen with desks all around the perimeter facing each other with bookcases in between. It was messy."

Staffers at the center showed them the programs that demonstrated that people with disabilities could function independently. "Ed Roberts taught us," Sheldon recalled. "He trained us how to run an independent living center. It was a great experience for us. A deaf woman there trained me on how she ran the deaf center. Then later, deaf specialists [from other independent living centers] came to see me, and I would teach them how to run a deaf program." Sheldon would later visit independent living centers in Massachusetts, Maine, New York, Japan, Thailand, China, and Mexico.[56]

For Jim Tuscher, the visit was even more profound. He set up a counseling center and learned how to face challenges and overcome them on behalf of consumers. "In the first few years," he recalled, "we got some people out of nursing homes, but it was like handcrafted independent living. We would hunt around, find an apartment for this person. We'd help them get their attendant, maybe get a two-bedroom where they have somebody get free room and board, and live there—maybe a college student or something . . . maybe get personal assistance through a regional center if they had a developmental disability. And then we looked at their lives and listened to what they were experiencing, and they were more isolated in the community than they'd been in the nursing home because they couldn't go have a beer with someone because there was no transportation.

"For me, it was a slow realization that the disability damages the person much less than society's impact through its architecture and attitudes. Those attitudes include all its discrimination and isolation, designing programs and architecture without a thought for people with disabilities. To survive you had to fit in. You had to fit into the jobs that were out there. You had to fit into the architecture that was out there . . . but you really had no rights as a person with a disability.

"That's what led me to [lobbying] in Jefferson City.

"The real thing was to open the doors to opportunity through advocacy. I remember Ed Roberts saying, 'The three most-important things that a center for independent living should be doing are advocacy, advocacy, and advocacy . . . and not necessarily in that order.'"[57]

·CHAPTER 11·
"WE'RE PARENTS!"

In 1980 another of Max and Colleen's dreams, having children, was also about to come true, but like everything else, not without trial. "We discussed having children during the two years we dated," Colleen would recall later in an interview with a magazine writer.[1] "I'm the oldest of twelve children and for me it wasn't even a fantasy; it was a given that I would be a mother. Max had explained about SCI (Spinal Cord Injuries) and infertility and I said fine and dandy, so let's adopt. He was very pro that idea. We didn't think it would be a problem. The big issue was how many."

Colleen started calling adoption agencies a few months after the wedding. "I called every adoption agency in the phone book. None of them would even take our application until we had been married for five years, so that was very frustrating.

"When we had been married three years, I went back and started pushing at it hard," Colleen said. Registration with adoption agencies was a long process requiring mountains of paperwork, interviews, home visits, gathering references, completing forms. It took Colleen and Max a year to complete the registration process with one agency, Catholic Charities, before they were told they didn't qualify. "We got a big fat no from them."[2]

"Mary Kay Vorbeck from Catholic Charities came for a home inspection," Max recalled. "Wrapping up the interview, she said, 'The babies are our clients, and we're here to meet their needs, not those of people wanting to adopt. We can't help you.'"

"When we asked her why, she said it was because Max can't play ball with a child," Colleen said. "They felt that Max could not possibly be an effective father because he couldn't play catch," she repeated, incredulously. "She also told us that a doctor had told her that because of Max's disability, he would probably die early of renal [kidney] failure. Max said, 'Get her coat, sweetie, she's leaving.' He threw her out of the house."

Reliable, data-based psychological research on the subject of disabled parents raising children was scarce at the time. In the late '70s, Frances Buck, Ph.D., of the Veterans Administration Medical Center in Wood, Wisconsin, and George Hohmann, Ph.D., of the Department of Psychology at the University of Arizona, were early pioneers in the scientific study of the relations between parental physical disability and children's adjustment. In one Buck-Hohmann article, published in the *Archives of Physical Medicine and Rehabilitation* in September 1981, they summarized the prevailing professional opinion at the time: " . . . the presence of a parent with a disability in the home poses many threats to normal child development and adjustment. Children's personality adjustment, sex role development, physical health patterns, athletic interests, interpersonal relations, and parent-child relations *have all been thought to be adversely affected* by parental disability."[3]

Vorbeck from Catholic Charities had given Max and Colleen a typical response at the time. Hohmann wrote in an article published in *Clinical Orthopedics and Related Research* in 1975 that "adoption agencies believed that a disabled father was less able to model appropriate masculine behavior, such as financially supporting the family, expressing aggression, and engaging in physically oriented activities. As a result of identifying with the more 'passive' father, it is believed that the boy will fail to develop a masculine self-concept and appropriate adult role behavior."[4]

Social workers and professionals in the fields of child psychology in the 1970s were not shy about filling the data-based research gap with nothing more than their educated opinions about the effects on children raised by a disabled parent. It was widely believed that a disabled parent was less able to discipline and maintain control of the child, often leaving it to the spouse. Professionals also commonly felt that the disabled parent's lack of ability to manage the physical care of children interfered with the normal bonding processes between parent and child.[5]

In 1979 the bulk of the studies on paternal influence on children defined a "good father" as exhibiting "competence, high achievement, motivation, self esteem, successfulness, internal control, and, to a lesser extent, creativity."[6] Given that people with disabilities were generally thought to exhibit few if any of those qualities, it was naturally assumed among professionals that disabled people generally did not make good parents. Interestingly, "nurturing" and "loving" were not on the list.

In a series of scientific studies supported by a grant from the Technology and Research Foundation of the Paralyzed Veterans of America, Buck and Hohmann concluded that "the most well controlled and comprehensive studies to date" in fact showed "no evidence to support any of the speculated ill effects of parental disability on children."[7] In one study they concluded, "Young adult children reared by fathers with spinal cord injuries (SCI) were compared with a matched group of children with able bodied fathers on numerous objective tests. No significant differences emerged between the two groups in their psychologic adjustment, sex role orientation, body image, or physical health patterns. Nor was SCI in fathers associated with problems in children's relationships with peers or recreational pursuits. Finally, affectional ties between parents and children, parents' discipline and decision-making effectiveness, and family socialization were not impaired by the presence of paternal disability."[8]

After being turned down by Catholic Charities, and just before moving into the Boulevard Apartments, Max and Colleen sent a letter to a Jesuit priest they knew, the Reverend Ray Pease, who was working in a mission in South America. Max's idea of contacting Rev. Pease, like his idea for the Boulevard, had come to him in a dream. He dreamed that Ray helped them adopt a child. Pease responded to their letter immediately, saying that Max and Colleen should contact Sister Carmen Garantia, a nun from his mission, who was in St. Louis and had helped a St. Louis couple adopt a child from El Salvador. The Starkloffs wasted no time making an appointment to see her.

HOPE SPRINGS ETERNAL

Then something unexpected happened. Cindy Webster from Children's Home Society of Missouri called. Children's Home had previously turned down the Starkloffs, but this time she was calling to tell Max and Colleen that she wanted to talk to them about their adoption application. Puzzled about the agency's change of heart, but excited about the possibility, Colleen and Max agreed to come to her office to talk to her. "It was about two weeks after Max was awarded the St. Louis Award," Colleen recalled. "We figured it had something to do with that. We were hopeful, but we'd been burned before."

Before talking to Webster, however, they met with Sister Carmen, who gave them a lot of hope. "She was going [to bring us a child], and all we had to do was to find a social worker here to handle the details," Colleen said. The following day, Colleen called Webster to cancel the meeting. She told Webster that they had found a source in Latin America for a child and had decided to pursue that. "And stunningly, and I mean stunningly, instead of her saying, 'Well, OK, good luck,' and hanging up, she says, 'Can I ask you a question? Are you going to adopt a child from South America because you want a Latin American child or because you think that no agency in St. Louis would place a domestic child with you?'"

Colleen replied, "Well, to be honest, we've been around the bushes in St. Louis with several agencies, and it is our opinion that nobody will work with us. You seem like a very nice person, but the reality is we really don't want to have to do antidiscrimination work over the personal issue of building our family, and Sister Carmen was very nice, and I guess to us a baby's a baby."

"Well not necessarily," Webster replied. "First of all, our reason for calling you was because we intend to pursue your application." At this point, Colleen recalled her jaw dropping to the floor. "I'm thinking at this point, 'Why is she willing to do this? Nobody else would.'" Webster continued, "We base our decisions on the individuals and whether or not they would be a good home for a child. I'd really like to talk to you about this. Would you be willing to do that before you make a final decision with Sister Carmen?" Colleen said yes. She and Max could barely contain their curiosity. Why was Children's Home Society suddenly so interested?

At the meeting, "We found [Webster] to be absolutely delightful, very positive," recalled Colleen. "But we kept wondering, why the change of heart?" Then came another surprise.

"You know," Webster explained, pulling out a large, bulging file, "I feel I already know something about you. Your friend,

Kathleen Hamilton, has been sending me all this information." The Starkloffs' friend, who herself had adopted a child through the Children's Home Society, had been secretly advocating on their behalf, sending Webster numerous newspaper articles about Max, Colleen, the Boulevard Apartments, the work they were doing for Paraquad and, most recently, Max's prestigious St. Louis Award honor. "You seem to be very good, solid citizens," Webster said.

"So we came away from that meeting with a totally different attitude," Colleen recalled. "We couldn't believe that somebody was actually going to work with us, and was going to deal with the disability in an up-front, honest way. We had had so many turn-downs . . . Max and I came away looking at each other and going, 'Wow!'" With a pledge from the Children's Home Society, Max and Colleen wrote to Sister Carmen, who had returned to South America, thanking her for her time and letting her know that they had found a domestic source.

In January 1980, Max and Colleen had a series of meetings with Webster. "We were gathering our letters of support, and she was doing our profiles and all the necessary paperwork. She made a house visit. We were living in the apartment in the Boulevard, but we took her over to our house and she could see that we were rehabbing it. It looked like it was a go."

In late February, Webster called to say it was not too early to begin gathering things for a nursery. Colleen got on the phone to friends who had promised to pass along their baby equipment, and she arranged to borrow everything she would need.

FINALLY

On a cold day in early March, the Starkloffs were wrapping up a weekend visit to Kansas City, where they were attending a conference. Colleen was in the hotel room packing to leave while Max was giving the closing address. The phone rang. It was Cindy Webster. Colleen remembered the moment in every detail: "And the voice on the phone says, 'You know you shouldn't leave town without telling your social worker where you're going.' And all I could think of was, 'Oh my God, I forgot to turn in those two documents! Why is she calling me all the way in Kansas City to tell me this?' And I say, 'Hi, Cindy, how are you? Why shouldn't we tell our social worker where we're going?' I'm clueless. Clueless. And she says, 'Well, because you are the mother of a beautiful baby girl. Congratulations.' The water works went on.

"I said 'Oh my God! Oh my God!' Then I said, 'I have to tell Max,' and I hung up the phone and ran out of the room. I went running through the hotel, tears streaming down my face and ran down to the ballroom area where Max was just finishing this speech. And I'm standing in the back of the room—there were several hundred people there—he is just finishing his last paragraph—I know it because I edited it and helped him write it, and I'm standing in the back sobbing, and he says, 'Thank you very much,' and everyone's clapping, and he starts to come back to me, and as he's approaching me, he sees that I'm crying, and he comes up and he says, 'Sweetie, what's the matter?' and I said 'We're parents!' and his face drained and he stared at me and said, 'What?!' and I threw my arms around him and I said, 'We're parents!' And he said, 'What do we have?' and I said, 'We have a daughter,' and he said, 'When do we get her?' and I said, 'Oh my God, I hung up on her!' And he said, 'You did what?!' And I said, 'Oh my God, I hung up on her. I got so excited I hung up the phone and came running to tell you.'

"So we go running back to the room, and by this time the meeting is over and people are coming out and seeing us and asking

'What's going on?' and we say, 'We're parents!' and we're running through the hotel saying, 'We're parents!' and people are looking at us, I mean, people we didn't even know. They're looking and they're seeing there's something wrong with these poor people. I mean tears are streaming down my face and I have this big grin on my face, and people are just looking at us, and we're saying, 'We're parents. We have a baby!'

"I ran back to the room and called Cindy, and she starts laughing. She said, 'Oh, I get these kind of reactions.' I said, 'Cindy we don't even know . . . we're in Kansas City!' She says, 'I know, I tracked you down, remember.' I said, 'Cindy, when do we pick her up?' and she says, 'When will you be coming back?' And I said, 'Well, now! I was packing when you called.' And she said, 'Well come on back and pick up your daughter tomorrow. Don't worry. She's waiting for you, and she's absolutely beautiful.'"

Colleen and Max quickly left the hotel and began their four-hour drive to St. Louis. In the van with Max, Colleen chattered away excitedly as she drove, reviewing their list of possible names for the baby and planning how she was going to relate the news to the future grandparents, aunts, uncles, and friends. "We're parents. We're going to have a baby!" she kept saying to herself.

Max, however, was having different thoughts. As the reality of what they were about to do started to sink in, Max's excitement began to surrender to worry, self-doubt, then panic. "What are we doing!?" he blurted out after almost an hour of silence.

Colleen's eyes met Max's in the rearview mirror, smile fading. "We're driving home to pick up our baby."

Max asked, "Do you think that you can just go home and go to the nursery and just go and pick this baby up on Monday and just bring her home?"

Colleen said nothing.

"We don't have any clothes for this baby. We don't have a bedroom for this baby. We don't have a bed. We don't have food. We don't know how to take care of a baby!"

Colleen, sensing a meltdown, said simply, "I know how to take care of a baby, trust me."

"You think you're just going to walk into that nursery, pick up that baby, and bring her home to nothing?"

"No, I don't think that. Sully Boyce and Nancy Moore are saving these things for me . . . they promised . . . everything's ready. All I have to do is pick up the phone and call them, and go by and pick 'em up and bring everything home and set it up."

"You're gonna set up an instant nursery?!"

"Yes, I am."

"This is the craziest thing I ever heard of. This is the most outrageous, irresponsible thing. You must be out of your mind."

Colleen, thinking that Max must be out of his mind—they'd only been discussing this for the last five years—began to grow angry. But she decided not to react. As she recalled, "At that point, my guardian angel came to me and said, 'This would be a good time to shut your yap, because you have a woman's perspective and men don't get it, and you're going to have to give him time to absorb this. And, by the way, you have the weekend.'

"The next three hours were pretty quiet," Colleen recalled. "Because I thought, the man's freaking out. He's one of three. I'm the oldest of twelve. Having kids is nothing to me. All I knew growing up was changing diapers and washing diapers and feeding babies and bathing babies. If there was an old hand at it by the age of thirty, it was me. So I had absolutely no misgivings whatsoever . . . cuz *he* had 'em all. And he was just spilling 'em out.

And so periodically when he would talk, he would say, 'You know, sweetie, this is a big responsibility . . .' and I could hear all these fears of instant fatherhood suddenly hitting him, and I'm sitting here thinking, 'This is not a big deal. We've planned this. This is our baby, so you better get with it.' But I had the good sense to just zip it. So he sweated and fretted, and we got home and got into our apartment, and, man, I was on the phone immediately."

Colleen called her parents first. "My mother was delighted . . . of course, she didn't quite know how to deal with all of this because in our family, babies came easily and quick, so adoption was a new thing, but she was very happy for us.

"But then I told my father. I said, 'Congratulations! You're a grandparent,' and he goes 'What? What are you talking about?' and I say, 'Dad, we've adopted a baby' . . . and my father, who is the ace of making wisecracks says, 'Is she hot?' I was terribly offended. Like where did we steal her from? I said, 'Dad! Put mother back on.'"

Colleen's second call was to Max's mother, Hertha. "Hertha was just deliriously delighted." When Colleen told her about Max's reaction and the long, silent car ride home, Hertha said, "Well, Max would react like that. He's being responsible." Colleen said, "I know, but it just irks the hell out of me. I was pretty quiet in the car the last three hours coming home."

Colleen made more calls. First she made an appointment with a pediatrician for a checkup. Then she called Sully Boyce. "Sully said, 'Oh, this is fabulous!' Sully had one biological child and three adopted kids. She had a beautiful little antique baby bed, and she had sheets and blankets, and onesies and T-shirts and undershirts and clothes. I called my friend Nancy, and she had the same wad of stuff. And so we made arrangements that we were going to go by

Sully's house and Nancy's house on our way to Children's Home, so we had everything we needed for the baby in the van."

The next day, Colleen and Max were prepared. "Cindy met us, and she took us into her office and she spoke to us, and I have no idea what she said, because all I could think was, 'OK, let's quit talking, and where's the baby?' Finally, she says, 'Would you like to meet your daughter?' Yes we would!"

But Colleen was soon to have her own moment of hesitation. As Cindy was placing her hand on the nursery door, Colleen stopped her. "'Cindy, could you hold on just a minute?' I walked into the bathroom across the hall . . . I didn't have to go to the bathroom. I had to take a breath. I went in there and looked in the mirror. I looked at myself and said, 'You are about to become a mother. In one minute, your life will change. You will be a mother.' And I stood there and wondered for one second, 'Will I love her? Will she love me? Will I bond with her? Will she be my child?' And I stood there just looking in the mirror, just staring at myself, and I thought, 'Yes,' and I said it. I was in there talking to myself in the mirror . . . very low so nobody would hear me and think I'd flipped my lid . . . which I had, and I said, 'Yes, you are about to meet your daughter. You're about to meet her. Go . . . get . . . her.' So I went back out in the hall, and said, 'OK, I'm ready.'"

They were led into a tiny room furnished with two comfortable chairs. At the opposite end was the door to the nursery. Through a window in the door they could see several small bassinets. Colleen remembered every moment: "A nurse, Mrs. Ernie, who was . . . probably in her sixties in a white nurse dress, with her white, curly hair and her broad, smiling face, came in with this little bundle, little pink blanket wrapped up in the typical, traditional, papoose-style wrap, and she comes in—Max and I were

MEAGHAN KATHLEEN'S TWO-MONTH BIRTHDAY,
1980.

standing next to one another—I was wearing a brown camel-hair blazer and a plaid skirt to match—Max had on a navy blue jacket and a tie, and khaki pants—he always wore khaki pants—and she came up to us and she held this child out to us and she peeled back this little pink blanket, and she had her nestled in her arms, and there was this adorable little baby with dark hair and perfect complexion and she's just there in a little diaper. Just this little, tiny, five-day-old baby. And we just looked at her. We didn't cry. We were so excited . . . to stare down at this . . . wonderful miracle . . . that had just happened to us. And I said, 'Hi, Meaghan. I'm your mommy. And this is daddy.' And I took her from Mrs. Ernie, and I put her in Max's lap and held her. And we just stared at her. It was an unbelievable defining moment. It was powered by every emotion a new parent could have. Love. Pride. Acceptance.

"It was as though I had carried her," Colleen continued. "We looked at her, and then I looked at Cindy and I said, 'This is our daughter. Thank you.' We were so ecstatic. And Mrs. Ernie said, 'Did you bring her clothes?' and, of course, we'd brought a little outfit, and she said, 'Would you like to put it on her?' and of course I laid her in my lap and started dressing her. It was the most fabulous moment in my whole life."

"It was love at first sight," Max remembered. "For me, she was a dream come true, the daughter I was never supposed to have." They named the baby Meaghan Kathleen. "We named her Kathleen," said Colleen, "because Kathleen Hamilton did all that advocacy . . . we probably never would have had her if it weren't for Kathleen." Max and Colleen brought Meaghan home on March 13, 1980.

·Chapter 12·
Pitched Battles

The Disability Rights and Independent Living movements emerged in the 1980s as bona fide civil rights movements and were chronicled by their own tabloid-sized newspaper, the *Disability Rag*. Described as "the movement's *Village Voice, Rolling Stone,* and *Mother Jones* all rolled into one small powerfully written tabloid,"[1] the newspaper was founded by a young, nondisabled aspiring journalist, Mary Johnson, who became "appalled that nobody seemed to be aware" of the housing, transportation, and accessibility issues faced by people with disabilities. She printed the first issue on an eleven-by-seventeen-inch piece of paper folded in the middle and was surprised when "people really took to it."[2]

Stories appearing in the *Rag* were quoted by mainstream publications such as the *Boston Globe* and the *Wall Street Journal*. In 1993, the last year of Johnson's editorship, the *Disability Rag* won the Utne Reader Alternative Press Award for Best Special Interest Publication.[3]

Bolstered by the successful advocacy for the promulgation of Section 504 in 1977, people with disabilities began to believe that their voices could make a difference. Now, with the federal funding of independent living programs and services, signed into law by President Carter in 1978, Max and other disability rights leaders began to impress upon others the need for advocacy.

In a keynote speech on May 12, 1980, to members of the American Coalition of Citizens with Disabilities, an organization he helped found, Max said,

> There is a need to educate, train and promote self-advocacy
> among disabled individuals. It has been very difficult to ac-
> complish this in the past, because most of these grassroots
> disability organizations were run by volunteers. So there
> was not much money and very little time that people had
> to give to the movement. But now with IL [independent
> living] money, disabled people who run IL programs can
> more fully dedicate themselves to advocating equality for
> all disabled people. Through IL services—counseling, one-
> on-one advocacy, public education, IL Programs will begin
> to generate that leadership we so badly need.[4]

By 1980, Max had earned a reputation as a solid leader. An impec-
cable dresser, Max always attended meetings looking businesslike
and professional. He learned to listen to others' ideas first and to
know what he wanted to say before speaking. He didn't speak often, but when he did, people listened. Max's longtime friend and
fellow disability rights leader Charlie Carr respected Max for his
ability to draw people in and get them to work together. "To me,
he was a role model," said Carr. "He just exemplified someone I
wanted to be like. He was a gentle giant. He was a warrior."[5] Often described as "low key," Max never raised his voice. His ideas
were presented with clarity and reason. An article about Max in
the *St. Louis Post-Dispatch* described him as "a powerful speaker
and sensible planner. He has emerged at the top of a movement
looking for its own Martin Luther King."[6]

It wasn't long before the Rehabilitation Services Administration
(RSA) called Max and the directors of the other nine new independent living centers (ILCs) to Washington in June 1980. Currently
part of the U.S. Department of Education, the RSA was established
by Congress as the principal federal agency authorized to oversee

grant programs that help individuals with physical or mental disabilities obtain employment and live more independently. Now that the independent living centers were to receive federal funding, the RSA needed more information. What services did an ILC provide? And how would the ILCs be measured? How would RSA know if they were doing the jobs they said they were doing?

"Our basic philosophic guiding principal was always consumer direction and consumer control," said Colleen, meaning that the disabled people themselves directed and controlled the programs. At a time when the medical model was king (that is, when doctors and the medical community were regarded as "the experts" and the patients were expected to do what they were told), the idea of the patients running an organization was anathema to the entire medical system. The RSA argued that the ILCs should be controlled by "traditional service agencies," which were run by people without disabilities.

The initial meeting in Washington was long and cantankerous as Max and his ILC cohorts tried to explain the basic tenets of the Disability Rights Movement, answer questions, and fend off the federal government's powerful urge to measure, report, and control an organization that defied any traditional definition. Peer counseling, for example, an important part of the ILC program for the newly disabled, was particularly difficult for the RSA to understand. "Peer counseling is not something you can measure with units of service or through an evaluation system," Max said. Added activist Marca Bristo, who helped found Access Living in Chicago that year and would later go on to help draft the Americans with Disabilities Act in 1990 and chair the National Council on Disability from 1994 to 2002: "There is a very fine line between a client and a professional within an independent living center. I contend that oftentimes the clients become the service providers even though they may not be on our payroll."[7]

"How the hell did we know how to report stuff?" recalled Jim Tuscher. "We were just making it up as we went along." The meeting started to turn sour. RSA people were shaking their heads. "They were asking us questions that we couldn't answer," recalled Max, "and we were asking them questions they couldn't answer."

The ILC directors felt frustrated and threatened . . . as did the RSA administrators. But Max and Bristo saw an opportunity. "We decided that if we didn't set our own policy," recalled Max, "that the RSA would do it for us. We had an opportunity here to determine our own future." Max, Colleen, and Bristo met later in a nearby Washington coffee shop. They decided they needed to quickly form an organization with national influence that would represent all ILCs nationwide. Max offered to host its first planning meeting in St. Louis in July.

A month later, the ten ILC directors met at the small Paraquad office in St. Louis. Directors came from Colorado, Illinois, Kansas, Maine, Massachusetts, New York, North Carolina, Rhode Island, and South Carolina.[8] All were disabled, strong, determined people, and some, like Max, had spent time in institutions. They decided to form a planning committee and asked Max to be the chair. Their charter was to be a not-for-profit organization, headquartered in Washington, D.C., with three goals:

1. To set standards for how ILCs should operate
2. To break away from the medical model—to be consumer directed and consumer controlled
3. To emphasize advocacy and the right of people with disabilities to live independently in the community

MARCA BRISTO AND MAX, 1980.

The St. Louis meeting was the first of many intense sessions held in most of the ten ILC cities. The group ultimately formed the National Council on Independent Living (NCIL), a national organization that today represents thousands of people with disabilities from centers for independent living and Statewide Independent Living Councils in every state and territory of the United States.

Well into the group's planning process in 1981 (ironically, during the International Year of Disabled Persons), it faced an unexpected challenge. After the inauguration of Ronald Reagan on January 20 came an intense effort to trim the federal budget. Reagan believed disability programs should be funded by corporate and private sources, and he didn't want the government funding advocacy groups.

The Rehabilitation Services Administration, with its large vocational rehab budget plus other programs for elderly and disabled people, was hit hard. RSA commissioner George Conn, himself a paraplegic, assumed that people with disabilities would be the "weakest link," and he focused his budget-cutting efforts on the Title VII funding of the independent living centers. RSA notified Paraquad and three other ILCs in 1982 that their funding would cease, effective immediately. They were forced to lay off staff and reduce programs. Worse, it meant some 150 ILCs around the country could not count on receiving federal money to establish themselves and determine their futures. Disability rights advocates across the United States responded with aggressive lobbying efforts and grassroots campaigns.

On November 8, 1982, the newly formed NCIL issued the final draft of its bylaws. The bylaws articulated the purpose of NCIL, listed eleven objectives, and defined the criteria for membership. Max paid a visit to an old friend, U.S. Sen. Tom Eagleton. Eagleton agreed to draft an amendment guaranteeing funding to Paraquad and the other three ILCs. It was passed on December 21, 1982. But by February 1983, Paraquad and the other three ILCs had still not received the funding that Eagleton's amendment had guaranteed. RSA commissioner Conn was stalling.

One week before the Senate subcommittee hearing, Max sent U.S. Sen. Lowell P. Weicker Jr. stories and statistics illustrating the cost-effectiveness—not just the humanitarian side—of the independent living programs and asked that copies be distributed to all members of the subcommittee. On the day of the hearing, Max was prepared. Having participated in and led hundreds of meetings discussing ILCs, he was one of the country's foremost experts on all aspects of independent living. He had also established a reputation within Washington as a "sensible planner." From doing years of advocacy work, he had come to know many members of Congress personally, and they had come to know and respect him.

As members of the subcommittee strolled in and took their seats, many of them recognized Max and Colleen and came over to say hello. One of them was U.S. Sen. Ted Kennedy, a longtime supporter of independent living. Last to arrive was Weicker. As he entered, everyone quieted. An imposing man standing six feet seven inches and weighing 280 pounds, Weicker was respected as a powerful senator. Max considered him "the Lord protector of ILCs." Max's friend Sen. Eagleton sat beside him. Eagleton introduced Max and Colleen. Max's testimony lasted approximately three minutes, after which he answered a few questions. While it was weeks before the final Senate vote, one immediate victory for Max was Weicker's closing comment instructing Commissioner George Conn, also present at the hearing, to release the funds for the four ILCs that he had withheld.

At the first annual meeting of NCIL on March 25, 1983, Max was elected the first president and subsequently re-elected in 1984 and 1985.

On Wednesday, May 18, 1983, the Senate Labor and Human Resources Committee, by a vote of 18 to 0, approved reauthorization of the Vocational Rehabilitation Act, guaranteeing funding of all qualifying ILCs at $200,000 each per year. It continues to fund ILCs today.

The NCIL bylaws, which both Max and Colleen supported, stipulated that any ILC that owned housing could not qualify for membership in NCIL. After passing the bylaws, the couple returned to St. Louis not knowing what to do about the Boulevard Apartments. They spoke with real estate and legal experts and decided to retain and manage the Boulevard under a separate company, and later sold it to pay off their HUD loan. "We never made any money off the Boulevard Apartments," Colleen said. "But it got Max out of the nursing home and was a huge learning experience."

In 2007, NCIL awarded Max its first annual lifetime achievement award, named fittingly the Max Starkloff Lifetime Achievement Award.

DAWN OF A NEW ERA

"Well here it is 7 a.m., the family is asleep, and I can let my thoughts wander as I tap away at my computer."[9] This was Max Starkloff writing in April 1993. He was quadriplegic to be sure, but as a thinker he was ambidextrous, at once looking backward and forward:

> I have been electronically rummaging through some of my old Paraquad files, projects that couldn't get funded or some that sounded good at one time but don't seem so great today.

> It's funny that I can't bring myself to erase a single file. On each one, there's a glimmer of hope worth saving. . . .

> I listen to the best thinkers in the disability community and their intriguing solutions. Fascinating dreams and hopes. One thing I'm sure of: The disability movement hasn't been raised to the level of sophistication that it should be. When you look at the economic impact and the number

of human lives affected, the movement is being neglected.

> We as a movement have yet to come together. There is still
> much fragmentation. There is also much naivete, apathy
> and despair. The subject of disability is so complicated and
> confusing that most people don't comprehend it.

Max was sharing his despair with readers of the *St. Louis Post-Dispatch* through a commentary piece—one of many he wrote after he founded Paraquad in 1970. This one stood out because it came at a time when the disability rights pioneer might well have drawn a great deal of satisfaction in all that had been accomplished over the previous decade.

For one thing, Max had become known not just as one of many in the disability community agitating for change, but also as a leader of international renown. He was among the first in the United States to forge ties with Japan, a country that would play a key role in the disability movement. Max attended the first Japan–USA Conference of Persons with Disabilities in 1985 and served as the U.S. chair of the event in 1991 and 1993. Eighteen years earlier, Max had been in a nursing home. And as he would later observe, "I went from wondering whether I should get up at 10 a.m. the next morning to worrying about getting to the airport on time for a flight to Tokyo."[10]

In Paraquad, Max was leading a pioneering organization, one of the first independent living centers in the nation, and one with a growing staff and budget. Many of those staff members were disabled. For all the world this demonstrated that people with disabilities could be job holders, not just passive recipients of services. And they could be managers, not just employees. Leading the organization at the time were Bill Sheldon, director of the deaf

PRESIDENT BILL CLINTON APPOINTED MAX TO SERVE AS A COMMISSIONER
ON THE PRESIDENT'S COMMISSION ON WHITE HOUSE FELLOWS IN 1993.

and hard-of-hearing program, and Jim Tuscher, vice president of
programs. Also employed at Paraquad were Kirk Francis, data specialist; Duane Gruis, Mary Gutzwiller, and Bob Hapka-Tracy, independent living specialists; Linda Baker Oberst, acting program
director; Kathy Skarstad, public policy secretary; Stuart Falk, information and referral specialist; and Juli O'Leary, youth and family program coordinator.

The nation had entered a new era the year before Max's article.
On July 26, 1990, the Americans with Disabilities Act took effect.
Paraquad was at the forefront locally in helping both the disabled
and nondisabled understand it and filing suits to make sure that

MAX AND COLLEEN IN 1993 WITH PRES-
IDENT GEORGE H. W. BUSH, WHO HAD
SIGNED THE ADA INTO LAW.

it was enforced. The ADA seemed to promise a sea change almost overnight. But that didn't happen, and perhaps that was the cause of the angst Max shared with *St. Louis Post-Dispatch* readers. Those who knew Max also recognized that he could never be satisfied with the way things were. If he had been, he would never have left that nursing home. He might have still been a painter, rather than a revolutionary. And yet over a dozen years beginning in 1981, Max, Colleen, and an indefatigable group of their supporters had come such a long way.

NEWBURGER BRINGS A NEW APPROACH

For most of his life, David Newburger never really thought of himself as disabled. He fell victim to polio as a child. But he never felt like a victim. For a time, his parents put him in a grammar school for "crippled children." But when they saw that he wasn't getting a very good education, they pulled him out. "And that was the last of my being associated with disabled people," Newburger recalled.[11] When it came to independent living, Newburger had been doing it all his life, getting around just fine with crutches and a wheelchair.

It wasn't until 1981 that Newburger renewed his association with disabled people. That's when he joined Paraquad's board. He said he was "enticed" by a Paraquad intern who also had polio, and he arranged a meeting with Max. "It seemed like a good place for a young lawyer to do his charitable work," he said. By this time, Newburger had gone through enough consciousness-raising that he recognized that he had a lot in common with others who had disabilities, including those who were deaf, or blind, or had spinal cord injuries or developmental disabilities, or were dealing with mental illnesses. All could be discriminated against. All deserved the chance to live independent lives to the extent that they were capable, which, of course, Newburger had been doing all his life.

Unlike many people associated with Paraquad, Newburger did not come of age agitating for change on the front lines of the Disability Rights Movement. But he was arguably the right man at the right time for Paraquad. In the first place, Newburger understood numbers and financial statements. When he first started looking at Paraquad's numbers, he did not like what he saw. As for financial statements, at Paraquad they didn't really exist. He recalled meeting a woman at Paraquad who was responsible for keeping

DAVID NEWBURGER, ESQ.

track of finances. "She walked into a room with some adding machine tape, and that was the extent of the financial statements," he said. "Later, we would find uncashed checks in her drawer. We were sitting on federal money and gifts from people. There was a complete lack of organization."

Along with Dan Feinberg, Newburger worked to put Paraquad's financial house in order. "We saw an organization that was going to die if it didn't have any administrative structure to it," he said. But, Newburger added, "I never had much concern about the program. The people at Paraquad knew what they were doing. What Paraquad does is turn the lightbulb on in people. Redefining independence and what it meant for people is clearly what we did."

IMPLEMENTING INDEPENDENT LIVING

In 1984, Colleen described the process of redefining independence in an interview with Mary Jane Brotherson for the *Independent Living Forum,* a publication of the Research and Training Center on Independent Living at the University of Kansas. It starts, Colleen said, not just with the disabled individual, but with his or her family. "For IL [independent living] programs to succeed, it is critical for us to work with families. If the family does not believe that an individual is capable of living independently, neither will the individual, nor will he or she be able to take steps toward independence. . . . When we help families realize what is possible, it strengthens the pursuit of the individual."[12]

So when a disabled individual comes to Paraquad, a family member is invited to participate in the intake activities. Paraquad workers, many of them disabled themselves, have to be active and sensitive listeners. "Sometimes," Colleen related, the disabled individual and the accompanying family member come "just because another agency told them to show up. Their hearts are not in it. Other times, [family members] will express deep concern about who is going to replace them and that they in turn need someone to take care of."

Often, Colleen said, family members say, "He can't take care of himself. Do you hear what I am telling you? He cannot get out of bed, dress himself, or subtract from a checkbook." To which Colleen and other intake workers say, "Fine, there are ways to deal with that." Paraquad looks at independent living as a process. "An individual doesn't just move out, become independent in six months, and have a perfect life," Colleen said. "Sometimes it takes several years."

"We want families to have a sense of what the future holds," Colleen told Brotherson. "Many disabled adults who have experienced independence say to parents [of young children with disabilities], 'Had I known that this was possible, I would have mapped out my education in a different manner. I would have had higher expectations.'"

·CHAPTER 13·

ADA AT LAST

At the time Colleen gave the *Independent Living Forum* interview, hardly anyone involved in disability rights saw an act of Congress on the horizon. To be sure, activists like the Starkloffs had been challenging societal barriers for decades, borrowing the strategies and tactics of the Civil Rights Movement, drafting legislation, participating in sit-ins, licking envelopes, testifying, and getting arrested. Like the civil rights protesters, they had gotten in the face of their adversaries and pricked the conscience of the nation.

The Civil Rights Act was passed in 1964 and signed by President Lyndon B. Johnson. It wasn't until passage of Section 504 of the 1973 Rehabilitation Act that the federal government barred discrimination on the basis of disability by recipients of federal funds. That was a big step forward, but many years were spent making sure the section was interpreted properly and enforced equitably. And all of this only had to do with matters in which federal funds were involved.

But what the fights over Section 504 did do was provide a toehold for activists. "For the first time, the exclusion and segregation of people with disabilities was viewed as discrimination," wrote Arlene Mayerson in a paper for the Disability Rights Education and Defense Fund. "Enactment of Section 504 evidenced Congress' recognition that the inferior social and economic status of people with disabilities was not a consequence of the disability itself, but instead was a result of societal barriers and prejudices . . . and that

MAX AND JUSTIN DART, THE "GODFATHER OF THE ADA," IN 1986.

legislation was necessary to eradicate discriminatory policies and practices."[1] In making the case for enforcement of Section 504, disability rights advocates learned how to litigate, how to lobby, how to move the levers of power, Mayerson wrote. "The disability community was taken seriously—it had become a political force to be contended with in Congress, in the voting booth, and in the media."[2]

With passage of the ADA in 1990 and its implementation in 1992, Paraquad yet again was able to increase its role and visibility in the community. It became unlawful for companies with twenty-five or more employees to discriminate against qualified individuals with a disability in the workplace or in hiring, training, or promotion. Companies were required to make "reasonable accommodations" for disabled workers. The act permitted disabled people to sue for punitive and compensatory damages.

In 1993, the year following implementation, businesses and government agencies hired Paraquad to provide accessibility consulting services. Paraquad held workshops to inform people with disabilities about their rights under the law and for companies that wanted to comply. At those workshops, Paraquad representatives were able to allay fears that small businesses would be driven to the wall with costly fixes. "Sometimes a simple change—like moving some display stand to make a wider aisle in a store—will make an area more accessible to a wheelchair," Max told the *St. Louis Post-Dispatch*.[3]

Still, Max noted, after just a year, interest had begun to ebb. This may have been the reason for the angst-ridden commentary that he wrote for the newspaper a few months later. "The problem," he said, "is lack of an enforcement body. Many will let things slide unless a suit is filed to force them to do something. It's a very complicated thing, and I don't think the Justice Department has figured out what to do about it."[4]

MAX TYPING A LETTER ON HIS COMPUTER.

David Newburger was also feeling frustrated. "I started trying to do a lot of lawsuits with ADA and I was not terribly successful with it," he recalled. "There's no limit to the number of complaints you can bring out there. But they turn out to be increasingly difficult cases. Your clients never had enough money. So what you are dependent on is having your defendants having to pay up in the end or you are just doing it as a public service."[5]

Newburger recalled a suit that he filed on behalf of disabled residents who were being evicted from units at the Darst-Webbe public housing project near downtown St. Louis. The suit called on the federal government to spend more money on providing accessible housing. "We lost that case on what I would consider legally sound technical arguments, but not on what I would consider the merits. The legal solution was just not there."

Still, in looking back, Newburger could say that if he lost the battle, he won the war. Federal housing became more accessible in part because of lawsuits, but also because the culture changed to the point where it was de rigueur to make public accommodations accessible. Newburger is now very cautious about the cases he takes: "We can still do things that are positive but maybe not as dramatic [in a courtroom]. It has to be solved at the level of society."

·CHAPTER 14·

RAISING MEAGHAN, MAXIM, AND EMILY

As Paraquad grew, so, too, did the Starkloff family. In 1986, Max and Colleen adopted a second child, naming him Max Carl. They called him "Maxim," which was the name Max's mother had called him when he was small. Three years later, they welcomed Emily Johanne.

Raising children was a dream that Max and Colleen shared. But they did not always see eye to eye. Max was raised with two siblings and mostly by a single mom. His father was neither present nor a positive influence in his life. After his accident, Max had to give up much that able-bodied people take for granted. Most people could expect to marry, have children, and build a family. For many years, that all seemed implausible to Max. Then Colleen came along and then Meaghan. Max had it all. He was happy.

Colleen came from a large family. She was the eldest of twelve kids. She expected to have a large family as well. Coming from such a large brood, Colleen had learned to multitask. She had no doubt that she could see to Max's needs and to her children's while also working a job.

Meaghan had been wonderful—an easy baby—from the day Max and Colleen laid eyes on her. That made Colleen want to have children all the more. She wanted Meaghan to know the joy of having younger siblings, just as she had had. Max looked at Colleen and Meaghan and wondered, why fix what's not broken?

Said Colleen, "I remember when we talked about having kids, Max asked how many I wanted, and I said ten and then asked, 'How many do you want?' 'Well, one,' Max said, and I said, 'Oh no, that can't be.' Max talked about the cost of raising kids. And I said, 'Love conquers all.' He said, 'No, it doesn't. It doesn't pay the bills.'

"When we got Meaghan, Max was absolutely content. She was a perfect child. She was easy to raise. And they were buddies. As soon as she was able, she would sit on his lap, and then when she was a little older she would stand with her feet inside of his and put her feet on his footrests. She would go everywhere with him. He thought that was a utopian existence. And I said let's get going on another one."[1]

Max and Colleen found they could not go back to the same agency that brought them Meaghan. The social worker there had

MAX AND MEAGHAN GROCERY
SHOPPING, 1983.

moved on, and they would have to start over again. For a time, Colleen tried to get pregnant through artificial insemination. It was not working, and her efforts and desire to have more children was putting what seemed like a permanent knot in her stomach. Meanwhile Max wanted Colleen to make peace with the idea of raising an only child. "Why do you want to have more children?" he would ask. Exasperated, Colleen would respond sharply, "Honey, I am not going to explain motherhood to you."

The knot in Colleen's midsection disappeared when Maxim arrived, and there was more joy three years later when Emily Johanne came along, remembered for her fiery red hair and nonstop chatter. But Colleen's anxiety would soon return. Just like with most families, Colleen and Max wrestled with a variety of child-rearing issues—discipline, academic pressures, knowing when to push and prod, when to let the kids take risks and set their own course. But, of course, rearing children when a parent is disabled is different. All the Starkloffs would agree, it's more challenging in some ways, but in other ways more rewarding.

It did not dawn on Meaghan for quite a while that her dad was so very different from any other adult. It probably did not occur to her either that she had a kind of physical intimacy that many children do not get with their dads, whether it was riding around with him on his wheelchair, feeding him dinner, or helping him comb his hair, which had to be done to her dad's exacting standard.

With Colleen taking on more of the physical tasks, Max played a greater role in the kids' emotional lives, both Emily and Maxim said. "My mom was so busy cooking and cleaning. All the physical stuff was on her," Meaghan said. "Dad could still give me hugs. He really wanted to know what you were feeling and thinking . . . and that to me was more important than any hug."[2]

MAX AND MAXIM (SIX MONTHS OLD)
IN 1986.

Max could also take on the role of disciplinarian and kindly drill sergeant when necessary. "It was my dad's job to keep after us," Meaghan said. "He would take the elevator to my room and make sure I was cleaning my room or doing my homework." Both Meaghan and Colleen remembered a confrontation Max had with Maxim that suggested this father, despite a physical disadvantage, was not to be messed with. "When Max was trying to talk with him," Colleen recalled, "Maxim would simply walk away. One time Max had had enough of this. So he literally charged him with his wheelchair and backed him into a corner and said, 'Now you will listen to me.' I heard this and I was in the kitchen, and I came in and there was Maxim in the corner. 'I have had it with you,'" Max said. To which, Maxim responded meekly, "OK, Dad. OK, Dad."[3]

MAX AND EMILY DINING TOGETHER.

More than twenty years later, Maxim laughed when asked about the incident. "He didn't do that just one time. I was such a bad little kid. He would full blast me into the wall with his chair. You smart off. You would start to see his teeth grind. You knew you were in trouble. He's taking it out on you."[4]

When Emily came along, the family dynamics became even more interesting. Meaghan, who has a background in early childhood education, believes that Emily became talkative and assertive in part to keep up with her brother. And, just like the other kids, she had an intriguing relationship with her dad. As Maxim recalled, "I remember when she was three or four years old, Emily at dinner would sit on the floor next to my dad's chair. Suddenly you would see a little hand snaking up through the chair and pick off a vegetable." This would happen again and again until Max had precious few vegetables left to eat. At the time, Maxim thought it remarkable that Emily wouldn't just swipe the vegetables but she'd eat them. What three-year-old likes brussels sprouts? he wondered.

Maxim said that his dad always made time to do things individually with his children. For Emily it was often lunch at a nearby Vietnamese restaurant. And they would get there with Emily riding on the chair by standing on the footrests. Max and Maxim would regularly engage in the "Great Cherry Pit Spit." As contestants succeeded in reaching certain marks, each would have to move back one inch until a winner was eventually declared.

Joint adventures included the so-called Fruit Safari that took place at Kathleen Duckett's farm in North Carolina. The kids would grab a basket and, perched on the armrests of Max's wheelchair, forage for berries and return to make a huge fruit salad. The family would also make regular trips to Fort Lauderdale where, among other activities, Max would referee the shuffleboard matches. "I would try to cheat, and my dad would always catch me," Maxim remembered.[5]

Meaghan said she was about five years old when it became apparent to her that the world looked at her father differently than

MAX AND MAXIM IN "THE GREAT CHERRY PIT SPIT."

she did.[6] "When we were in a store, even though I was just a little kid, people would talk to me instead of my dad. 'So what do you think he wants?' they would say. And I would say, 'I don't know. Ask him.'

"I started to realize that to other people he wasn't the norm. Everyone would look at him funny. And I would be looking at them funny. What's wrong with you? Why would you ask me that question? Why wouldn't you ask my dad?"

As in most families, the children followed their own paths. Meaghan, acknowledged by everyone as "the easy child," did well with her studies and participated in a variety of Paraquad youth group activities, traveled widely, and took up early childhood education. "I'm sure I went through that typical teenage thing of not wanting to be around your parents. But I couldn't be selfish. I couldn't tell my dad that I'm not going to help him if he's thirsty. He could get overheated really easily on hot days. Something bad could happen if I didn't help him out. I am really glad I had that. It kind of taught me to be more selfless. It helped shape me into a better person."

At age eighteen, as many adopted kids do, Meaghan began to wonder about her birth parents. Meaghan could not remember when her parents first told her that she was adopted, but she recalled them reading storybooks to her about adopted children and how they (and she) "came out of another lady's tummy." She said, "My parents did a great job with that."

Even so, there were difficult times. "When I was eighteen, I was bawling my eyes out and I just remember being so torn up," Meaghan said. "I wanted to know where I came from." At that point, Colleen shared more information with Meaghan. She was born to a young Catholic woman whose husband had left her.

"She didn't want to raise me without a father," Meaghan said. "She specifically requested a Catholic family with a couple who had a stable relationship."

When Meaghan was in her early twenties and pregnant with her first child, Maya, she learned that her birth mother also wanted to meet with her. She had launched a search of her own in the hope of finding out that she had done the right thing for her daughter. Meaghan was able to arrange a get-together at the Missouri Botanical Garden. At their meeting, "I told her she got everything she wished for," Meaghan said. "[My parents] were very devoted to each other through thick and thin, pulled through the stinkiest mud you can think of, and stayed together through it all. My father is amazing, and I can't imagine life without him."

Meaghan said her birth mother probably did not know that her adoptive father was quadriplegic. She guessed that if her birth mother had known, it might have given her pause at the time. But in the current circumstance, Meaghan said her birth mother seemed gratified that everything had turned out so well. Two years after that meeting, Meaghan's birth mother suffered a thrown blood clot,[7] which disabled her. She went to live in a nursing home. "It's ironic," Meaghan said.

Maxim has also met his birth mother and other relatives. The encounter also answered a lot of questions for him, including why he was such a hell-raiser. "I just realized how good of a life that I had. Their life was turmoil. My [biological] sister was in rehab for meth. My brother was on the run from the cops."[8] This made Maxim's transgressions seem tame in comparison. As a child, he was prone to tantrums. "I was defiant," Maxim said. "I had it my way or the highway." In some instances, literally. At times, Maxim wouldn't just blow a curfew; he wouldn't come home at all. He was arrested for drug possession. He had gotten kicked off his school's wrestling team.

A possible explanation for some if not all of his behavior was that his birth mother may have been abusing drugs and alcohol during the time that she was pregnant with him. "People say it's in your blood and in your genes. I believe it," Maxim said.

Maxim's issues were a huge concern for Max and Colleen. "I just adore my son," Colleen said.[9] "We are joined at the hip. But he was a real pain in the ass to raise. When he was a little kid, we didn't know what we were dealing with. We realized he had a short fuse, and that was challenging. He had no respect for authority. He would yell. He would throw things. He had night terrors. It just made us love him more and want to help him to grow to be a good kid and a good man."

Counselors at Maxim's school told Max and Colleen he had attention deficit hyperactivity disorder. "We told Maxim it was a disability," Colleen remembered. "And he adamantly said it was not."

"Well, we said, 'Your dad could own up to his disability, son.'

"And he would respond, 'Well I'm not disabled.'

"But you know, it doesn't matter whether you do or don't own up to it," Colleen said. "The issue is what are you going to do with your life. That's the way it is with people with disabilities. What choices are you going to make and how do you direct your life so it is successful."

Maxim said he could see the wisdom in Colleen's words. A few years before his father died, Maxim got a job at a corner gas station near the family home. Before then, he had been hired and fired from jobs "about every other month" for arguing with managers or yelling at customers.[10] He was also feeling the pressure

THE STARKLOFF FAMILY, FEBRUARY 1987.

of fatherhood, having had three children over the previous four years. But this new job took. "It did a lot for me," Maxim said. Until then, "I didn't have the confidence to keep a job. Here I got to interact with people, and they were people who I already knew from the neighborhood. After two years, they gave me a promotion, and I started learning how to work on cars. It made my dad really happy."

Up to that point, Maxim "had been depressed a lot, and my dad recognized that. He would always tell me, 'Maxim, I don't care what you do. I don't care if you want to be a mailman or a trashman or president of the United States as long as you are happy with it and you are doing something. That's all that I ask.'"

·CHAPTER 15·
THE BOULEVARD SHUTS ITS DOORS

Disabled people finding fault with Paraquad might qualify as man-bites-dog news. But in the late 1990s, many disabled residents living at the Boulevard Apartments were unhappy with their landlord. The Boulevard had fallen into disrepair, and federal officials wanted to move the tenants to facilities they considered safer.

Paraquad was ready to go along with this for a couple of reasons. Under federal regulations, the Boulevard's units were open only to disabled tenants. Max had long been philosophically opposed to segregated housing but, in Paraquad's early days, the Boulevard was seen as the best way to get disabled people out of institutions and into a neighborhood where they could lead normal and active lives.

The Boulevard had also become a financial albatross. Money had always been set aside for maintenance but, as it turned out, not enough to keep up with an aging and not particularly well constructed forty-year-old building. In 2000, HUD estimated that it would cost $1.1 million to $2.8 million to renovate the Boulevard and even more to maintain it in the years ahead.[1]

But Max was well aware of the anxiety that uprooting fifty-seven tenants would cause. Even if he hadn't been, the residents sure let him and federal officials know about it. HUD had proposed moving the tenants to Council Tower, a high-rise building about a mile away on Grand Boulevard. Those who didn't want to relocate there would be given vouchers to rent apartments. While the voucher concept would have made no sense twenty years earlier, there were now at least some buildings that were accessible to disabled tenants, thanks in part to Paraquad.

Still, the plan didn't sit well with the tenants. Council Tower had not been built with disabled tenants in mind and, since it was a high-rise, it seemed in some ways less safe for people with disabilities. Moreover, it lacked a sprinkler system. And then there was the issue of the neighborhood. While the Boulevard had deteriorated to some degree, the neighborhood had thrived. Tenants could find services like banks, cleaners, restaurants, and pharmacies right around the corner. They wanted to stay. Many, some with tears in their eyes, turned out at a public meeting to protest the plan. "You should stop and think about us before you move us out," Charlene Day, a thirty-eight-year-old tenant, lectured officials.[2]

But a little more than a year later, in September 2001, all the tenants did move. Paraquad sold the Boulevard in 2002 for a bit more than $2 million, which it used to pay off its mortgage to HUD.[3] Conrad Properties bought the site and redeveloped it, building a $32 million, three-building complex with 213 loft-style apartments. The complex has storefronts facing Forest Park Boulevard and blends in well with the neighborhood. Some units in that complex are accessible for the disabled, though how many disabled residents are currently living there is unknown. Rents as of 2013 ranged from twelve hundred dollars to twenty-two hundred dollars. Under the federal government's Low Income Housing Tax Credit Program, also known as Section 42, qualified tenants, including those with disabilities, are eligible for rent subsidies of up to five hundred dollars a month.[4]

THE NEWSPAPER'S POLITICAL CARTOON ABOUT MAX. COURTESY
OF THE *ST. LOUIS POST-DISPATCH*, COPYRIGHT JANUARY 6, 2002.

In the end, the Boulevard brouhaha created a result about
which everyone could feel proud. U.S. Sen. Christopher S. "Kit"
Bond, working with Paraquad, was able to get $1 million to fund
replacement housing in St. Louis. Another $650,000 came from
the St. Louis Affordable Housing Commission, where Colleen had
served as the founding chair. This led directly to construction of
6 North Apartments, an eighty-two-unit complex developed by
McCormack Baron Salazar and located on the corner of Laclede
Avenue and Sarah Street, not far from the Boulevard site. It features universal design, including extra-wide doorways, stepless
entries, adjustable kitchen counters, and light switches and electrical outlets that are easy to reach. Some of the units are eligible
for rent subsidies, meaning that people with disabilities and others
who have lower incomes can afford to live there.

Colleen beamed with pride when talking about 6 North.[5] She said she had recently seen Richard Baron, chair and CEO of McCormack Baron Salazar, at a restaurant where he introduced her to his daughter as "the godmother of 6 North." "That was a happy moment for me," Colleen said.

During the design phase, Baron had asked Colleen, Max, and Dan Feinberg how many units at the site should be built with accessibility standards. "We know we have to do 5 percent for people in wheelchairs," she recalled him saying. To which Colleen responded, "We don't want accessibility, we want universal design."

"OK," Baron said, "how many?"

"All of them," Colleen said.

That got Baron's attention. "What is universal design?" he asked. It's everything from the streetscape to the roof that makes the facility accessible to anyone, Colleen told him. Though taken aback at first, Baron hopped on board with the concept. "We worked with them on all the features that it needed," Colleen said, "and they did a really first-class job."

A NEW FOCUS

From all appearances, Paraquad was a thriving organization as it entered the twenty-first century. The organization's 1999–2000 annual report on its thirtieth anniversary listed assets of nearly $1 million, more than doubled from 1986, and a staff totaling seventy, up from twenty-three in 1986. The organization wore a halo as far as the media were concerned. Whenever any development occurred involving people with disabilities, reporters called Max to get his point of view. The *St. Louis Post-Dispatch* regularly printed his commentaries. And gossip columnist Jerry Berger made frequent mention of the successful fund-raising galas that Paraquad held that featured celebrities and attracted the A-listers.

But trouble was brewing within the organization. With the benefit of hindsight, board members and those who worked at Paraquad said discord was inevitable as the organization grew into a substantial, well-funded nonprofit. Some call it founder's syndrome. Max, Colleen, and a hardy band of advocates skilled in protests and persuasion founded Paraquad. They knew what it took to win attention, get people on their side, and move public policy in the right direction. But as Paraquad began to provide services and attract federal dollars, grants, and donations, it required managers with different skills. "Max didn't really want to be running a lot of employees," David Newburger said. "He wanted to continue to create and implement ideas."[6] Still, Max knew people were needed to run Paraquad in a businesslike fashion, by managing its resources, developing the staff's capabilities, and promoting its good works in the community.

When the Starkloffs learned that then-Paraquad board chair Gray Kerrick left Southwestern Bell Telephone, where he had served as vice president of advertising and communications since 1990,[7] they leaped at the chance to hire him as Paraquad's chief operating officer. Kerrick could be the yin to Max's yang—a hands-on, behind-the-scenes, capable manager working in tandem with a visionary, inspirational public figure. Kerrick took on the post in December 1993 and began instituting some of the same structural disciplines he had learned at Southwestern Bell, one of which was a performance appraisal system.

As the months passed, new hires were made and new processes put in place. Paraquad thrived in many respects, but Colleen said she began to see a divide developing.[8] She described it as a divide between people who "got it" and "people who didn't get it." The people who got it understood Paraquad's history of advocacy and its peer-counseling mission of employing people with disabilities (independent living specialists) to counsel people with disabilities in order to empower them to lead independent lives. The people who didn't get it—and these included people with disabilities— saw Paraquad as a nonprofit like many others that raised money, provided services, and above all needed to be run efficiently. Colleen had nothing against efficiency, but she also believed there needs to be a human factor, particularly in dealing with people who have disabilities. She found increasingly that disabled staff members were coming to her with complaints about their managers, most of whom were nondisabled.

"The [independent living specialists], all of whom were disabled, who were connecting with the consumers we were here to serve, were feeling like they didn't matter," recalled Colleen. "And they were the ones who empowered people to change their lives. It was a performance standard that worked at Southwestern Bell, but didn't work at Paraquad. Everybody became very demoralized over it because everybody got low scores . . . including me! That's when I threatened to quit. I thought, if I'm only a three, what do you need me for?"

Others saw the divide in a different way. There were those who were accountable for their work and behaviors and aligned themselves with the goals of the organization, and there were those who didn't. Some believed Colleen favored staff members with disabilities, whatever their abilities might be. Genny Watkins, a key manager at Paraquad beginning in 1996, looked at it this way, as did Kathleen Lee, who joined in 1991 as a senior employment specialist and moved up to director of the employment program in

1998. Another very much in the mix was businessperson Martha Uhlhorn, who joined Paraquad's board in 1994, later led its marketing committee, and served as chair from 2002 to 2005. These three would come to be seen by Max and Colleen as key engineers in a coup that led to Max's and Colleen's ouster in 2002. Watkins, Lee, and Uhlhorn look back at that time with a measure of regret. They admired and respected Max and Colleen, and for much of that time got along with them well. But they also acknowledged a culture clash and believed strongly that the organization had to move forward in ways that the Starkloffs found uncomfortable.

Watkins said she worked closely with Max as vice president of development and operations and reported directly to Gray Kerrick.[9] While different in the way they looked at the world, she said they were the two best bosses she had ever had. Max, she said with tears welling in her eyes, taught her to come to terms with her disability caused by a childhood spinal tumor—not so much in physical terms, because she had done just fine in leading a successful and independent life, but in the way she thought about her role as a standard-bearer. Like David Newburger, Watkins said she had grown up without really acknowledging that she was a member of a distinct group. She said Max counseled her that the disability "doesn't define you, but it is part of you. I had to be a role model and tell my stories to others. Max taught me all of that in a quiet, beautiful way."

Watkins said she certainly felt like she "got it" when it came to people with disabilities. Along with being disabled herself, Watkins and her husband, Jack, were raising a daughter, Kate, with a rare disease called Walker-Warburg syndrome, a form of congenital muscular dystrophy. Kate died of the disease at age six in 2002. As a manager and fund-raiser, Watkins enjoyed a great deal of success over the years. She felt confident in the role of managing change in a growing organization. "I don't see it as the people who get it or the people who don't," she said. "I see it as the people who want to be accountable and the people who don't want to be accountable." Some staff members at Paraquad, she believed, didn't want structure. "They wanted to be able to do what they wanted to do when they wanted to do it."

Newburger, who by then was no longer on the board but still in touch with what was going on at Paraquad, believed that managers were trying to "drive square pegs into round holes."[10] He remembered a conversation with Kerrick in which the executive groused, "You know, when I was working at Southwestern Bell and I told somebody to do something, they did it. When I tell someone around here to do something, they say, 'Well, why?'"

Said Colleen, "All the corporate structure was beginning to eat away at the life of the program. For an independent living center to be effective, you have to let the people in your program share of themselves [in order to] to empower the people they're connecting with; to empower them to see themselves differently than society sees them." Colleen described the work of the independent living specialists as "touchy-feely," not something whose outcome could be measured and analyzed.

On October 4, 1999, the same date as the Starkloffs' anniversary, Kerrick was asked to step down as chief operating officer at Paraquad after almost six years. The culture clash frustrated Uhlhorn, whose background was in international business management. She had gotten connected to Paraquad while working in St. Louis at subsidiaries for Anheuser-Busch.

Max was growing restless with day-to-day operations, Uhlhorn observed. At the same time, she said, he was hearing from

Colleen, who as a vice president for community affairs was very much in touch with the staff, some of whom were having difficulties adjusting to new standards and practices. Colleen would take sides, Uhlhorn and Watkins said, and not observe the chain of command. "Colleen would make decisions about people who get it or don't get it," said Uhlhorn, who is not disabled. "She never gave us the credit that we deserved because we were all capable of getting it."[11]

Stephen Leicht, the board chair at the time, felt similarly. Leicht is a quadriplegic who suffered a broken neck at age nineteen in a diving accident. He is an investment counselor with a background in both social work and finance. He admired both Max and Kerrick and called the latter analytical and a straight shooter. He thought it was regrettable when Kerrick left in 1999, but he understood why it happened. There were too many conflicts, particularly with Colleen.[12]

Colleen would agree that there were disagreements and plenty of them. "That's who I was fighting for," she said of the independent living specialists who were being demoralized by the new systems. "Because they were afraid to speak up for fear of losing their jobs." As board member Dan Feinberg recalled, Colleen was known for "coming in and undoing a lot of what Kerrick had done."[13]

Though Leicht had no say in Kerrick's departure, it made him reflect on what was going to happen with the organization when Max could no longer be in charge.[14] The urgency for such considerations increased as Max's health became increasingly fragile. In August 2001 while on a trip to Florida, Max's hip started to trouble him. Returning to St. Louis, Max's orthopedist discovered a large abscess beneath the skin, which he surgically removed, leaving what Colleen described as "an open sore large enough to insert a hand." Max was required to stay in bed through the rest of 2001, and he later contracted pneumonia in March 2002. Throughout this time, Max remained very much in touch with Paraquad via phone. Board and staff meetings were held as Max participated by speakerphone.

Uhlhorn said the board's decision to replace Max at the top of Paraquad should not have come as a total surprise to him, though it may have to Colleen, who she said was focused on her advocacy work and on Max's recovery. Feinberg recalled Max and David Newburger working out an arrangement that would put Max in an emeritus position with perhaps Newburger taking on the role of director.[15]

For her part, Colleen did remember that the board raised the notion of a succession plan at Paraquad in the late 1990s. She said Mark Sauer, a board member and then president of the St Louis Blues, told Max and Colleen, "You need to be grooming someone and thinking about who should take over." That made sense to Colleen, but she said she "couldn't imagine Max retiring. He was not the type. Retire and do what? He wasn't going to go fishing. He wasn't going to go back to painting. The idea of Max retiring was something that was foreign to him. And we didn't have an option to retire. We had never made a lot of money. He would say, 'I wish I had the *option* to retire, honey.'"[16]

In hindsight, Colleen said she might have recognized then that what she called a "coup d'état" was brewing. If that is what it was, it took some time to unfold. The first Max and Colleen learned that the board wanted to replace him was in late 2001. As Colleen recalled, Max was in the living room, which had been converted to a bedroom while he recovered from his hip surgery. They were awaiting a call from Paraquad's executive committee, which Max could listen to through a speakerphone. But the call never came.

Max called in to find out what was going on. He was then informed that the committee had been in a closed session, where it decided to name Kathleen Lee as interim director. "I was frantic watching my husband in total shock and disbelief and fighting for his dignity and role and being told, 'I am sorry this is the way it's going to be,'" Colleen remembered. "It was incredible. It cut him to the core. Everything he had worked for, everything he had invested. At this point, he was one of the world leaders in disability rights, and to have this done to him, to have this organization taken away from him. . . . We believed it to be a coup d'état."

"Sabotage," Max said.

The Starkloffs later learned that Watkins, Lee, and a couple of other members of the management team had taken their concern about Max's leadership to individual board members. Max and Colleen believe this was the first of an apparent effort to get Watkins into the leadership role of Paraquad. No one at the time saw Lee as the permanent replacement. But Watkins was among those who would be considered to lead Paraquad.

Leicht, Uhlhorn, Watkins, and Lee all expressed regret about the way in which Max received the news. In looking back, they said that perhaps succession discussions could have unfolded differently. But each had no regret about the need to replace Max at the top of the organization, and it wasn't because of his health. Colleen disagrees. "If it wasn't because of his health, why did they wait until he was down?"

Uhlhorn stated that Max's attentions were increasingly focused elsewhere, other than Paraquad operations. "Max was always about the cause," Uhlhorn said. She respected that. But Paraquad had become less about the cause and more about providing services and having to hit the mark in complying with regulations, drafting budgets, and raising the money necessary to meet them.

Watkins said communication broke down in part because of Colleen. "There was never an opportunity for reasonable conversation at the board level. We didn't have a way to resolve the problem. . . . We were trying to get things in place for communications and a chain of command, and it wasn't really followed by Colleen. We needed to make a change." Neither Watkins nor Colleen were on the board, nor were they on the management committee, so there was no management forum for Colleen to express her concerns other than on an impromptu basis to anyone who would listen. Watkins has no regrets concerning Paraquad. "But the way that it hurt Max and Colleen," she said, "I look back on that with great regret."

At that point, Max and Colleen had an important decision to make. They could go quietly or they could create a stir. There was no doubt that if they went public, the public would take their side. Max by then was already a near legendary figure in St. Louis. It would almost be as if the Cardinals had decided in the 1960s to send Stan Musial packing instead of allowing him to retire on his own terms. Newburger advised the Starkloffs to hire Chet Pleban, an attorney who had handled many controversial cases and would not be reluctant to bring them into the court of public opinion. Pleban, along with PR maven Richard Callow, also skilled in handling public spats, went to work on the Starkloffs' behalf.

But in this instance, the controversy barely bubbled into the public domain. In fact, if you read the *St. Louis Post-Dispatch* on the morning of January 12, 2002, you would have thought a nearly seamless transition had occurred: "This week, Starkloff relinquished the reins of [Paraquad], which he said had grown so large 'my days became a series of 10-minute meetings.' He plans to return to working at the forefront of the disability movement."[17]

In just a few weeks, the Starkloffs and Pleban had worked out a settlement with Paraquad's board. The terms are secret because of a nondisclosure agreement. But the result was that Paraquad got a new chief executive, Bob Funk, who was acceptable to the Starkloffs. They would continue to work with Paraquad for some months, then leave with a severance package that gave them a running start on setting up what would become the Starkloff Disability Institute. Funk, an attorney, had at one time served as chief of staff for the Equal Employment Opportunity Commission under the first George Bush and had spent the previous fifteen years in Washington, D.C., working in the public and private sectors. He was an amputee and also contended with bipolar disorder.

Much further down in the *St. Louis Post-Dispatch* story, the twenty-eighth paragraph, mention was made of "some schisms" that had developed in the organization concerning whether the new director should be more manager or more advocate. But that is as far as the story went concerning discord. The Starkloffs and everyone at Paraquad were glad about that. Yes, feelings were bruised, but the work Paraquad was doing was far more important. "We didn't want that ship to sink," Colleen said.[18] "There were people with disabilities who depended on Paraquad for their jobs. All of them would have been victims of an organization cracking apart."

·CHAPTER 16·
THE STARKLOFF DISABILITY INSTITUTE

Max and Colleen began meeting with David Newburger, Lance Carluccio, a dean at Maryville University, and Philip Ferguson, a professor at the University of Missouri–St. Louis, to talk about what to do next. Carluccio was leading Maryville's School of Health Professions and was also director and professor of rehabilitation counseling. He had taken a strong interest in the Starkloffs and their work in helping disabled people find jobs. Ferguson held the E. Desmond Lee Endowed Chair for the Education of Children with Disabilities at UMSL. The two professors worked together in recording the Starkloffs' thoughts and ambitions and created a white paper that articulated an approach.

Boiled down to its essence, the Starkloff Disability Institute would move from changing the lives and attitudes of people with disabilities to changing the attitudes of nondisabled people toward those with disabilities. Too often, Colleen said, well-intentioned people fail to recognize that people with disabilities also have abilities—particularly when it comes to doing a job. Too often, they only see people who need care. "The biggest battle is attitude," Colleen told the *St. Louis Beacon* in an interview in 2012.[1] "We have achieved lifts on buses, curb cuts [for wheelchairs], and education laws, housing laws and the Americans with Disabilities Act that fight discrimination. But we're still fighting the attitude that once you have a disability, [you lose] the ability to make decisions or function in the world."

Functioning in the world to a great extent means working at a job. For all the progress that has been made, the employment rate for people with disabilities has barely changed. More than seven of every ten people with disabilities in the United States do not hold jobs.[2] The Starkloff Disability Institute began working with employers by training their human resources directors and connecting them to disability service organizations. "We want employers to know they can come to us and ask questions," Colleen told the *Beacon*. "We promise we won't sue." By 2010, five companies had signed on as "Role Model Companies" that offer opportunities to disabled people: Nestlé Purina, Centene Corporation, Enterprise Rent-A-Car, Enterprise Bank and Trust, and SSM Health Care. More have signed up since.

Successes have been hard won. When the Starkloffs left Paraquad, they did not immediately find a great deal of support for their new vision. Colleen remembered a conversation that she had with a prominent St. Louis attorney and a longtime Paraquad supporter whom she approached for funding. "He said, 'Well, we need to see what you can do now.' And we said, 'Really?' We had to prove ourselves all over again."[3]

LOSING EMILY

The years 2007–2008 might well have been remembered as the best of times for the Starkloffs. By then they were deep into work with Robert Archibald at the Missouri History Museum on a multi-million dollar retrospective on the Disability Rights Movement. In summer 2007, Max received a lifetime achievement award from the National Council on Independent Living, and the next year would bring yet another honor, a star on the St. Louis Walk of Fame in the University City Loop. By this time, too, they were grandparents three times over. Meaghan had blessed them twice during the Christmas season with Maya on December 13, 2002, and Talia on December 11, 2005. Maxim's first child, Jade, arrived on April 9, 2008.

But there were challenges as well. Max took a spill at a movie theater in spring 2007 and, as a result of the injury, he punctured a lung and needed a ventilator to assist in his breathing. The machine inhibited his ability to speak, emitting a series of high-pitched beeps to warn him against straining too much. But Max soldiered on. He had to. He told a *St. Louis Post-Dispatch* reporter in 2007 that even after nearly four decades at the forefront of the movement, he was still finding so many people who misunderstood people with disabilities. "They regard them either as heroes or objects of pity," he said. "People think that [a disability] is worse than it really is."[4]

But then came an event that was far worse than anything Max or Colleen had ever experienced, including Max's accident. Meaghan recalled that her dad was "never the same" after the night of May 5, 2008. No one will ever learn exactly what unfolded on that moonless, cloudless early morning on Forest Park Boulevard near the Barnes-Jewish Hospital medical complex and just a few blocks from the Starkloff home. Maxim surmises that Emily was returning home by MetroLink train from a job she had at a sandwich shop in Maplewood. The walk home from the station would have taken her across Forest Park Boulevard. Sometime around 1 a.m., a St. Louis police officer found Emily's lifeless body in an eastbound lane, the apparent victim of a hit-and-run driver.

Emily, nineteen years old, had ambitions to be a nurse. And she would have been a good one, too, her sister Meaghan recalled. Meaghan had seen how Emily had increasingly played an active role in her father's care as her elder siblings moved on with their lives. "Emily was such a very sweet, helpful person," Meaghan said. "When dad got his trach [ventilator], she learned how to do the suctioning. She was able to help out with a lot of important medical stuff that he needed."

Colleen remembered the exact time that a police officer called her: 4:22 a.m. He asked if he could come and see them. "We both said, 'What has happened to Maxim?'" Maxim had recently been in a couple of automobile accidents. When the officer arrived at the Starkloff home, Colleen opened the door for him. "Mrs. Starkloff,

EMILY STARKLOFF AT THE SAINT LOUIS ZOO
IN 1996.

I am very sorry but I have to tell you there has been an accident. Do you have a daughter named Emily?" At that point, Colleen said, "I just hit my knees and came unglued. I sat on the steps trying to hear what he was saying. 'You have to come upstairs and tell my husband,' I said. 'I can't tell him . . . ' He came in and told Max. And Max burst into tears, too. I collapsed on top of Max."

A few hours later, Colleen and Max drove down to the city Medical Examiner's Office to identify Emily's body. For the rest of the day, Colleen said she felt numb as friends gathered at her home. There was never a time that she needed her husband more. "I had Max to get through it," she recalled. "He was strong in the sense that he had been through more than I had. He was able to hold on to his emotions. After that morning when Emily died, he didn't cry and I think he felt that he needed to be strong for me."

Emily's memorial Mass was celebrated on May 8, three days after the accident, at St. Francis Xavier College Church, where Max and Colleen were married. Max's brother, Carl, delivered the homily. Maxim spoke, and Colleen gave a blessing. Colleen was sitting at the front of the church during the Mass and did not look back to see who might have attended. When she arrived at the altar and looked out at those in attendance for the first time, she was stunned. The church was full. More than four hundred people turned out to celebrate Emily's life. Afterward, the family met with many well-wishers at nearby Busch Memorial Center. But there were so many that they decided to continue receiving people at their home.

The Starkloffs were both bereaved and exhausted. But Colleen and Max agreed that on the following Tuesday they would go back to work. "We couldn't stay at home," Colleen said. "We would be overcome all the time." But it proved to be too soon. "That Tuesday morning, I was going to start getting Max up and he was very quiet. He burst into tears. And, I said, we aren't going to work today. That was his meltdown, and he needed to do that."

On May 29, the *St. Louis Post-Dispatch* ran a short item saying that police were looking for the public's help in finding the vehicle that struck and killed Emily. Police were looking for a light-colored, two-tone Jeep Grand Cherokee that was headed east from the scene. The police never found the vehicle or its owner.

More sadness followed in August when Colleen's sister, Christine Smith, died at age fifty-four. Carl again presided at the service. Carl, then seventy-five years old and a Jesuit for fifty-six years, died ten days later as he was undergoing a stem cell transplant to treat the lymphoma he had been battling for years. The service for Carl was again held at the college church.

"They were so close," Colleen said of Max and Carl. "They were best buddies." "The losses took a toll," Meaghan said. "My dad was always such a fighter. But losing a child is so difficult. He was never the same after losing Emily. It wasn't as easy to fight anymore."

MAX'S LEGACY

If there was balm for Max's soul, it came in the form of the Missouri History Museum's exhibition devoted to the Disability Rights Movement. It opened in June 2010 to mark the twentieth anniversary of the Americans with Disabilities Act and remained open and free to the public until January 2012. The exhibition attracted more than 160,000 visitors, who gained an appreciation of what it meant to live with a disability in the United States over the last century, particularly in the Midwest.

There was so much to cover and so many materials to curate that mounting the exhibition took five years.[5] To jump-start the effort, the Museum held a two-day conference where disability rights advocates gathered. "Everyone [was there] from visually impaired [people] to [people who are] post-polio to psychiatric survivors, as well as historians studying the [independent living] movement," Robert Archibald, president of the Missouri History Museum, told an interviewer writing for *Independence Today*, a publication produced by an independent living center in Troy, New York.[6] "We got more issues than we could possibly deal with," Archibald said. They ranged from "fissures within the disability rights movement [such as] the lack of identification between people who are deaf and people who are in wheelchairs" to the geographical focus of the project.[7]

The planners kept their eyes on the Midwest and how the movement there had a national impact. The narrative the Museum provided was powerful as it showed how far the disability movement had come from the days when so many were institutionalized and all but forgotten, to a time when just a few, then thousands and tens of thousands could hold jobs and lead independent lives.

The artifacts drew a great deal of attention. They included everything from a TTY device (introduced in St. Louis in the late 1960s), which enables people who are deaf, hard of hearing, or speech impaired to use the telephone to communicate by sending text messages, to an iron lung that provided a lifeline for people who contracted polio. Paraquad's Jim Tuscher called the History Museum the best place for such a showcase. "This museum doesn't collect history . . . like so many dried flowers," he said. The Museum's curators research movements "so they can take that knowledge, learn from it and create social justice in our society in the future."[8]

"Hopefully 163,000 people will think more positively about disabled people, but also our role in history," Colleen said in looking back at the effort. "We have changed history. We have changed the view of disability."[9] That effort continues today in a variety of ways, not the least of which is a joint effort involving the Starkloff Disability Institute and Maryville University.

Since 2005, Maryville has offered an undergraduate degree in rehabilitation services, which gives graduates a chance to help people with disabilities develop work skills and lead independent lives. As part of the program, the Starkloff Disability Institute provides a host of courses, including disability rights history, public policy, the history of independent living, and an independent living service delivery course.[10] "With every student we teach, we are changing attitudes toward people with disabilities," Colleen said. "And these are the people who plan to go out and work with [people with disabilities] as careers."[11]

FAREWELL

While Max took the deaths of so many of his loved ones hard, Colleen said it was the physical challenges that were beginning to get the best of him. The spirit was always willing, she said. Max could never be alone after he suffered the punctured lung and went on the ventilator. "He hated that," Colleen said. "He would say, 'Quit hovering over me.'" But if something happened to the ventilator, Max would have at best just five minutes before he would go into respiratory arrest. Getting Max up and going also became a more arduous process. Where once it took seventy-five minutes, after the punctured lung it took two and a half hours. Max rarely complained, but Colleen could tell that he was getting depressed. She said Max increasingly turned inward or became irritable.

Max Starkloff, disability rights pioneer, role model, husband, and father died December 27, 2010, at his home in St. Louis. He was seventy-three years old. It was a total shock to Colleen and his family. "Max and I had been out shopping for new clothes for him a few weeks before, and he had promised to take me out for dinner on my birthday, December 24. But on that night, he said he didn't feel well so we stayed in. It didn't seem to be anything more than the flu," said Colleen. "On Christmas day, he still didn't feel well, so we had our Christmas dinner around his bed. The flu can run for several days, so I wasn't surprised when he still didn't feel well on the twenty-sixth, but I started to worry when he began chattering [talking compulsively], which he does when he has a fever. But he had no fever. At 5 a.m. after Max had had a really rough night, I called the doctor and said I thought Max was dehydrated. They agreed to send over some [intravenous] fluids. We had dealt with the flu before, and there wasn't anything to say that this was different. But by 9 a.m. the fluids hadn't come, and when I called the [doctor's] office, they told me there had been a snafu. I told them we need to get this done. Nobody said to call an ambulance, which we've done before. By noon [on December 27], Max was sleeping, and I didn't want to wake him." Colleen, who had not left Max's side since the evening of December 24, decided to run down one floor to switch laundry. When she returned a few minutes later, she noticed a change in Max's countenance. "As I walked in the room, I didn't want to disturb him. But then I looked back again. There was just something different about the way he looked. His composure had changed. The vent was pumping so there was breathing going on, but it didn't look like he was an active player in it. Suddenly I thought, 'This can't be.' I ran over and looked at him and pulled his eyelids up, his pupils were dilated, and I knew. I couldn't do mouth-to-mouth. He already had respiration. So I pounded his chest to restart his heart. And I just knew . . . he was gone."

A week later, hundreds packed St. Francis Xavier College Church to hear eight of Max's friends, colleagues, and family members remember him in different ways.[12] There was Charlie Carr, who recounted how Max helped him get a grip after a diving accident put him in a wheelchair. "I met Max at a time when I needed to look up to someone. He was someone who shared my pain and then used that pain as a tool for change." And there also was Marca Bristo, a fellow disability rights pioneer, who said Max demonstrated that "disability is a normal part of the human condition. He carried that message to those of us with disabilities in everything that he did."

Colleen did not speak at the Mass. But her thoughts were included in the program for the service:

> Max had a way of drawing people to him. He had wisdom about human nature and knew how to communicate a message in very compelling ways.
>
> Not everyone was comfortable around him, though, because his disability intimidated them. His dignity showed on his face and the set to his jaw was firm, which made him seem formidable at times. He used this to his advantage with policymakers and others who seemed resistant to his message about equality and independence for all people.
>
> But to his family, friends and people with disabilities, he was warm and welcoming, understanding and approachable, witty with a great sense of humor. . . .

I've lost the love of my life, my best friend, my confidant, my mentor, my strength, my hero. He has left us with a tremendous gift and legacy—to continue the work he has started. I invite all of you to join me in continuing his righteous and noble work, and achieve true independence and equality for all persons with disabilities and their families. I count on you . . . I love you! Lead On!

EPILOGUE

While one might imagine that the loss of its founder, leader, inspiration, and moral force would mean a temporary setback for the Starkloff Disability Institute, the organization instead gathered steam. On April 28, 2012, nationally renowned broadcaster Bob Costas led a sold-out celebration of Max's life at the Pageant theater, just a stone's throw from Max's star on the St. Louis Walk of Fame. On hand to discuss disability issues and Max's influence were movie star John Goodman, baseball legend Ozzie Smith, and Washington University chancellor emeritus Dr. William H. Danforth, as well as Ray Hartmann, former *Riverfront Times* publisher and former Paraquad board member, and Judy Heumann, who has advocated for the disabled at the State Department and at the World Bank. The event raised ninety thousand dollars.

Meanwhile Colleen, David Newburger, and the SDI staff were forging ahead on a number of initiatives. In 2012 and 2013, St. Louis played host to the fourth and fifth Universal Design Summits. Hosted in St. Louis since 2002 and coordinated by the Starkloff Disability Institute and the RL Mace Universal Design Institute, the summits focused on housing that is accessible to everyone and featured exhibits, workshops, and tours of universally designed housing and neighborhoods. The idea for the summits was Colleen's.

Max's vision for a "future that welcomed all people with disabilities" has started to become a reality with the institute's signature program, the Next Big Step, driven by Max himself. "The biggest issue facing people with disabilities," Max would say, "is jobs. Jobs drive independence, self-esteem, everything. We have to find a way to help people with disabilities get mainstream jobs." That was the impetus that led to SDI's Next Big Step program, a program that could be described as truly revolutionary.

Efforts to "hire the handicapped" have met with limited success since World War I. Max pushed to create a program that did not duplicate previous unsuccessful approaches. It was an ambitious push, an effort to unravel huge complexities and break new ground in a positive way with both corporations, which were "gun shy" and misinformed about hiring people with disabilities, and with the disabled themselves, many of whom had largely given up trying.

As a first step, the author and SDI board member Bill Durham met with the senior-most human resource executives at several large multinational companies in St. Louis, such as Nestlé Purina and Enterprise Rent-A-Car. They wanted to know how receptive these companies would be to hiring qualified people with disabilities. Every executive with whom they met expressed interest and enthusiasm for the program. They all understood that people with disabilities represent an untapped source of talent and that they demonstrate increased loyalty and appreciation for their jobs, thereby reducing employee turnover and improving morale. Steve Degnan, vice president for human resources at Nestlé Purina, was the first to embrace the program. "Many of our employees either have people in their families with disabilities or know people with disabilities," he said. "This [program] reflects our values as a company."[1]

Through in-kind donations from SDI's initial Role Model Companies, the institute was able to conduct focus group research among twenty corporate hiring managers and HR professionals to uncover attitudinal barriers to employing people with disabilities. This helped SDI design a more effective program that addressed real-world challenges. The Next Big Step program involves educating employers, leveling the playing field for job seekers with disabilities through intensive preparation, and bringing these two groups together to facilitate hiring. Focusing first on the community, SDI prepares receptive employers to interview and hire qualified job seekers with disabilities. Companies that are extremely receptive to such employment are invited to serve as role models. Then, to connect these employers with appropriate job applicants, SDI collaborates with Partner Organizations working with disabled job seekers.

To prepare the candidates to compete, SDI provides a fourteen-week training course, which meets weekly for three-hour workshops with SDI staff, Partner Organizations, and hiring managers from Role Model Companies. Here, job seekers study and practice job acquisition skills. SDI is unique in its ability to expose candidates to HR professionals from major companies where there is a commitment to hiring qualified individuals with disabilities. The class addresses needs for both constituencies, as job seekers and employers learn what it takes to achieve their goals.

Though the program is only three years old at this writing, it is meeting with success. SDI is working with five major corporations as Role Model Companies.[2] Ten Partner Organizations have joined SDI in an effort to identify and train qualified people with disabilities.[3] The Next Big Step program has trained over two hundred hiring managers in how to effectively use the skills

Colleen and Max in 2005.

of disabled employees and how to retain and promote individuals with disabilities. In just two years, the Next Big Step work-readiness training course has assisted twenty-seven people with disabilities in securing competitive jobs and internships.

Max's "next big step" has the potential to expand across the country with dramatic results. "And of course, with every person we place," said David Newburger, "they are our best advocates for hiring more people with disabilities as their nondisabled teammates learn what value they bring to the workplace."

Colleen Starkloff and David Newburger, co-directors of SDI since Max's death, stepped into their new leadership roles without missing a beat. Colleen as the dynamic, charismatic advocate. And David as the disciplined strategist and expert in disability law. Between them, they have over eighty years of experience, much of which they gained while working together. They are each recognized nationally as pioneers, leaders, and advocates in the Disability Rights Movement. The institute they direct has a staff of seven and a board of directors consisting of twenty-one civic and business leaders, many with disabilities.

"Max's life was an example of what we should be doing," said Colleen. "He never wanted to be called a hero. When people tried to make a hero out of him, he denied it. Because if he's a hero, then the everyday Joe will think he can't do what Max did. The everyday Joe has to believe that this dream is possible. Otherwise, it's only for the heroes. And we can't accept that. We don't accept that. This life is for everybody, and our people have to be raised out of poverty, and out of isolation, and out of second-class citizenship, to where they belong: a first-class citizenship and living the dream like we all do. That's what Max did. He lived the dream."

·ACCOMPLISHMENTS·

Through Max Starkloff's accomplishments, people with disabilities in St. Louis have gained the opportunity to live independently. Below are a few of his achievements.

- Co-founded Paraquad in 1970, with his wife, Colleen, as a privately funded Independent Living Center
- Secured first-ever stateside, barrier-free legislation for local and state curb cuts
- Acquired disabled parking legislation
- Established Paraquad as one of the original ten federally funded Independent Living Centers in the nation
- In 1970, founded the St. Louis Chapter of the National Paraplegia Foundation
- Labored for access to public buildings and schools
- Received a commitment from the local transportation authority to adopt a policy that all new buses be wheelchair lift–equipped
- Organized and spearheaded a large coalition of people with disabilities, volunteers, and community leaders to support the above transportation policy, making St. Louis the first city in the nation to have lift-equipped buses on its streets
- Influenced St. Louis's new light-rail system to endorse and include total accessibility
- Co-founded and was founding president of the National Council on Independent Living
- Served on the board of directors of the World Institute on Disability, Berkeley, California; Blue Cross/Blue Shield of Missouri; and Gazette International Networking Institute, St. Louis

APPOINTMENTS/PUBLIC SERVICE

- Research & Training Center on Independent Living and Public Policy: advisory committee
- World Institute on Disability, Berkeley, CA; Blue Ribbon Panel, National Project for Telecommunications Policy: adviser
- Leadership St. Louis: recruitment/selection committee
- SSM Rehabilitation Institute: advisory board
- American Institute of Medicine, Washington, D.C.: Committee for National Agenda for Prevention of Disability
- Rehabilitation Institute of Chicago, Chicago: Research and Training Center Advisory Committee on Secondary Disabilities
- Rehabilitation Services Administration, Washington, D.C.: National Advisory Panel for evaluation of standards for Independent Living
- Fourth Japan/USA Conference of Persons with Disabilities, 1991: chairperson of the U.S. delegation
- Fifth Japan/USA Conference of Persons with Disabilities, 1993: chairperson of the U.S. delegation
- National Council on the Handicapped, Washington, D.C.: official advisor
- County Commission on Disabilities, St. Louis: chairperson
- President's Commission on White House Fellowships by President Clinton: commissioner

AWARDS

- President's Distinguished Service Award—President George H. W. Bush
- Community Leadership Award—Leadership St. Louis
- Commissioner's Distinguished Service Award—Rehabilitation Services Administration, Washington, D.C.

- Mayor's Arch Award for leadership in disability rights—St. Louis
- Annual Civic Service Award—Maryville University
- Human Rights Award—United Nations Association, St. Louis
- Humanitarian Award—Human Development Corporation, St. Louis
- St. Louis Award
- Sold on St. Louis Award
- Sword of Ignatius Loyola Award, Saint Louis University's highest honor
- Missourian Award—Missouri Hall of Fame
- Doctor of Humane Letters—Webster University, St. Louis
- Doctor of Humane Letters, University of Missouri–St. Louis
- Recognized by National Council on the Handicapped and St. Louis Unit of NASW
- "Max Starkloff Lifetime Achievement Award"—National Council on Independent Living, Washington, D.C.
- St. Louis Walk of Fame, inducted June 20, 2008

·Family Tree·

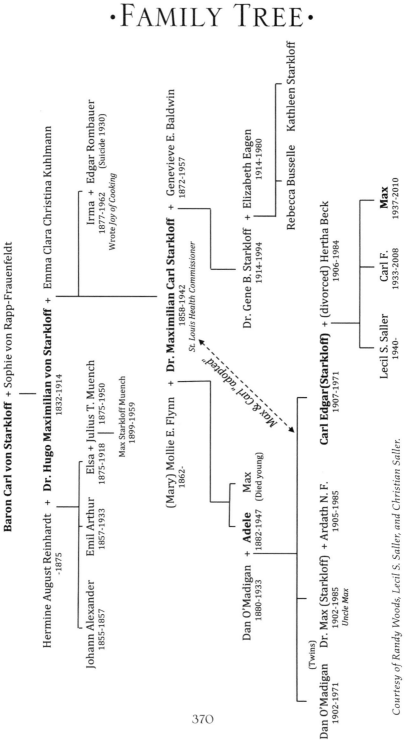

Baron Carl von Starkloff + Sophie von Rapp-Frauenfeldt

Hermine August Reinhardt + **Dr. Hugo Maximilian von Starkloff** + Emma Clara Christina Kuhlmann
        -1875   1832-1914

Johann Alexander   Emil Arthur   Elsa + Julius T. Muench   Irma + Edgar Rombauer   (Suicide 1930)
1855-1857   1857-1933   1875-1918 | 1875-1950   1877-1962
                                           | *Wrote Joy of Cooking*
                                  Max Starkloff Muench
                                  1899-1959

(Mary) Mollie E. Flynn + **Dr. Maximilian Carl Starkloff** + Genevieve E. Baldwin
1862-   1858-1942   1872-1957
                          St. Louis Health Commissioner

                          Dr. Gene B. Starkloff + Elizabeth Eagen
                          1914-1994   1914-1980

                                    Rebecca Busselle   Kathleen Starkloff

Max & Carl "adopted"

Dan O'Madigan + **Adele**   Max
1880-1933   1882-1947   (Died young)

Carl Edgar (Starkloff) + (divorced) Hertha Beck
1907-1971   1906-1984

Lecil S. Saller   Carl F.   **Max**
1940-   1933-2008   1937-2010

(Twins)
Dan O'Madigan   Dr. Max (Starkloff) + Ardath N. F.
1902-1971   1902-1985   1905-1985
                 Uncle Max

Courtesy of Randy Woods, Lecil S. Saller, and Christian Saller.

·ACKNOWLEDGMENTS·

Many people have contributed to this book since I began researching it ten years ago.

I am particularly indebted to Richard Weil, without whose help and support the manuscript would still be a manuscript. Also to Dick Weiss, friend and journalist, who helped me finish the job, and to my wife, Katie, who edited the edited version.

Thanks to a number of people at the Missouri History Museum: to Robert R. Archibald, former president of the Museum, who, after hearing me talk about the book in 2005, had enough respect for Max's story to volunteer to publish it sight unseen; to Museum staffers Victoria Monks, Lauren Mitchell, Keri McBride, and Leigh Walters.

The late Ralph Kalish, Arkadia Olson, and Mark Sableman gave help and advice throughout the publishing process.

Most of the details of Max's accident and recovery came from an unpublished manuscript titled "From Nothing On," written by his mother, Hertha Beck Starkloff. I dedicate my book to her and to all mothers of children with disabilities.

Max's wife, Colleen, worked tirelessly to recall memories, provide information, check facts, and retrieve hundreds of photographs; Max's sister, Lecil Saller, his late brother Carl, and his children Meaghan Breitenstein and Maxim Starkloff provided memories, photos, and details.

Many medical professionals, reference librarians, and archivists contributed their time and expertise: Mary M Krieger, Martha Riley, Stephen Kinstler, William Fischetti, Dr. Bill Stoneman, Dr. Katherine McMullin Jones, Ray Spencer, Dr. Henry Betts, Dr. Tom

Lieb, Sister Marylu Steuber. Thanks also to Mirka Fete, daughter of Dr. Otakar Machek; Genie Cannon Newport, daughter of Dr. Edward Cannon; and Dr. Robert H. Lattinville, son of Dr. Henry Lattinville.

Additional background information on St. Joseph's Hill Infirmary was provided by Brother Bernardo, Donna (Oberkramer) and Gary Brocato, Margaret Hinkle, Joanne Bright, Stacey Geddis, and Bob Huskey.

Max had myriad friends and associates, many of whom shared their experiences, stories, and insights with me. I'm sorry I couldn't include everyone's name and story. For those I did, I hope I got it right.

·Notes·

Chapter 1

1. Reminiscences are from author interviews and Hertha's manuscript.
2. J. White, "Injuries to the Cervical Cord," *The Cervical Spine* 41-A, no. 1 (January 1959): 13. See also E. A. Comarr, "Laminectomy in Patients with Injuries of the Spinal Cord," *Journal of International College of Surgeons* 31, no. 4 (April 1958).
3. White, "Injuries to the Cervical Cord," 11.
4. T. Gucker III, "Rehabilitation in Injuries of the Spinal Cord," *Journal of Occupational Medicine* (January 1962): 61–62.

Chapter 3

1. T. Gucker III, "Rehabilitation in Injuries of the Spinal Cord," *Journal of Occupational Medicine* (January 1962): 61.
2. H. Rusk and E. Taylor, *Rehabilitation Medicine: A Textbook on Physical Medicine and Rehabilitation* (St. Louis: C.V. Mosby, 1958), 19.
3. Association of Academic Physiatrists, physiatry.org.

Chapter 4

1. google.com/search?hl=en&lr=&q=catheter+irrigation+&btnG=Search.
2. C. S. MacCarty, "The Treatment of Spastic Paraplegia by Selective Spinal Cordectomy," *Journal of Neurosurgery* 11 (1954): 539.

Chapter 6

1. Nell Gross, "How a Courageous Former Marine, Paralyzed from the Neck Down in Auto Crash, Found a New Interest in Life—in Painting," *St. Louis Globe-Democrat*, February 23, 1964.
2. alvensleben-photography.de/052/text.html.

CHAPTER 7

1. The Civil Rights Act of 1968 is now known as the Fair Housing Act. The prohibition of discrimination based on gender was added in 1974.

2. en.wikipedia.org/wiki/Gini_Laurie. The other "grandmother" was Mary Switzer, who was in charge of vocational rehabilitation at the national level from 1950 to 1970.

3. Post-Polio Health International, postpolio.org/hist-gini.html.

4. Charles Childs, "From Vietnam to a VA Hospital Assignment to Neglect," *Life*, May 22, 1970, 22–35.

5. Joseph P. Shapiro, *No Pity: People with Disabilities Forging a New Civil Rights Movement* (New York: Three Rivers Press, 1994), 238.

6. Mary Johnson, *Make Them Go Away: Clint Eastwood, Christopher Reeve and the Case against Disability Rights* (Avocado Press, 2003), 188.

7. Gay Chadeayne Noonan, interview with the author, May 12, 2004.

8. Thomas E. Drennan, letter to Hon. James W. Symington, July 10, 1970, Starkloff Disability Institute Archives.

9. Laurent Torno, interview with the author, March 21, 2006.

10. Ibid.

11. Richard Ward had just graduated from Washington University in St. Louis with a second of three graduate degrees, this one in architecture and urban design. He received his bachelor of architecture at Virginia Tech University in 1964, a first master's degree in urban and regional planning at Virginia Tech University in 1965, and a third master's degree in business administration, finance, and strategic planning from Washington University's Olin School of Business in 1991.

12. The National Paraplegia Foundation (NPF) was founded in 1948 by members of the Paralyzed Veterans of America (PVA), which was founded one year earlier. PVA is a congressionally chartered nonprofit veterans' service organization whose members are honorably discharged veterans of military service with spinal cord injury or

dysfunction. The NPF is the civilian arm of its movement. Both the NPF and PVA chapters in many cities and states have taken a leading role since their inception in advocating for civil rights and equal opportunities for people with disabilities.

13. Bob Huskey, interview with the author, ca. 2005.

14. Southern Illinois University in Carbondale is not to be confused with the University of Illinois (U of I) in Champaign, a separate system. U of I was an early pioneer in accommodating students with disabilities. As early as 1947, the university converted a former VA hospital in Galesburg, Illinois, into a satellite campus in order to accommodate the many World War II veterans seeking to use the funding of the GI bill to earn their college degrees. The unit was closed one year later. However, the director, Timothy Nugent, along with students, staged protests and eventually won minimal support from the U of I Champaign campus. Steven E. Brown, *Freedom of Movement: Independent Living History and Philosophy*, ILRU Bookshelf Series (2000), 21, 22, 24. After many setbacks, by the 1950s the program included nonveterans and offered accessible transportation and housing to undergraduate, graduate, and married students; peer counseling; specialized medical care; and individually designed assistive devices. Charlene DeLoach, "The Independent Living Movement," in *Region V Rehabilitation Continuing Education Program ADA Train the Trainer Program* (Carbondale, IL: Southern Illinois University at Carbondale Rehabilitation Institute, 1992).

15. Bob Huskey, interview with the author, ca. 2005.

16. Dr. Howard Rusk, "Home for Handicapped: An Analysis of the Special Features Found in House Designed for Disabled," *New York Times*, April 5, 1959.

17. This was Max's second trip on an airplane since his accident, as he had visited the Montreal World's Fair in 1967 with his mother, Carl, and another Jesuit.

18. Eric Dibner, interview in *Builders and Sustainers of the Independent Living Movement in Berkeley*, vol. 3, an oral history conducted from

1997 to 1998, Regional Oral History Office, Bancroft Library, University of California–Berkeley, 2000.

19. "Highlights from Speeches by Ed Roberts," as collected by Jon Oda [Ed Roberts's attendant for three years), World Institute on Disability, wid.org/about-wid/highlights-from-speeches-by-ed-roberts (February 14, 2008).

20. Julia Sain, "History of the Disability Rights Movement" (ILNET Teleconference, April 4, 2004).

21. Joan Leon, "Reminiscences of Ed Roberts," Ed Roberts Campus, Berkeley, CA, edrobertscampus.org/er_03.html.

22. Ed Roberts speech from "Highlights from Speeches by Ed Roberts," as collected by Jon Oda, World Institute on Disability, wid.org/about-wid/highlights-from-speeches-by-ed-roberts (February 14, 2008).

23. Ibid.

24. Brown, *Freedom of Movement*, ILRU Bookshelf Series (2000), 30.

25. Sain, "History of the Disability Rights Movement."

26. Ibid. According to Steven E. Brown, *Freedom of Movement*, 31, "During Ed's first academic year, 1962–63, the same year that the African-American James Meredith integrated the University of Mississippi, Ed was the only student with a disability at Cowell, and, as far as we know, the first student with a disability of this significance to attend an American university."

27. Ed Roberts speech (February 14, 2008).

28. Independent Living USA, "Ed Roberts, the Father of Independent Living," ilusa.com/links/022301ed_roberts.htm.

29. Sain, "History of the Disability Rights Movement."

30. Eric Dibner, "Advocate and Specialist in Architectural Accessibility," an oral history conducted in 1998 by Kathy Cowan in *Builders and Sustainers of the Independent Living Movement in Berkeley*, vol. 3 (Berkeley: Regional Oral History Office, Bancroft Library, University of California–Berkeley, 2000, 8.

31. Nancy M. Crewe and Irving Kenneth Zola, *Independent Living for Physically Disabled People* (Lincoln, NE: iUniverse.com, 2001), 17.

32. Joseph P. Shapiro, *No Pity: People with Disabilities Forging a New Civil Rights Movement* (New York: Three Rivers Press, 1994), 51.

33. Max, Colleen, and other disability rights leaders still apply this "law" today to organizations serving the disabled.

34. Ed Roberts speech from "Highlights from Speeches by Ed Roberts," as collected by Jon Oda, World Institute on Disability, wid.org/about-wid/highlights-from-speeches-by-ed-roberts (February 14, 2008).

35. Independent Living USA, "Ed Roberts, the Father of Independent Living," ilusa.com/links/022301ed_roberts.htm.

36. San Francisco State University, "Chronology of the Disability Rights Movement," www.sfsu.edu/~hrdpu/chron.htm.

37. Ibid.

38. Ann Gailis and Keith M. Susman, "Abroad in the Land: Legal Strategies to Effectuate the Rights of the Physically Disabled," *Georgetown Law Journal* 61, no. 6 (July 1973): 1507, footnote 47.

39. "Some of the statutes provide that accessibility is required only if economically feasible and not unreasonably complicated. Others require that the building have one entrance which is accessible while ignoring other barriers." Source: Ann Gailis and Keith M. Susman, "Abroad in the Land," *Georgetown Law Journal*, 1509, footnote 59.

40. Ibid., 1509.

41. Ed Roberts speech from "Highlights from Speeches by Ed Roberts," as collected by Jon Oda, World Institute on Disability, wid.org/about-wid/highlights-from-speeches-by-ed-roberts (February 14, 2008).

42. Max Starkloff, "Disability Rights Movement: Toward Independence" (speech, City Club, 1986, p. 3, Starkloff Disability Institute [SDI] Archives).

CHAPTER 8

1. Ann Gailis and Keith M. Susman, "Abroad in the Land: Legal Strategies to Effectuate the Rights of the Physically Disabled," *Georgetown Law Journal* 61, no. 6 (July 1973): 1501, footnote 2. Jim Tuscher Archives.

2. Frank Bowe, *Equal Rights for Americans with Disabilities* (New York: Franklin Watts, 1992), 117.

3. Ibid. See pages 228–229, in which this is discussed in more detail. Today, as defined by the ADA, an individual with a disability is "a person who has a physical or mental impairment that substantially limits one or more major life activities, a person who has a history or record of such an impairment, or a person who is perceived by others as having such an impairment." The ADA does not specifically name all of the impairments that are covered.

4. Ibid.

5. In Bowe, *Equal Rights for Americans with Disabilities,* 62.

6. Marilyn Hamilton, a paraplegic, designed the first ultralight manual wheelchair in 1978 out of the same aluminum tubing used in ultralight gliders. She designed the chairs to fold quickly for portability, manufactured them in "screaming neon colors," and named her company Quickie. According to Joseph P. Shapiro in his book *No Pity: People with Disabilities Forging a New Civil Rights Movement* (New York: Three Rivers Press, 1994), "Hamilton's proud chairs struck a chord with the emerging disability rights movement. For one thing, there were more wheelchair users, up from half a million in 1960 to 1.2 million by 1980, most of whom were no longer living in nursing homes or institutions as they had been just a couple of decades before. This new generation of wheelchair users was newly politicized and wanted maximum independence. They were demanding curb cuts, lifts on buses, and handicapped parking spaces. They had come to expect that they would go to college, take jobs, get married, and sometimes even start families. . . . She took a universal symbol of sickness and turned it into a symbol of disability self-pride."

7. This information is from Max's "Initial Statement" to the Greater St. Louis Chapter of the National Paraplegia Foundation, given on Wednesday, October 13, 1971. SDI Archives.

8. Dr. Saul Boyarsky (speech to the National Paraplegia Foundation, October 13, 1971, SDI Archives).

9. Ibid.

10. Max Starkloff (speech to the National Paraplegia Foundation, October 13, 1971, SDI Archives).

11. Ibid.

12. Jim Tuscher, interview with the author, June 27, 2006.

13. Ibid.

14. Ibid.

15. The *Journal of Rehabilitation* is the official publication of the National Rehabilitation Association, a private, nonprofit corporation dedicated to the rehabilitation and well-being of handicapped persons.

16. James Tuscher and Gary C. Fox, "Does the Open Door Include the Physically Handicapped?," *Journal of Rehabilitation* (September–October 1971): 11.

17. Ibid.

18. Patricia Rice, "Quadriplegic Planning Center for Disabled," *St. Louis Post-Dispatch*, ca. 1971.

19. Jake McCarthy, "View from the City. A Personal Opinion . . .," *St. Louis Post-Dispatch*, January 31, 1972.

20. Max Starkloff and Mike Dahl, *Para-Quad: A Normal Environment for the Physically Disabled* (prospectus, sect. 3, part B), February 1, 1972.

21. Ibid., sect. 3, part C.

22. Patricia Rice's article, estimating the cost at $15 million, is undated but is believed to have been published in the *St. Louis Post-Dispatch* before Torno's February 1, 1972, estimate in the prospectus. Ibid., sect. 3, last page.

23. Colleen and Max Starkloff, interview with the author, May 29, 2004.

24. Max Starkloff, letter to editor, *American Journal of Nursing* 72, no. 7 (July 1972).

25. Reporter Dave Dorr gives 1972 as the year of the first curb cuts in St. Louis. Dave Dorr, "No Retreat," Everyday, *St. Louis Post-Dispatch*,

December 13, 1995. Max remembered being interviewed by Julius Hunter about a curb cut at Busch Stadium.

CHAPTER 9

1. The Colleen Starkloff quotes are from interviews with the author, 2004–2014.

2. Brown, *Freedom of Movement*, 42. Section 504 made it illegal for "any program or activity receiving Federal financial assistance" to discriminate against an "otherwise qualified handicapped individual."

3. Joan Headley quoting Gini Laurie (1997 Region V Independent Living Conference, Oak Brook, IL, October 1997), Post-Polio Health International Archives, St. Louis.

4. *Rehabilitation Gazette, International Journal of Independent Living by and for Persons with a Disability* 30, no. 1 (January 1990): 2, 3. SDI Archives.

5. Joan Headley, executive director, Post-Polio Health International, publisher of the *Rehabilitation Gazette*, founded by Gini Laurie in the 1950s.

6. Max Starkloff, interview with the author, February 27, 2006.

7. The second independent living center opened in Houston, Texas, in 1972. Residents lived in a dormitory-style building near the downtown area. Lex Frieden, "IL Movement and Programs," *American Rehabilitation* (1978), 3, 6–9. Found in Nancy M. Crewe and Irving Kenneth Zola, *Independent Living for the Physically Disabled* (Lincoln, NE: iUniverse.com, 2001), 43.

8. Doris Zames Fleischer and Frieda Zames. *The Disability Rights Movement: From Charity to Confrontation.* (Philadelphia: Temple University Press, 2001), 43.

9. Lex Frieden (keynote speech, St. Louis, April 10, 2006).

10. Max Starkloff, "Advocacy: A Change-Centered Occupation— Disabled Individuals as Change Agents" (keynote address, American

Coalition of Citizens with Disabilities Rehabilitation Training Workshop, May 12, 1980, pp. 3, SDI Archives).

11. Wikipedia, "American Coalition of Citizens with Disabilities" (November 16, 2006).

12. Ibid.

13. Eunice Fiorito became the second president of the American Coalition of Citizens with Disabilities in 1976.

14. Wikipedia, "American Coalition of Citizens with Disabilities."

15. Frank Bowe, *Equal Rights for Americans with Disabilities* (New York: Franklin Watts, 1992), 98.

16. Joseph F. Shapiro, *No Pity: People with Disabilities Forging a New Civil Rights Movement.* (New York: Three Rivers Press, 1994), 57.

17. Judy Heumann, interview with the author, April 20, 2006.

18. Quoted in Shapiro, *No Pity*, 57.

19. Torri Minton, "Disabled Crusader Takes Fight National," *San Francisco Chronicle*, March 17, 1993.

20. Sharon Barnartt and Richard Scotch, *Disability Protests: Contentious Politics 1970–1999* (Washington, D.C.: Gallaudet University Press, 2002), 59.

21. Torri Minton, "Disabled Crusader Takes Fight National," *San Francisco Chronicle*, March 17, 1993.

22. Section 504 was a single sentence at the end of the Rehabilitation Act that defined "qualified individual with a disability" as stated in Section 7 (6) of the Rehabilitation Act. See Richard K. Scotch, *From Good Will to Civil Rights: Transforming Federal Disability Policy*, 2d ed. (Philadelphia: Temple University Press, 2001), 52.

23. Section 504.

24. Richard K. Scotch, *From Good Will to Civil Rights: Transforming Federal Disability Policy*, 2nd ed. (Philadelphia: Temple University Press, 2001), 75.

25. Ibid., 65, in which he quotes the definition of the term "handicapped individual" as stated in the Rehabilitation Act of 1973, Section 7 (6)

as, "any individual who (A) has a physical or mental disability which for such individual constitutes or results in a substantial handicap to employment, and (B) can reasonably be expected to benefit in terms of employability from vocational rehabilitation services provided persuant to Titles I and III of this Act."

26. Ibid., 66, in which he quotes a passage from H.R. 17503, 93rd Congress, 2nd session (1974). " . . . such term (handicapped individual) means any person who (A) has a physical or mental impairment which substantially limits one or more of such person's major life activities, (B) has a record of such impairment, or (C) is regarded as having such an impairment."

27. HR 17503, 93rd Cong., 2nd sess. (1974).

28. Quoted in Richard K. Scotch, *From Good Will to Civil Rights: Transforming Federal Disability Policy*, 2nd ed. (Philadelphia: Temple University Press, 2001), 71.

29. Ibid., 72.

30. Ibid., 93.

31. *Paraquad Corporate Background and Capabilities* (SDI Archives, ca. 1978, p. 8).

32. Richard Ward and Mary Breuer memo to Max Starkloff, June 27, 1975, "Results of First Phase Survey" p. 1, SDI Archives.

33. Richard Ward and Jack Pyburn memo to Max Starkloff, June 27, 1975, *Paraquad Site Analysis*, Appendix A, SDI Archives.

34. Dr. William H. Danforth, interview with the author, July 19, 2006.

35. www.fundinguniverse.com/company-histories/HOK-Group-Inc-Company-History.html (April 23, 2008).

36. Jerry King, interview with the author, March 7, 2006.

37. Dr. William H. Danforth, email to the author, June 12, 2014.

38. Jerry King, interview with the author, March 7, 2006.

39. http://www.civicprogressstl.org/, June 16, 2014.

40. Dr. William H. Danforth, interview with the author, July 19, 2006.

41. Jerry King, interview with the author, March 7, 2006.

42. Norm Parish, "Federal Housing Officials Tell Disabled They Have to Move," *St. Louis Post-Dispatch*, July 11, 2000.

43. Richard Ward and Jack Pyburn, memo to Max Starkloff, June 27, 1975, *Paraquad Site Analysis*, sect. 3.0, table 1.

44. Richard Ward and Jack Pyburn, *Paraquad Site Analysis*, memo to Max Starkloff, June 27, 1975, Sect. 4.2.

45. Max Starkloff, "Advocacy: A Change-Centered Occupation—Disabled Individuals as Change Agents" (keynote address, American Coalition of Citizens with Disabilities Rehabilitation Training Workshop, May 12, 1980, 6, SDI Archives).

46. The Bi-State Development Agency was an interstate compact formed by Missouri and Illinois in 1949. Since February 2003, the agency has been doing business as Metro.

47. Max Starkloff, "Disabled Individuals as Change Agents," p. 6.

48. Bob Baer, interview with the author, November 2, 2006.

49. Mary Johnson, *Make Them Go Away: Clint Eastwood, Christopher Reeve and the Case against Disability Rights* (Louisville: Avocado Press, 2003), 86.

50. Ibid., 87.

51. Ibid., 88.

52. Quoted in ibid., 86, but attributed in a footnote to Douglas B. Feaver, "Equipping Transit Lines for Disabled Would Cost Billions, Group Testifies," *Washington Post*, September 20, 1978, A6.

53. While Max was the leader, he and Colleen share credit with many others, including Jim Tuscher and Bill Sheldon, who worked alongside him during this period.

54. Mary Johnson, *Make Them Go Away: Clint Eastwood, Christopher Reeve and the Case against Disability Rights* (Louisville: Avocado Press, 2003), 112.

55. Ibid., 93–94.

56. Max Starkloff, interview with the author, May 12, 2004.

57. "Since the inception of Paraquad in July, 1970, all administrative

expenses have been borne by my family, my friends, and myself, at a cost of thousands of dollars, until the fall of 1975. At that time, several foundations, including the Louis D. Beaumont Foundation, the H.B.S. Fund, the McBride Foundation, and the Roblee Foundation had contributed enough monies to meet administrative expenses through June, 1976." Max Starkloff, Corporate Background and Capabilities (St. Louis: Paraquad, March 1978, p. 15, SDI Archives).

CHAPTER 10

1. Laurent Torno, interview with the author, March 21, 2006.

2. Patricia Degener, "Struggle for Independence in a Hostile Environment," *St. Louis Post-Dispatch*, June 24, 1977.

3. *Paraquad History and Purpose* (St. Louis: Paraquad, ca. 1976, SDI Archives).

4. Laurent Torno, interview with the author, March 21, 2006.

5. James L. Young, Department of Housing and Urban Development, Washington, D.C., letter to Max Starkloff regarding Application No. 1342, September 3, 1976, SDI Archives.

6. Max Starkloff, interview with the author, July 28, 2006.

7. Thomas Newsome, "The Newest Minority . . . The Disabled," Features, *St. Louis Globe-Democrat*, sec. F, December 8–9, 1979.

8. B. Teixeira, F. Varker, and R. Bowlin, *Accessible Bus Service in St. Louis: Final Report UMPA/TSC Project Evaluation Series*, February 1, 1980.

9. J. A. Lobbia, *Riverfront Times*, October 9–15, 1985.

10. "Handicapped Hold Rally in Favor of Curb Cuts," *St. Louis Globe-Democrat*, ca. 1976.

11. "The first systematic installation of curb-cuts occurred at the Urbana-Champaign campus of the University of Illinois in the late 1940s, as the result of advocacy by Timothy Nugent and students at the school's disabled students' program. The city government of Minneapolis installed 9,000 curb-cuts between 1968 and 1974, under the direction of William B. Hopkins, director of public affairs of the Min-

nesota Society for Crippled Children and Adults, Inc." Fred Pelka, *The ABC-CLIO Companion to the Disability Rights Movement* (Santa Barbara, CA: ABC-CLIO, 1997), 82.

12. According to Doris Zames Fleisher and Frieda Zames in their book *The Disability Rights Movement* (p. 99), a group called Disabled in Action in Philadelphia and twelve individual plaintiffs filed two Title II class-action lawsuits against the Philadelphia Streets Department in 1992. They won both, mandating curb cuts whenever streets were repaired and constructed and also on every corner in the downtown business district of Philadelphia. In 1994, noting that New York City had not prepared the required schedule for constructing curb cuts at all sidewalk corners mandated by Title II of the ADA by July 26, 1992, the Eastern Paralyzed Veterans Association filed suit against the New York City Department of Transportation.

13. Degener, "Struggle for Independence in a Hostile Environment."

14. Scotch, *From Good Will to Civil Rights*, 103.

15. Quoted in Doris Zames Fleischer and Frieda Zames, *The Disability Rights Movement: from Charity to Confrontation* (Philadelphia: Temple University Press, 2001), 55–56.

16. "Nondiscrimination on Basis of Handicap: Programs and Activities Receiving or Benefiting from Federal Financial Assistance," *Federal Register*, May 4, 1977, 22676–22702.

17. Richard Bryant Treanor, *We Overcame*, 1st ed. (Falls Church, VA: Regal Direct Publishing, 1993), 82.

18. Patricia Degener, "Dignity for Disabled. Struggle for Independence in a Hostile Environment, *St. Louis Post-Dispatch*, June 24, 1977.

19. Quoted in Treanor, *We Overcame*, 82.

20. Quoted in Shapiro, *No Pity*, 70–71.

21. "Conway, Democrat for Mayor," press release, March 31, 1977, SDI Archives.

22. Section Nine of the ordinance, Board Bill #115, reads "The passage of the ordinance being deemed necessary for the immediate preser-

vation of the public health and safety, it is hereby declared to be an emergency measure which shall take effect and be in full force immediately upon its approval by the Mayor." SDI archives.

23. Amended Board Bill Number 115, Section 3, Paragraph B, SDI Archives.

24. Patricia Harris was the first African American woman to serve in the United States cabinet and the first to enter the line of succession to the presidency.

25. Patricia Degener, "Dignity for Disabled. Struggle for Independence in a Hostile Environment," *St. Louis Post-Dispatch*, June 24, 1977.

26. The Paraquad 1979 annual report, enclosure no. 2, "Chronology Statement of the Development of the Paraquad Housing Project," lists the facilities visited as Creative Living in Columbus, Ohio; 2100 Bloomington in Minneapolis; New Horizons Manor in Fargo, North Dakota; and Independence Hall in Houston.

27. Torno attributes this to "Making Facilities Accessible to the Handicapped," State University of New York, 1967, p. 13.

28. Handwritten document from Laurent Torno, ca. 1977, SDI Archives.

29. The Boulevard sales brochure, SDI Archives.

30. Max Starkloff, interview with the author, January 29, 2004.

31. Paraquad 1979 Annual Report, Enclosure no. 2, "Chronology Statement of the Development of the Paraquad Housing Project."

32. David Fink, "Project Gives Handicapped Housing Hope," *St. Louis-Post Dispatch*, October 6, 1977, 10A.

33. Lex Frieden (speech to students at Saint Louis University School of Occupational Therapy, April 11, 2006).

34. Ibid.

35. Lex Frieden, "Independent Living Models," special article, *Rehabilitation Literature* 41, no. 7–8 (July–August, 1980): 169–173, A-289, independentliving.org/docs6/frieden1980.html.

36. The Independent Living Research Utilization program "is a national center for information, training, research, and technical assistance

in independent living. Its goal is to expand the body of knowledge in independent living and to improve utilization of results of research programs and demonstration projects in this field." Source: www.ilru.org, April 11, 2009.

37. In an early Paraquad document titled "Corporate Background and Capabilities," dated March 1979, Paraquad is described as a "corporation which deals directly with the issue of greatest concern to the disabled, i.e., the integration of disabled persons with the rest of able-bodied society. To establish this objective the staff has worked in the specific areas of housing exploration, development of criteria necessary to barrier-free design, accessible housing development, totally accessible public transit in the role of consumer advocate, civil rights, development of workshops covering disability-related issues, and many other concepts designed to improve the quality of life for disabled persons."

38. All of Lucy Dolan's recollections are from "Rebuilding My Life," a panel discussion that was part of "Rebuilding People and Communities: Life after Disabling Injuries," a disability workshop put on by SDI, St. Louis, April 21, 2006.

39. The Paraquad board consisted of seven prominent St. Louisans: Max, Samuel Aftergut, John Boyce, Mrs. Ernest Eddy, Dr. Elizabeth Stoddard, William McBride Love, and Charles E. Claggett (father of the author).

40. Jake McCarthy, "Disabled Liberation," *St. Louis Post-Dispatch*, October 18, 1978, 2H.

41. Katy Gurley, "New Apartments Built for Needs of Disabled," *St. Louis Globe–Democrat*, September 3, 1979.

42. Max and Colleen Starkloff, interview with the author, August 25, 2006.

43. Colleen Starkloff, email to the author, December 1, 2013.

44. Max Starkloff, interview with the author, March 22, 2006.

45. Degener, "Housing for the Disabled," *St. Louis Post-Dispatch*, November 15, 1979.
46. Dan Feinberg, interview with the author, June 22, 2009.
47. "The St. Louis Award and Previous Recipients," Washington University Public Relations Information Office, November 15, 1979.
48. Max and Colleen Starkloff, interview with the author, May 6, 2009.
49. Thomas Newsom, "The Newest Minority . . . the Disabled," *St. Louis Globe-Democrat*, p.1 of Features; December 8, 1979.
50. Courtesy of Title VII, the Rehabilitation Act Amendments of 1978, which for the first time authorized funding of Independent Living Centers. Though the original amendment sought $80 million, only $2 million was granted to test the program. The money was divided evenly between ten independent living centers.
51. SDI archives.
52. Bill Sheldon did not learn to use sign language at Central Institute for the Deaf (CID), because it is an oral school. No American Sign Language or finger spelling is allowed at CID—to this day. He learned to use his hands to form words after coming to work for Paraquad.
53. Max and Colleen Starkloff, interview with the author, May 29, 2007.
54. Bill Sheldon, interview with the author, August 30, 2007.
55. The National Captioning Institute (NCI) was established in 1979 as a nonprofit corporation with the mission of ensuring that deaf and hard-of-hearing people, as well as others who can benefit from the service, have access to television's entertainment and news through the technology of closed captioning. http://www.ncicap.org/index.asp
56. Bill Sheldon, interview with the author, August 30, 2007.
57. Jim Tuscher, interview with the author, June 27, 2006.

CHAPTER 11
1. *Accent on Living Magazine*, Summer 1993, 80–84.
2. "The Trials and Triumphs of Adoption," *Progression* 2, 1992, 3.

3. Frances Marks Buck and George W. Hohmann, "Personality, Behavior, Values, and Family Relations of Children of Fathers with Spinal Cord Injury." *Archives of Physical Medicine and Rehabilitation* 62, September 1981, 432. Italics added by author.
4. Frances Marks Buck, "The Influence of Parental Disability on Children: An Exploratory Investigation of the Adult Children of Spinal Cord Injured Fathers," Ph.D. diss., University of Arizona, 1980, SDI Archives. 7–8. Buck attributes this to George W. Hohmann, "Psychological Aspects of Treatment and Rehabilitation of the Spinal Cord Injured Person," *Clinical Orthopedics and Related Research*, 1975, 81–88, 112.
5. Ibid., 8.
6. Ibid., 19. He attributes this to M. Hamilton, *Father's Influence on Children* (Chicago: Nelson-Hall, 1977, 140).
7. Frances M. Buck and George W. Hohmann, "Child Adjustment as Related to Severity of Paternal Disability," *Archives of Physical Medical Rehabilitation* 63, June 1982, 249.
8. Ibid.

CHAPTER 12

1. Fred Pelka, *The ABC-CLIO Companion to the Disability Rights Movement*, (Santa Barbara, CA: ABC-CLIO, 1997), 99.
2. Mike Ervin, "Mary Johnson: 'Write' Stuff for the Disability Movement," *Independence Today News*, June 30, 2014.
3. Pelka, *The ABC-CLIO Companion to the Disability Rights Movement*, 99.
4. Max Starkloff, "Advocacy: A Change-Centered Occupation. Disabled Individuals as Change Agents" keynote address at the ACCD rehabilitation training workshop, May 12, 1980, SDI Archives.
5. Colleen Starkloff, interview with Charlie Carr, January 10, 2014.
6. Judy J. Newmark, "Disabled Americans: A Question of Rights," *St. Louis Post-Dispatch*, Sunday Magazine, January 29, 1984, 7.

7. Marca Bristo, interview with author, December 4, 2009.
8. The names of the original ten ILCs and their directors have not been recorded as far as I know. This list was provided by Max from memory at an interview on January 29, 2004.
9. Excerpted from a commentary Starkloff wrote for the *St. Louis Post-Dispatch*, April 13, 1993.
10. Jennifer LaFleur, "New Executive Director Takes Over Management Duties at Paraquad," *St. Louis Post-Dispatch*, January 3, 2002.
11. David Newburger, interview with the author, March 4, 2006.
12. Mary Jane Brotherson, "Families and Independent Living," *Independent Living Forum* 2, no. 2, 1984.

CHAPTER 13

1. Arlene Mayerson, *The History of the ADA: A Movement Perspective* (Berkeley, CA: Disability Rights Education and Defense Fund, 1992), http://dredf.org/news/publications/the-history-of-the-ada/
2. Ibid.
3. Sue Ann Wood, "Progress Toward Accessibility Is Slow, Paraquad Reports," *St. Louis Post-Dispatch*, January 12, 1993.
4. Ibid.
5. David Newburger, interview with the author, April 4, 2006.

CHAPTER 14

1. Colleen Starkloff, interview with the author, August 6, 2013.
2. Meaghan Starkloff-Breitenstein, interview with the author, July 18, 2013.
3. Colleen Starkloff, interview with the author, January 16, 2011.
4. Maxim Starkloff, interview with the author, August 24, 2013.
5. Maxim Starkloff, interview with the author, September 26, 2013.
6. Meaghan Starkloff-Breitenstein, interview with the author, July 18, 2013.

7. This figure of speech, not a medical term, refers to a blood clot that breaks away from its original source and causes damage elsewhere in the body.

8. Maxim Starkloff, interview with the author, August 24, 2013.

9. Colleen Starkloff, interview with the author, August 6, 2013.

10. Maxim Starkloff, interview with the author, August 24, 2013.

CHAPTER 15

1. Norm Parish, "Federal Housing Officials Tell Disabled They Have to Move," *St. Louis Post-Dispatch*, July 11, 2000.

2. Ibid.

3. Phyllis Librach, "Paraquad Apartments Sell for Over $2 Million," *St. Louis Post-Dispatch*, February 14, 2002.

4. Jodie Kopp, property manager for Conrad Properties, interview with the author, December 3, 2013.

5. Colleen Starkloff, interview with the author, September 9, 2013.

6. David Newburger, interview with the author, September 9, 2013.

7. Gray Kerrick did not make himself available for an interview. Before becoming VP of advertising & communications, he was VP of corporate communications for Southwestern Bell Telephone. Jerry Berger, "St. Louis Magazine Is Bringing Its New Art Director from KC;" *St. Louis Post-Dispatch*, November 19, 1990.

8. Colleen Starkloff, interview with the author, August 8, 2013.

9. Genny Watkins, interview with the author, September 20, 2013.

10. David Newburger, interview with the author, September 9, 2013.

11. Martha Uhlhorn, interview with the author, August 21, 2013.

12. Stephen Leicht, interview with the author, October 15, 2013.

13. Dan Feinberg, interview with the author, October 28, 2013.

14. Stephen Leicht, interview with the author, October 15, 2013.

15. Dan Feinberg, interview with the author, October 28, 2013.

16. Colleen Starkloff, interview with the author, August 6, 2013.

17. Jennifer LaFleur, "New Executive Director Takes Over Management at Paraquad," *St. Louis Post-Dispatch,* January 3, 2002.
18. Colleen Starkloff, interview with the author, August 6, 2013.

Chapter 16

1. Virginia Gilbert and Barry Gilbert, "Starkloff Institute: Fighting a World That Says, 'You Shouldn't Be Here,'" *St. Louis Beacon,* October 10, 2012.
2. Bureau of Labor Statistics, U.S. Department of Labor, June 11, 2014: "A large proportion of persons with a disability—about 8 in 10—were not in the labor force in 2013, compared with about 3 in 10 persons with no disability."
3. Colleen Starkloff, interview with the author, August 6, 2013.
4. Stephen Deere, "He Personifies Freedom on Wheels: Max Starkloff, Founder of Paraquad, Is Honored for His Work," *St. Louis Post-Dispatch,* July 11, 2007.
5. The exhibition, called *Action for Access: Changing Perceptions of Disability in American Life,* lives on in cyberspace at actionforaccess.mohistory.org/.
6. Kathi Wolfe, "Missouri Museum to Tell Disability Story," *Independence Today,* June 2008. http://www.itodaynews.com/june_2008/museum.htm.
7. Ibid.
8. Ibid.
9. Colleen Starkloff, interview with the author, September 9, 2013.
10. SDI website, http://starkloff.org/s/home/disability-studies/.
11. Colleen Starkloff, interview with the author, September 9, 2013.
12. Richard Weiss, "Starkloff Remembered as Force for Change, Example for Many," *St. Louis Beacon,* January 4, 2011.

EPILOGUE

1. Steve Degnan, interview with author, spring 2010.
2. Centene, Enterprise Bank & Trust, Enterprise Holdings, Nestlé Purina, SSM Health Care (as of June 2014).
3. Alternative Opportunities, Inc.; Life Skills; MERS Goodwill; Missouri Rehabilitation Services for the Blind; Missouri Vocational Rehabilitation; Paraquad; Rochester Institute of Technology/National Technical Institute for the Deaf; Special School District (St. Louis); St. Louis VA Medical Center; St. Patrick Center (as of June 2014).

·Index·